What
Birds
Eat

What Birds Eat KIM LONG

HOW TO PRESERVE THE NATURAL DIET AND
BEHAVIOR OF NORTH AMERICAN BIRDS

SKIPSTONE

Published by Skipstone, an imprint of Mountaineers Books—an independent, nonprofit publisher. Skipstone and its colophon are registered
trademarks of The Mountaineers organization.

Printed in China
23 22 21 20   1 2 3 4 5

Design: Kim Long and Heidi Smets
Layout: Heidi Smets
Cover design: Mountaineers Books and Heidi Smets
Cover photograph: *Bohemian Waxwing*, © iStock/Ornitolog82
Back cover, top: *Black-billed Magpie* © Coulanges/Shutterstock; back
cover, bottom: *Lesser Goldfinches at feeder* © Kim Long
Frontispiece: *Juvenile Chipping Sparrow* © Tarpan/Shutterstock

All photographs and illustrations by author unless credited otherwise.

A record for this book is available at the Library of Congress.

Printed on FSC®-certified materials

ISBN (paperback): 978-1-68051-300-4
ISBN (ebook): 978-1-68051-301-1

Skipstone books may be purchased for corporate, educational,
or other promotional sales, and our authors are available for a
wide range of events. For information on special discounts or
booking an author, contact our customer service at 800.553.4453
or mbooks@mountaineersbooks.org.

Skipstone
1001 SW Klickitat Way Suite 201
Seattle, Washington 98134
206.223.6303
www.skipstonebooks.org
www.mountaineersbooks.org

LIVE LIFE. MAKE RIPPLES.

CONTENTS

INTRODUCTION

Birds are powerful symbols. For many people in the modern urban environment, birds are highly visible representatives of a natural world that is increasingly remote. They are also the most common, and welcome, form of wildlife found where most people now live, in cities. A recent national survey by the US Fish and Wildlife Service reports that more than 38 million Americans consider themselves bird-watchers.

In a modern world where the majority of the human population lives in cities and suburbs, an understanding of birds must include one point of interaction most people will have with these wild animals: bird feeders. Thus, the behavior of birds at or near feeders is often their most visible activity to many bird lovers. Why do birds choose certain foods? How do they find it? Do they share it or hoard it? What is the impact of dwindling natural food sources on how birds feed and what they feed on? Are birds a threat to agriculture or an ally?

Birds and their food sources are a major focus of human interest, spanning traditional ornithology, environmental science, evolutionary theory, animal behavior, and other professional and amateur interests. Yet most bird lovers and gardeners understand birds only from watching them at backyard feeders and may never have seen an American Goldfinch perched on a native thistle in the wild, pulling out tiny seeds one at a time.

In a wide range of habitats, from backyards to parks, from oceans to mountaintops, birds depend on an extraordinary variety of food sources, and evolution has improved their effectiveness at finding food. As birds adopted various diets, their anatomy and behavior evolved in response, equipping each species with a distinctive array of bill, tongue, and talons, a range of specialized senses, and characteristic feeding practices.

Food has a significant influence on bird behaviors such as territorial defense, flocking, migration, and breeding. These activities are linked to birds' anatomy and physiology, which have fundamental similarities from the smallest species to the largest, as well as uniquely different characteristics that can vary even among individuals of the same species.

To appreciate both the similarities and differences among birds, anatomy and physiology is an essential starting point. This book focuses on how birds' anatomy and physiology affect eating: structures and processes to identify food and then capture and digest it. The signature movement of birds—flying—is left to other resources, as are plumages and mating behaviors.

But while birds are well established in their niches, a warming climate, agricultural chemicals, pollution, and the loss of habitat from human development threaten their food sources. Declining insect communities and dwindling seed availability are among the consequences of these threats that are already underway. The fallout from these trends poses direct and indirect perils for the future health of bird populations.

In the past, bird feeders have been criticized as a threat to birds, luring them away from the natural food sources they would otherwise rely on for survival. Scientific studies (see resources), however, now support the value of these popular backyard amenities as supplemental sources of food, especially critical for the rising number of species threatened by changes to their environment.

To most humans in modern society, the most visible wild animals they encounter on a daily basis are birds. Bird-watching and maintaining bird feeders are activities that are accessible for all ages, from individuals to families. Thus, birds are the most effective starting point for people to turn a passive activity (bird-watching) into committed involvement and additional action in support of birds.

Lawns and gardens represent territory that is in the control of home owners and renters, property that can be put to use in support of the diminishing natural habitats that support birdlife. Lawn and garden chemicals not only pose significant risks to insects that are important components of bird diets, they are also a barrier to healthy, sustainable backyard environments that support birds. The selection of plants for lawns and gardens usually favors grasses, plants, shrubbery, and trees that are either not native to the continent or do not grow naturally in a local ecosystem. Backyards can be havens for birdlife, and bird feeders can supplement their natural diets—both goals that are in the control of most home owners and renters.

Citizen science already capitalizes on popular interest in birds. The FeederWatch program from the Cornell Lab of Ornithology relies on a large network of bird lovers in North America to observe,

American Robin eating a chokecherry
(*Photo by Gray Photo Online*)

note, and share data from bird feeders in backyards, school yards, and nature centers. The information from this widely dispersed volunteer community helps tracks changes in bird populations from year to year, a variable with increasing importance as risks to birds' survival expand.

With the environment increasingly under threat, birds deserve our attention. They stand unrivaled as a widely observable subject that engages both scientists and citizens, a focus for continuing advances in knowledge about their anatomy and behavior, a highly visible bellwether for environmental change, and an accessible symbol of the wild nature of our planet.

HOW BIRDS EVOLVED

Birds are often described as living dinosaurs. We know this connection is valid thanks to an ever-growing pool of fossil evidence that provides credible links between these modern flying animals and their dinosaurian roots from millions of years ago. There were other flying dinosaurs in addition to birds, notably pterodactyls, but birds followed a different branch of development. Their size, structure, and behavior turned out to be the right combination, for the living birds that fascinate us today are the descendants of creatures that survived the catastrophic event that ended in extinction for all the other dinosaurs. Living birds are part of a lineage that dates back to a very remote ancient past.

DINOSAURS WITH FEATHERS

Before there were dinosaurs, there were reptiles, amphibians, fish, and mammals. The earliest known reptiles emerged in an age known as the Middle Pennsylvanian epoch, between 312 million and 307 million years ago. These early reptiles produced numerous variations. Some branches became extinct, but others have survived to this day.

During the Triassic period, reptiles developed a branch called archosaurs, which generated the dinosaurs. The fossil evidence uncovered to date includes at least 130 genera and at least 700 species of dinosaurs. By the beginning of the Jurassic period, dinosaurs had developed into a wide variety of forms, including both four- and two-legged variations. The latter type was characterized by long hind legs and short forelegs, engineered to provide an upright posture and bipedal locomotion.

The evidence from known fossils illustrates numerous shared characteristics between living birds and the theropod branch of the dinosaur family. Theropods were carnivorous animals in a range of sizes that included velociraptors and *Tyrannosaurus rex*, iconic images in popular culture thanks to the success of films such as *Jurassic Park*. Essential features of many theropods relate directly to characteristics of modern birds, including their upright stance, hollow bones, elongated (though relatively short) forelimbs, elongated foot bones (metatarsals), and a unique pelvis.

Unlike other dinosaurs, such as the giant *T. rex*, the ancestors of modern birds began shrinking in size at least 200 million years ago, a practical contribution to their flying capability. The closest links to modern birds were theropods called coelurosaurians, birdlike animals that walked on two legs and ranged in size from 100 to 500 pounds (45–225 kilograms). The first known ancient dinosaur with a full complement of bird characteristics is the Archaeopteryx, a reptilian creature with feathers. The fossil record for this creature dates to 155 million to 135 million years ago, during the Jurassic period. About the size of a modern raven, it had wings and flight feathers, although it may not have been capable of flight, or at least prolonged flight. It also had teeth, the better to manage its carnivorous diet.

The first fossilized skeletons of Archaeopteryx that have been uncovered to date also feature other characteristics common in modern birds. At the end of their long legs were feet with three strong clawed toes, able to grasp onto perches, and

ARE BIRDS DINOSAURS?

These are among the shared characteristics of living birds and some dinosaurs:

> External covering of feathers
> Hollow bones with thin walls
> Elongated leg bones
> "Hands" with three fingers
> Feet with four toes and elongated bones between the ankle and toes (metatarsals)
> Ankle joint hinged for limited front-to-back motion
> A wishbone (furcula) formed by the fusion of the collarbones (clavicles)
> Scapula reduced to a simple strap
> Pectoral structure able to produce a power stroke in the forelimb or wing
> Pubis (one of three bones on the vertebrae side of the pelvis) oriented to the rear, with a characteristic expansion on its farthest (distal) end
> System of distributed air sacs
> Large eye openings
> Long S-shaped neck
> Standing position with feet under the body and ankles elevated
> Reproduction by laying eggs

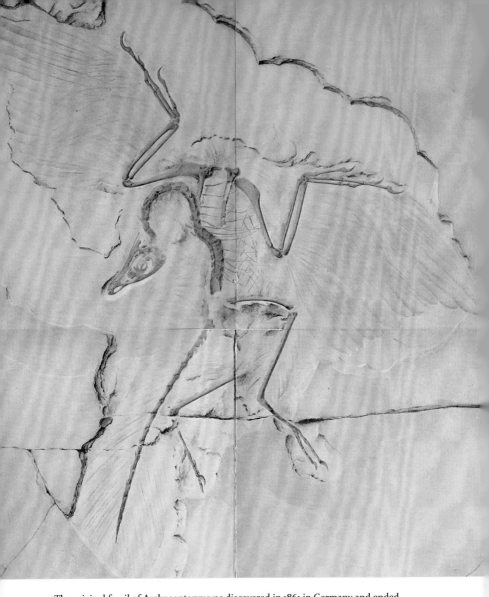

The original fossil of Archaeopteryx was discovered in 1861 in Germany and ended up in the London Natural History Museum, about the same time as the publication of Charles Darwin's *On the Origin of Species*. This image is of another specimen, also found in Germany, which joined the collection of the Humboldt Museum für Naturkunde, in Berlin. It was reproduced in a large fold-out insert in the monograph "Uber Archaeopteryx," published in 1884.

AVIAN TREE OF LIFE

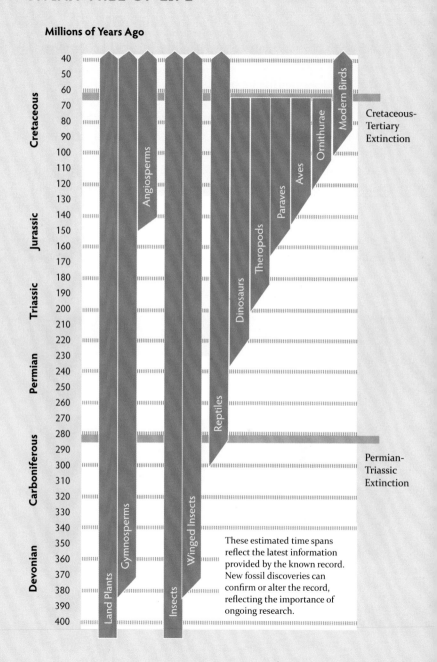

Millions of Years Ago

These estimated time spans reflect the latest information provided by the known record. New fossil discoveries can confirm or alter the record, reflecting the importance of ongoing research.

they had pronounced bills. Though many paleontologists consider Archaeopteryx the earliest known ancestor of birds (see the Avian Tree of Life chart), others believe that this branch of development led to a dead end.

During the age of the dinosaurs, before the emergence of birds, some early reptiles also developed flying forms; early avian dinosaurs coexisted with these. The pterosaurs were one such group, a diverse collection of reptiles that thrived for an estimated 150 million years, overlapping the era of dinosaurs. The reptilian pterosaurs could be quite large but were also capable of flying, though without feathers or other characteristics common to the early birds. The smallest pterosaurs were about the size of modern songbirds, and the largest, *Quetzalcoatlus*, had a wingspan of about 35 feet (10.7 meters), roughly the same width as an F-16 fighter jet and as tall as a giraffe. The most familiar pterosaur in popular culture is *Pterodactylus*. Smaller than *Quetzalcoatlus*, *Pterodactylus* had a wingspan of about 5 feet (1.5 meters).

Birds as we recognize them today are flying dinosaurs, but not all dinosaurs that flew survived and not all animals that flew in the Jurassic and Cretaceous periods were dinosaurs. This fossil is of a pterosaur, a flying reptile. Some pterosaurs were as small as sparrows, and others had wingspans comparable to that of modern airplanes. *(Photo by Akkharat Jarusilawong)*

Some pterosaurs were capable of flying by flapping their wings; others could only glide. Both actions were possible because of a leather-like webbing of skin stretched between their bodies and elongated digits at the end of their forelimbs.

Over millions of years, pterosaurs grew, evolving to be larger and larger, much like dinosaurs. These flying reptiles did not evolve into birds, and though they thrived alongside dinosaurs, they were not dinosaurs themselves. Pterosaurs became extinct about 66 million years ago, at the same time as dinosaurs and possibly from the same cause.

One of the key features of birds as they evolved, according to paleontologists, is that they persisted because they grew smaller over time, likely a major factor in helping them survive in a changing, calamitous world. Not only could they sustain life with less food, but they were likely able to outcompete their closest competitors: the sixty genera of pterosaurs known from the fossil record that were smaller forms.

Birds are alive today because of their unique characteristics. They are living dinosaurs, true, but they adapted to survive conditions that wiped out their larger reptilian cousins.

THE FIRST REAL BIRDS

The direction of development for wings began on the ground. As some four-legged animals became bipedal, walking upright on two legs, their smaller forelimbs' role in locomotion changed. What was the evolutionary advantage to this development?

In small animals that depended on bipedal running to hunt for food and escape from predators, small forelegs provided an effective counterbalance, as with the modern Ostrich. The small non-flight-worthy appendages on these large terrestrial birds provided balance and stability when they ran, yielding an evolutionary clue to their value, which contributed to their development over time into appendages that generated a better way to chase food and escape from predators.

Feathers, which came before the forelimbs developed into wings large enough to provide lift, provided insulation as well as visual cues associated with mating. Feathers are a key requirement in birds' distinctive engineering of flight. Recently, evidence has been found that pushes back the date for feathers earlier than the appearance of Archaeopteryx, previously the only known precursor to modern birds. Several dinosaur specimens with filamentous feathers have been found that date to the Triassic period, which preceded the Jurassic. By the Cretaceous period—beginning about 145 million years ago and following the Jurassic—most of the characteristics that define modern birds were evident, including the signature keel on the modified sternum (essential for anchoring flying muscles), fused vertebrae (the pygostyle) that support the tail, and wings large enough to generate lift.

Fossil evidence from 130 million to 115 million years ago, during the Cretaceous period, marks the appearance of birds with wings large enough to provide flight. Fossil discoveries include anatomical variations in both sizes and shapes of wings as well as the proportional association with body size. These variations suggest the beginning of specialization for survival in different ecological niches, as well as dependence on food sources—from insects and larger animals to seeds and tree sap—that influenced flight behaviors.

Along with feathered wings, birds also developed a signature element that improved their success with feeding: the avian bill. The bills on modern birds evolved from a simpler form over millions of years; the variety of bills that now characterize different species arose later and in shorter time spans. Various studies have shown that bill sizes and shapes within a single species can change in only a handful of generations, a fast-change strategy in response to fluctuating feeding opportunities.

The evolution of bills paralleled another dramatic change in birds: the loss of teeth. Teeth and the heavy jaws needed to support them represented a weight penalty for animals that flew. The switch from toothed jaws to toothless bills reduced weight, improving flight effectiveness.

Hummingbirds, which have the most distinctive bills among North American birds, probably fed on insects as this form developed. Over time, the insects they hunted led them to a new, highly charged source of food—plant nectar—and in response, their bills gradually adapted to take advantage. Insects are still part of hummingbird diets as an important source of protein before the seasonal abundance of flowers is available for foraging.

How did some birds develop structures that made water a suitable medium? The earliest fossil of an aquatic bird is dated to 100 million years ago. Diving and swimming underwater require adaptations rather than radical changes. Wings that were already developed as effective forms of propulsion in the air adapted over time to generate propulsion in the denser medium. In general, wingspans became shorter and narrower. Feet that developed to grip perches and prey adapted to generate propulsion through water as well, with the development of webbing, as in ducks, and lobes, as in grebes. Water environments also had an effect on other elements of bird anatomy and physiology. Complex feathers, down, subsurface fat, and oil glands provided insulation from cold temperatures; for diving birds, metabolisms and blood circulation changed to accommodate the pressure of water under the surface.

One of the oldest species yet found of a birdlike dinosaur is *Confuciusornis*. This fossil was uncovered in China and is held at the Shanghai Natural History Museum. *Confuciusornis* had flight feathers that were longer than its body and is the oldest known bird to have a beak. It lived about 124 million years ago and measured about 10 inches (25 centimeters) long. *(Photo by Akkharat Jarusilawong)*

ANCIENT FOOD

Birds developed as carnivorous dinosaurs. Since they were relatively small, unlike *T. rex* and other giants, their food sources were also small. Insects, arthropods such as spiders and mites, amphibians, and small reptiles and mammals provided a broad menu of feeding opportunities. All of these prey animals were well established during the Jurassic period.

The earliest insects found in fossil records date back almost 500 million years, to the Early Ordovician period, although initially they did not have wings. At about the same time, the first plants developed on land, and these two milestones have been evolving in step ever since.

Wings appeared on insects about 400 million years ago, a period of rapid diversification and also about the time that plants became part of insects' diet. Wings allowed insects to exploit more ecological zones as well as avoid predators. At about the same time that insects developed wings, plants underwent their own period of rapid diversification, growing taller, which rewarded insects that could fly and thereby reach new heights. About 400 million years ago, the first plants that reproduced by pollination also appeared.

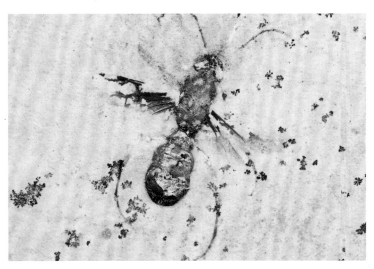

This fossil of an ancient wasp dates from the Cretaceous period, 108 million to 92 million years ago. The creature was about 0.5 inch (1.3 centimeters) long with a wingspan of about 0.75 inch (1.9 centimeters). *(Photo by Bjoern Wylezich)*

Some ancestors of modern insects followed the same path of development of most dinosaurs, evolving to extreme size. Giant insects included the dragonfly-like meganeuras, with wingspans of more than 2 feet (0.6 meter). As with others of these extinct animals, the path to extreme size may have been fueled by the composition of the ancient atmosphere—up to 35 percent oxygen compared to about 21 percent now. Animal cells use oxygen to produce energy; in general, higher levels of atmospheric oxygen promote larger bodies.

One of the theories that explains the strong diversification in bird species in ancient times points to the parallel expansion in the diversity of insects: the more insects moved into new habitats and increased in numbers, the more opportunity it presented for birds to benefit by accessing them through flight.

Insects' and plants' coevolution led to a codependence that remains in modern times and continues to have considerable impact on the health of bird populations. Any change that affects one group has an impact on the others. As flowering plants developed, for example, they not only provided a significant new source of food for insects and the insect species that diversified to take advantage of them, but the plants also diversified in turn to depend on these insects for reproduction.

Plants that suffered from insect predation developed systems in defense, primarily through chemical weapons that repelled or poisoned the threats to their survival. In turn, most insects evolved to become specialists. Their digestive systems developed countermeasures to allow them to digest toxic plant materials, but typically they were effective for only a narrow range of host plants.

This ever-evolving relationship is often localized, with continents and ecological zones marking natural boundaries established by unique links between plants and insects. In the modern world, as more and more plants, insects, and birds are accidentally or purposely transported to geographical regions where they are nonnative, these natural links are disrupted, with dire consequences.

Aside from providing a widespread—in both geography and range of habitats—menu of food options for birds, insects and other arthropods also diversified in response to the emergence of birds. Lice, for example, first emerged about 53 million years ago as parasites of birds and mammals.

One of the key features of modern insects, metamorphosis, was also involved in a growing interdependence with birds. The first insects hatched directly from eggs in their adult forms, although not full-sized. The complicated phases of development we now recognize as the signature metamorphosis process developed about 300 million years ago, with a beneficial outcome for insects. In effect, the different life stages of the same insect are independent of one another. Young and mature phases of most insects rely on different sources of food, which reduces competition and increases the chance for survival for each stage.

As an extended consequence, birds also benefit. This evolutionary change provides additional varieties of food that often live in segregated zones. Mosquito larvae feed on algae and plankton in bodies of water, for example, while adult mosquitoes fly to locate sources of animal blood.

SURVIVORS OF THE CRETACEOUS-TERTIARY EXTINCTION

About 66 million years ago, a cataclysm known as the Cretaceous-Tertiary (K-T) extinction most likely occurred when a large asteroid slammed into the earth. The force of the impact had a huge immediate impact on the environment over a wide area and for hundreds, perhaps thousands, of years. The result was the death of most life-forms on the planet, encompassing as much as 70 percent of all animal species, including all of the dinosaurs. Some types of birds survived. Paleontologists believe that before the K-T extinction there were relatively few distinct lineages of birds, mostly just ratites (ostriches and relatives) and ancestors of modern ducks and geese.

About the same time, a series of violent volcanic eruptions further disrupted the atmosphere and added to the catastrophic effects that culminated in the extinction of many species. The theories that tie these events to the end of the dinosaurs are based on increasing bodies of evidence and the application of sophisticated computer models. Some theories also suggest that many dinosaur species may have already been in decline at the time of the K-T event. As with many scientific theories, the debates and disagreements may not be resolved without more evidence and additional computer modeling, but the prevailing opinion currently favors the K-T event as the main trigger.

THE DIVERSIFICATION OF BIRDS

Roughly around the time of the K-T extinction, birds rapidly diverged into many different species. Almost all bird species we recognize today emerged within a window of 10 million to 15 million years, a relatively short evolutionary time span.

The postextinction birds that were part of this dynamic expansion are known as the Neoaves, and they represented 90 percent or more of all bird species alive at the time. They were mostly land-based. Among the earliest clusters of similar species within the Neoaves were hawks and vultures, which have one of the clearest links to dinosaur ancestry. Among other raptors, owls have closer taxonomic ties to hornbills and toucans, and falcons have more in common with songbirds and parrots than other living raptors. DNA comparisons have also indicated that hummingbirds and swifts evolved from an ancestor of the nightjar and most likely were nocturnal for millions of years.

These and other revelations have come from a recent global project that compared DNA from bird specimens representing all modern branches of the avian family. The results of this comprehensive study have rearranged previous theories about birds and their taxonomic relationships, a traditional scientific method of grouping organisms through similar characteristics (see the Taxonomic Classification of Birds sidebar). Modern taxonomy relies more and more on DNA analysis, which reveals shared patterns that do not always reflect physical characteristics.

Based on the latest known evidence, the Hoatzin, a species native to South America, has the oldest lineage of all modern birds. Whether or not it is considered "primitive," the Hoatzin does have the most highly specialized of all digestive systems among modern

TAXONOMIC CLASSIFICATION OF BIRDS

The taxonomic system groups organisms in a traditional hierarchy, first developed by Carl Linnaeus in the eighteenth century, beginning with the most general classification (kingdom) and concluding with the most specific (species). Each animal or plant, living or dead, is assigned a scientific name that reflects this hierarchy, using Latin as a universal language; the genus and species are always italicized, with the genus capitalized and the species name lowercase.

The naming convention for birds in the United States is governed by the American Ornithological Society (AOS), which periodically reviews and renames known species to reflect updated knowledge about their relative taxonomic position. Thus, the example below represents *Spinus tristis*, the current taxonomic entry for the American Goldfinch, which traditionally was classified as *Carduelis tristis*. The AOS, in alignment with the International Ornithological Union, recommends capitalizing the common names of individual species: thus, American Goldfinch, not American goldfinch.

Kingdom: Animal
Phylum: Chordata
Class: Aves
Order: Passeriformes
Family: Fringillidae
Genus: *Spinus*
Species: *Tristis*

birds: it feeds on leaves and buds, which it ferments in its crop using microbes and bacteria, much like cows and other ruminants. All other birds rely on digestion based in a two-part stomach to process food. Another uncommon characteristic of the Hoatzin is a set of claws on the wings of young birds, a vestige of ancient predecessors that likely used them to climb trees, before such birds were capable of flight.

A fossil found in New Mexico represents another early ancestor of living birds, called *Tsidiiyazhi abini*, which has been dated to about 62.5 million years ago. Its structure is linked to modern mousebirds, but with kinship to kingfishers and woodpeckers as well. *Eofringillirostrum boudreauxi* dates to the Early Eocene epoch, about 52 million years ago. The shape of its bill indicates that it was a seedeater, one of the first perching birds to adapt to this diet.

Also based on the latest evidence and scientific interpretation, the perching birds (passerines)—about 60 percent of all living bird species—are thought to have emerged as a group about 47 million years ago from a base in the Southern Hemisphere, most likely what is today Australia. The oldest North American fossil of a passerine, which was unearthed in Wyoming, is the earliest known example of a bird with a bill similar to that in modern sparrows and finches.

Though the first birds developed as small carnivorous dinosaurs, most passerine species evolved to be insectivorous, but there is great diversity in what insects they favor, how they find and eat their prey, and which habitats they favor. These passerines hunt in the air, on the ground, in foliage, on tree trunks and branches, and on and under the water. Other passerine species have diets that favor nectar, leaves, seeds, and a wide variety of other invertebrates, small vertebrates, and mammals.

The ability to fly must have given birds a significant survival edge when they lived alongside nonflying dinosaurs, as well as flying reptiles, species that did not survive the K-T extinction. Something about the first birds represented an advantage that kept some of them alive through an era of extremes and made them an ideal base from which thousands of new species could emerge to populate the postextinction world (see the North American Bird Species table, for example).

Adaptation is one of the keys to birds' survival of the K-T extinction. Birds have adapted to fit into almost every ecosystem on the planet, with modifications to their anatomy, physiology, and behavior to take advantage of almost every type of food available, becoming specialists or generalists in order to survive. Flight also

NORTH AMERICAN BIRD SPECIES

The species counts listed here are from the latest American Birding Association list for Canada and the continental United States.

SPECIES	NUMBER
Accipitriformes (hawks, eagles, allies)	28
Acrocephalidae (reed warblers)	2
Aegithalidae (bushtits)	1
Alaudidae (larks)	2
Alcedinidae (kingfishers)	4
Alcidae (auks, murres, puffins)	46
Anhingidae (anhinga)	1
Anseriformes (ducks, geese, swans)	68
Apodidae (swifts)	9
Aramidae (limpkins)	1
Ardeidae (bitterns, herons, egrets, allies)	20
Bombycillidae (waxwings)	2
Calcariidae (longspurs, buntings)	6
Caprimulgiformes (nighthawks, allies)	10
Cardinalidae (cardinals, allies)	18
Cathartiformes (New World vultures)	3
Certhiidae (creepers)	1
Charadriidae (lapwings, plovers)	17
Ciconiidae (storks)	2
Cinclidae (dippers)	1
Columbiformes (pigeons, doves)	19
Corvidae (jays, crows)	20
Cracidae (curassows, guans)	1
Cuculiformes (cuckoos, roadrunners, anis)	8
Diomedeidae (albatrosses)	9
Emberizidae (sparrows, allies)	53
Estrildidae (waxbills)	1
Falconiformes (caracaras, falcons)	11
Fregatidae (frigatebirds)	3
Fringillidae (finches, allies)	25
Gaviidae (loons)	5

Glareolidae (Oriental pratincoles)	1
Griodae (cranes)	3
Gruidae (thick-knees)	1
Gruiformes (rails, gallinules, coots)	17
Haematopodidae (oystercatchers)	3
Heliornithidae (sungrebes)	1
Hirundinidae (martins, swallows)	15
Hydrobatidae (storm-petrels)	15
Icteridae (blackbirds)	25
Jacanidae (jacanas)	1
Laniidae (shrikes)	3
Laridae (gulls, terns, allies)	49
Locustellidae (grassbirds)	2
Mimidae (mockingbirds, thrashers)	12
Motacillidae (wagtails, pipits)	10
Muscicapiidae (Old World flycatchers)	15
Odontophoridae (New World quail)	6
Pandionidae (ospreys)	1
Paridae (chickadees, titmice)	12
Parulidae (warblers)	57
Passeridae (Old World sparrows)	2
Passeriformes (tyrant flycatchers, allies)	46
Pelecaniformes (pelicans)	2
Phaethontiformes (tropicbirds)	3
Phalacrocoracidae (cormorants)	6
Phasianidae (partridge, grouse, turkeys)	17
Phoenicopteridae (flamingos)	1
Phylloscopidae (leaf warblers)	8
Piciformes (woodpeckers, allies)	25
Podicipediformes (grebes)	7
Polioptilidae (gnatcatchers)	4
Procellariidae (shearwaters, petrels)	31
Prunellidae (accentors)	1
Psittacidae (parakeets, macaws, parrots)	7
Psittaculidae (lories, lovebirds, allies)	1
Ptiliogonatidae (olive warblers)	1
Pycnonotidae (bulbuls)	1
Recurvirostridae (stilts, avocets)	3

Regulidae (kinglets)	2
Remizidae (verdin)	1
Scolopacidae (sandpipers, curlews, allies)	66
Sittidae (nuthatches)	4
Stercorariidae (skuas, jaegers)	5
Strigiformes (owls, not including Barn Owl)	22
Sturnidae (starlings)	2
Sulidae (boobies, gannets)	5
Sylviidae (sylvid warblers)	2
Thraupidae (tanagers)	5
Threskiornithidae (ibises, spoonbills)	5
Tityridae (becards, tityras)	3
Trochilidae (hummingbirds)	23
Troglodytidae (wrens)	11
Trogoniformes (trogons)	2
Turdidae (thrushes)	26
Tytonidae (Barn Owls)	1
Upupidae (hoopoes)	1
Vireonidae (vireos)	16

gave some bird species a significant opportunity in migration, the ability to move in response to seasonal changes.

The question for this class, Aves, of the animal kingdom is whether birds' capability to adapt will allow them to overcome the extreme threats to reproduction and sustenance represented by climate change and increasing effects of human activity. Hazards generated by humans include development, which has greatly reduced and fragmented natural spaces; agriculture, which increasingly limits the natural variety of plant sources of food for birds; toxic agricultural controls, which destroy insect sources of food; and pollution, which disperses a range of toxicity across many natural habitats. More than ever, birds' survival depends on what they eat.

THE ANATOMY AND PHYSIOLOGY OF HOW BIRDS EAT

The fundamental imperative—the core mission and reason for being—for all life-forms on Earth is to increase their kind. All species exist to reproduce. Birds, like all animals, have evolved to follow this imperative.

Food fuels birds' (like all animals) ability to survive, which leads to a never-ending cycle of looking for more food to digest for energy and sustenance. Searching for and managing food, reproducing, competing for food, avoiding predators, and (for many species) migrating, all depend on a complex system of anatomy and physiology. Some attributes are common to all birds, and others are specialized adaptations.

When foraging, birds use their feet to uncover insects and seeds in the litter on a forest floor and they are also handy for preening. But the primary function of feet for most passerines is perching, with toes locking around branches. For most species, feet are not very effective for walking. As a result, many birds hop instead of walking when on the ground. The hopping gait may also be a development from their time spent on tree limbs, where hopping and flying are the only practical methods to move around. *(Photo by Mike Truchon)*

HOW BIRD TOES ARE ARRANGED

Bird toes may be positioned in a variety of ways, but almost all are variations on three basic styles tailored to the primary activities of a species.

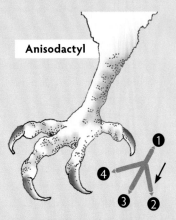

Anisodactyl

The most common foot arrangement for birds, found in about three-fourths of all species, consists of a smaller toe pointing back and three toes pointing forward.

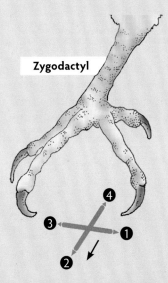

Zygodactyl

This arrangement, in which toes 1 and 4 point backward and toes 2 and 3 point forward, bolsters the ability to climb tree trunks, as well as adds strength for perching.

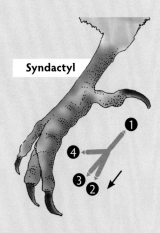

Syndactyl

In this arrangement, the number 1 toe points to the back and toes 2 and 3 or 3 and 4 are mostly fused together, which adds gripping strength for perching and grasping prey.

EXTERNAL ANATOMY

Elements of birds' anatomy that are easily visible, such as feet and toes, claws, bills, and tongues, play a role in their ability to capture and swallow their food. These essential tools may be specialized to make these tasks more effective in dealing with different kinds of food sources, such as flying insects, nectar, or tiny seeds.

FEET AND TOES

Birds' feet and toes do double duty, standing in for the lack of paws and fingers of mammals. Feet and toes are birds' go-to tool when it comes to perching, moving on the ground and in the water, and foraging—and, for raptors, grasping prey. Modifications in different species represent adaptations specialized for specific environments and ecosystems, survival strategies, and diet. Wings cannot grasp, making feet and claws (along with bills) the primary food handlers.

The part of a bird leg we recognize as its foot is much less complex than a mammal's foot. Other than the toes, it is made up of a single bone (the tarsometatarsus). Attached directly to it are toes that make contact with surfaces such as the ground or tree limbs. Much like mammals' variations in the number and shape of toes, bird species exhibit considerable diversity in the size, number, and configuration of their toes.

The size of toes varies according to how a species perches, climbs, wades, and grasps, and webbing is an added feature of the toes of aquatic birds. The number of toes ranges from two to four, but most birds have four; a spur higher on the leg is not actually a toe though it might seem to be one.

These toes are arranged in different configurations depending on the type of bird (see the How Bird Toes are Arranged sidebar), though most birds have three toes pointing forward and one pointing to the rear (anisodactyl). Other toe configurations include a two-and-two configuration (zygodactyl), like that of owls and woodpeckers. Ornithologists number the toes from the inside (medial) position to the outside (lateral), with toe number 1 the equivalent of the thumb or big toe in humans. This first toe is called the hallux. In most North American bird species, the hallux is the toe facing to the rear.

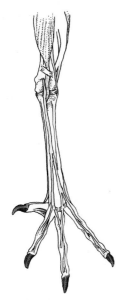

Specialized tendons enable birds' toes to clasp when perching.

As with other animals, the flexibility of the toes greatly improves birds' ability to walk, swim, search for and grasp prey, groom, climb trees, and perch. The ability to adjust the position of each toe independently is an essential asset for birds. The hallux has two segments (called phalanges), while the other toes have three segments, corresponding to the same bones in humans and some other mammals.

In humans and some other mammals, a single toe can have more than one set of muscles and tendons controlling its movement. Birds, however, have only a single muscle and tendon for each of the two principle actions made by a single toe: flexion (bringing two or more bones toward their inner, or anterior, surfaces) and extension (spreading two or more bones toward their outer, or dorsal, surfaces).

Perching: Over time, birds developed a key anatomical feature that allows them to perch above the ground and away from predators. Between the bones of their thigh (femur) and foot, tendons connect the flexor muscles at both ends, automatically closing the toes around a branch or other object. The action is reinforced by tiny barbs along the surfaces of the tendons, locking them together to provide mechanical reinforcement.

Perching birds are among the taxonomic order known as Passeriformes, which represents more than half of all the world's bird species. The ability to perch evolved to provide an effective mechanism for safety from predators while resting above the ground and may be one of the most significant adaptations for the survival of these birds over time. Like an opposing thumb, the backward-facing toe curls forward when a bird perches, locking in place in conjunction with the other three toes that curl down and to the back. When birds perch, this combination of flexed rear and front toes allows passerines their well-known pose.

Gripping: Bones, muscles, and tendons in the leg are links in a chain of supporting mechanisms, a system that contributes to the gripping capabilities of birds' feet and toes (and claws). The full strength of the grip of a Bald Eagle is estimated to be about 400 pounds per square inch (180 kilograms per 2.5 centimeters square), more than ten times greater than that of a mature human hand.

Woodpeckers can climb vertical surfaces because of their toe arrangement: two toes forward and two back. This Downy Woodpecker uses its toes to scale trees in search of insects.

Gripping strength is transmitted by tendons from muscles higher up on the leg. These muscles act like the hands of a puppeteer, pulling strings that manipulate the toes. Compared to humans, which have the same basic "puppeteer" arrangement, birds produce more gripping strength than the equivalent in mammals.

Specialization: To move on the ground or in the water, bird feet are specialized in size, shape, and the addition of webbing. Most of these attributes primarily support movement, but they also help birds acquire food. The two-by-two configuration of a woodpecker's toes, as well as its highly curved sharp claws, allow it to move securely up and down tree trunks and branches, essential movement in the bird's hunt for insect prey. The perch-grasping ability of finches supports their feeding activity by allowing them to hold awkward positions on plant stalks while extracting seeds.

CLAWS

Claws are an extension of the outermost section of the toes (the distal, or terminal, phalanx). The core of the claw is covered with a layer of connective tissue and a compact outer layer of hardened keratin—the same material that makes up human fingers and hair, as well as feathers, nails, hoofs, and horns in other animals. Each claw has a dorsal plate (the unguis) covering its back and sides and a ventral plate (the subunguis) closing the gap underneath. The dorsal plate is the harder of the two.

Keratin, a fibrous protein, comes in two forms: alpha keratin and beta keratin. Alpha keratin is commonly found in vertebrates, including birds, but beta keratin occurs only in birds and reptiles. Keratin varies according to application: in bird feathers it is more fiber-like than that found in claws or the outer sheath of bills (which is composed mostly of thin, parallel sheets). Within the family of birds, aquatic species and raptors have a greater percentage of beta keratin.

Claws (like bills) grow continuously. Growth occurs at the base in a conical zone that spreads outward from the end of the last toe bone. This growth is normally offset by use: pecking, stabbing, probing, and other actions wear down the tip of the claw. Studies of songbirds estimate that the rate of growth is from 0.001 to 0.002 inch (0.03 to 0.05 millimeter) a day. The rate of growth can vary between the backward-pointing toe and the other three toes and varies from season to season, possibly due to changes in metabolism or diet.

Birds can sense vibrations and pressure changes through their claws. This important sensory information is provided by mechanoreceptors, specialized groups of cells similar to those in human fingers and toes. These sense organs are highly sensitive to even weak stimulations, providing critical information relating to food sources and potential threats.

Technically, all claws can be called talons and all talons are claws, although many birders are used to the convention of limiting the term *talon* to the claws on raptors. Larger and stronger than the claws on most birds, raptor talons are an essential tool for grabbing and holding prey, from birds caught in midflight or rodents and reptiles captured on the ground.

Evolutionary biologists believe that raptor talons developed primarily as a tool to immobilize large prey while it is dismembered. The absolute size as well as the comparable sizes of each talon on a

RAPTOR TALONS

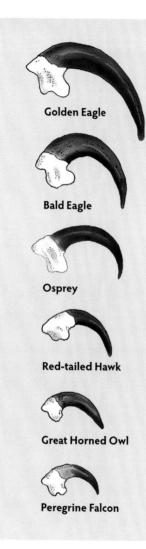

Golden Eagle

Bald Eagle

Osprey

Red-tailed Hawk

Great Horned Owl

Peregrine Falcon

Raptors do not all prey on the same animals, hunt in the same habitats, or capture their food the same way.

Eagles and hawks, among the largest raptors, have extra-large talons on their number 1 and number 2 toes. This gives them added security when grasping larger prey animals that often are not killed immediately at the point of capture. The greatest curves in raptor talons are found on Ospreys, which use them as hooks to snag fish just below the surface of the water. Talons are attached to relatively short bones in owls compared to other raptors, which increases the leverage of the muscles that control them. Falcons, which often strike and capture smaller birds, depend on their initial strikes to stun their prey and typically use their bills instead of talons to kill.

foot relates to the most common behavior that different species use to hunt and eat (see the Raptor Talons sidebar).

Falcons, for example, depend on striking their prey feet first with great force, sometimes killing on impact, and have less-developed talons than owls, whose talons are shaped to grip small prey tightly,

A few species of birds in North America have a claw-like spur that grows on the outside of the tarsometatarsus bone in males, as illustrated on this Wild Turkey leg. Turkeys (domestic and wild), domestic roosters, and Ring-necked Pheasants have this feature, which is used for fighting.

crushing it to death. When prey is captured alive, falcon talons function like a cage while the prey is killed with the bill. Falcon talons are also relatively long compared to those of other raptors because falcons mainly hunt other birds and the added length of their talons helps to extend their reach through layers of feathers.

Osprey talons are large and highly curved, the better to catch and hold their primary prey, slippery fish. Their talons, not coincidentally, are similar in shape to fish. Unlike most other raptors, ospreys also have the ability to rotate their outside toes backward, creating a two-by-two configuration that amplifies their gripping power. Owls also benefit from this physiological advantage. Unlike the talons of eagles, hawks, and falcons, vultures' talons are typically smaller because they eat carrion, which does not require killing or holding.

The largest raptors are not always quick to dispatch their prey, but depend on their larger size and weight to immobilize prey. Once some raptors, especially eagles and large hawks, capture prey, they rely on their second or third talon as a tool to rip it open. Larger prey is not swallowed whole but is dismembered with the bill while the talons firmly hold the prey.

Claws on some types of birds are adapted for other uses. The backward-pointing first toe is elongated on a few land-dwelling species, such as marsh birds, including rails. This feature helps with stability and support while walking or running across floating vegetation. The Horned Lark also has elongated claws, to support walking across the open expanses of ground it favors.

BILL

A bill, also called a beak, is to a bird what jaws are to a mammal: the entry point for food destined for the digestive system. Lacking hands, a bird uses its bill like fingers to sense, probe, preen, and manipulate objects, especially food. Bird bills are made up of an upper (the maxilla) and a lower (the mandible).

The bill is covered by a sheath composed of keratin. In some scientific use, the outer covering of the bill is called the bill sheath (rhamphotheca: *rhampho* means "rod" or "beak" in Latin), and it is constantly growing, unlike the underlying bony structure, which reaches its full size at maturity.

The keratinous sheath usually conforms to the size and shape of the underlying bone. The Red Crossbill (*Loxia curvirostra*) is a rare exception. It is commonly identified by curving upper and lower bills that cross over each other in opposing directions. This visible feature is created by the outer sheath alone; minus the sheath, the bone underneath is similar in shape to that of other small seed-eating species. The American White Pelican's beak has another unique characteristic: during breeding season, both males and females develop an irregular growth on their upper bill, which later falls off. Similarly, Puffins' and some auklets' bills have an additional basal part that's even more complex and interesting.

Bills, like other bony structures in avian bodies, have a lightweight open framework with passageways for nerves and blood vessels. In almost all bird species, the upper bill is a single unit, but the lower is formed of two distinct sections that are side-by-side mirrors of each other and fused at the tip in a conjunction known as the gonys (see the Avian Bill Terminology sidebar). In most North American bird species, both bills are the same length, or the upper bill is slightly longer than the lower.

The inside edges of both the upper and lower bills, called tomia, are typically simple crests that run from the front to the back. When

AVIAN BILLS

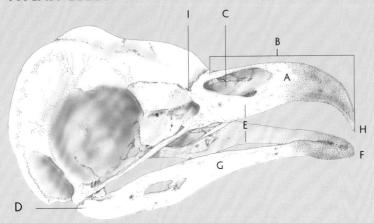

A. Upper bill (maxilla); B. Culmen; C. Nare (nostril); D. Rictus (gape); E. Tomia; F. Gonys; G. Lower bill (mandible); H. Tip (nail); I. Craniofacial hinge

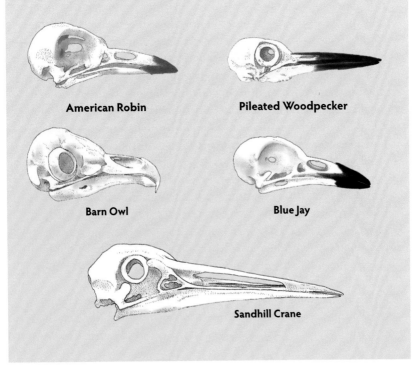

American Robin

Pileated Woodpecker

Barn Owl

Blue Jay

Sandhill Crane

bills are closed, these edges come together to create a cutting tool, though the edges are not particularly sharp in most species.

Several additional bones are part of a flexible connection joining the upper bill to the skull, although the upper does not have anything close to the mobility of the lower. These bones and paired bony protuberances on the skull are important attachment sites for the muscles used to open and close the bill.

Movement of the upper bill is a reflexive action called rhynchokinesis. The ability to move the upper bill is useful because it increases the width of the gap between the open upper and lower bills, an angle called the "gape." It also allows birds to open only a small section of bill to grasp food while the head and lower bill remain still. This ability is minimal in most species and is most extreme in parrots, boosting their crushing strength with very hard nutshells. Waterbirds such as sandpipers also benefit from this specialized action because they can grab prey from under the surface of sand or mud without taking in much of the inedible substrate.

The muscles that control bills have various attachment sites on the skull, and as in most animals, the larger the muscle, the more pronounced the ridge or protrusion where the muscle attaches. Because muscles can only contract, it takes at least one set of muscles to open a lower bill and another set to close it; the number of sets varies by species. With rhynchokinesis, muscle control is more complicated due to the engineering required to manipulate all or part of the upper bill. Some birds open this bill in a simple up-and-down motion (though typically not by much); others can also open just the outermost (distal) end and/or move the upper bill tip from side to side. These movements are possible because of the thinness and flexibility of the underlying bone and a set of lever-like bones called the Pterygoid-Palatinum Complex, which transfers the contractions of muscle sets into directional movements of the bill.

Bills (like claws), grow over time. Foraging, probing, raking, dabbling, and other actions involved with feeding erode the outer surface. Just as with hair and skin in humans, an ongoing process adds keratin to the outer surface, helping maintain the critical function of this appendage as use wears down its surface. Biologists

VARIATIONS IN BILL SHAPE

Raptors have large hooked bills, effective for tearing apart the bodies of their animal prey. The bills are specialized in different species to deal with a range of prey sizes and activities.

Seed-eating birds have conical bills that are shaped to effectively break open seedpods and husks. These bills provide strength and leverage. Bills with tips that cross each other are effective for prying open pinecones.

Some insect-eating birds have thin, pointed bills they use to probe for insects among leaves and twigs and in soil litter. Other insect-eating birds have very strong pointed bills used to hammer and drill into tree trunks.

Nectar-seeking birds have very long bills that they use to probe within flowers.

In ducks and other waterfowl, bills are long and flattened to allow them to effectively scoop through mud and aquatic vegetation. Aquatic birds that prey on fish and other animals in and near the water have bills like daggers, but most of the time, they snatch rather than spear their prey.

studying some bird species believe that the loss of bill length due to wear and its subsequent replacement by new tissue can be as much as a 1–2 inches (2.5-5 centimeters) a year, with up to 3 inches (7.6 centimeters) for some parakeets. But because the wear and replacement cycle are concurrent, bills do not normally appear to lose or gain length. Bird skeletons found in nature are often missing the outer sheath, which degrades much more quickly than bones.

Variations: The shape, size, and relative importance of the bill varies from species to species and is directly related to how a species

AVIAN BILL TERMINOLOGY

Beveled: chisel-like at the tip

Cere: featherless fleshy structure at the base of the bill

Compressed: flattened from side to side

Conical: cone-shaped, with a broad base

Craniofacial hinge: flexible joint at the juncture with the skull that allows the upper bill to be raised

Culmen: lengthwise ridge along the top of the upper bill

Curved: curved downward

Depressed: flattened from top to bottom

Gonys: junction of the two halves of the lower bill

Hooked: curved down at the tip

Lamellae: ridges across the inside surfaces of the upper and lower bills

Maxilla: another name for the upper bill

Nail: plate of hard tissue at the tip of the upper bill

Nares: nostril openings in the upper bill

Nasal bristles: bristle-like feathers that extend from the forehead to cover the nares

Operculum: membrane attached to the base of the bill and covering the nares

Recurved: curved upward

Rhamphotheca: layer of keratin covering the bill; also called the bill sheath

Rhynchokinesis: movement of the upper bill

Rictal bristles: bristle-like feathers at the gape

Rictus (gape): hinge of the upper and lower bills, characterized by a fleshy bulge

Serrate: resembling the teeth of a saw; usually refers to tomia; *see* tomium, toothed

Spatulate: flattened and wider toward the tip

Terete: round in cross section

Throat pouch: loose sac of skin attached underneath the lower bill and used to hold food

Tomial tooth: projection on the bottom edge of the upper bill, fitting with a corresponding notch on the lower bill

Tomium: edge of a bill; plural, tomia

Toothed: serrated; usually refers to tomia on the upper bill

The female Ruby-throated Hummingbird (top) demonstrates its ability to flex open only the tip of its bill, a feature called rhynchokinesis that is useful for some birds when acquiring food. *(Photo by Donald T. Devine)*

Many other birds, including Dunlins, Sanderlings (middle), sandpipers, and Bar-tailed Godwits (bottom) have this ability. *(Photo of Sanderling by Ray Hennessy; photo of Bar-tailed Godwit by Imogen Warren)*

BILLS OF NORTH AMERICAN HUMMINGBIRDS

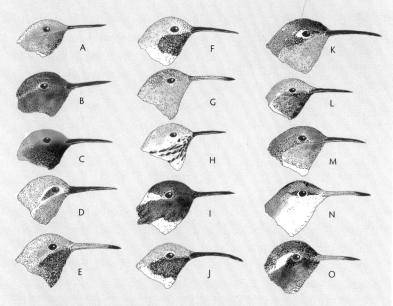

A. Allen's; B. Anna's; C. Black-chinned; D. Blue-throated; E. Broad-billed;
F. Broad-tailed; G. Buff-bellied; H. Calliope; I. Costa's; J. Lucifer; K. Magnificent;
L. Ruby-throated; M. Rufous; N. Violet-crowned; O. White-eared

The bills of North American hummingbirds exhibit a range of lengths, adaptations that reflect a specialization for targeting different sources of nectar. These variations are relatively small compared to hummingbird species from Central and South America, where competition for food and a greater variety of food sources have influenced the development of bills that match the specific flower sizes and shapes.

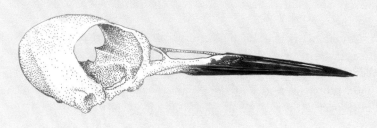

House Finches and other seed-eating passerines have a groove in their upper bills that they use to open seeds. Pressure from the lower bill pushes up on a seed as it is held steady in this groove, helping to pop open the hull. These small birds can remove the hulls from dozens of seeds a minute.

acquires and manipulates its food sources (see the Variations in Bill Shape sidebar). Not surprisingly, raptors have stronger bills and stronger bill muscles than songbirds, the better to grasp and tear their prey. Songbirds that eat seeds have shorter and stouter bills than those of birds that eat insects. Woodpecker bills are among the toughest, reflecting their roles in pounding through bark and wood.

In many bird species, bills are longer or larger in one sex or the other; for example, the female Long-billed Curlew's bill is much longer than the male's. Another sex-related difference, though rare in North American species, is seen in a few species such as the American Avocet: females have bills that curve upward more than those in males. The young of birds with elongated beaks, such as hummingbirds and curlews, hatch with much shorter bills that then grow as the birds mature.

Variations in bill sizes and shapes reflect the preferred foods of different species. The bills of hummingbirds found in North America vary in length from $9/_{16}$ inch to almost 1 inch (1.4-2.5 centimeters) but differ little in shape, reflecting a relatively similar diet throughout their geographical range (see the Bills of North American Hummingbirds sidebar). Bills of Central and South American hummingbirds vary much more in both length and shape due to more variation in plant food sources and species, so these species have become specialists relying on a narrow range of flowers year-round. Their bills' shape and size vary according to the structure of the blossoms they favor.

Although their primary diet is nectar, hummingbirds feed on insects during some parts of their annual feeding cycles, especially early in the year before sources of nectar are widely available and more protein is needed for their young. The bills of a few hummingbird species (though not any species found in North America) have tiny serrations along the edges of the bills to help catch and hold insects.

Many seedeaters, such as the American Goldfinch, use their short cone-shaped bills to select single seeds. The upper bill has grooves along each side that fit with the convex edge of the lower bill as the bills come together. The groove holds the edge of a seed in place as the lower bill's sharp edge pushes against the husk and cracks it to

Depending on the species, birds have different capabilities in how wide they are able to open their bills, an adaptation related to their primary food source. Swallows, such as this Tree Swallow, are noted for their extreme gape, a helpful adaptation as they forage for insects on the wing. *(Photo by Gerald A. DeBoer)*

extract the seed. This groove varies in width, with the widest part to the rear. Larger husks fit here and smaller husks fit farther forward, where the groove is narrower.

In general, though bills in seedeaters are primarily cone-shaped, they vary in depth and width according to the size of the seeds in a bird's primary diet. These measurements correlate with the musculature that powers the bill. The wider and deeper the bill, the greater the force capable of being exerted to remove a seed from its husk.

The bills of swallows, flycatchers, and similar insectivores are relatively broad, a profile well adapted to snatch individual smaller insects when the bird is on the wing. Swallows have fairly small bills that can open wide, which is effective for scooping insects out of the air although not as precisely as the larger bills of flycatchers, a group of birds that typically target individual insects, requiring more precise aim. In many species that specialize in catching insects in the air, their bills are also equipped with ligaments that accelerate the speed that the upper and lower bills close, improving the trap rate. Wood Storks, which mostly forage for ground- and water-dwelling prey, also have fast bill reflexes, among the fastest reaction time for vertebrates.

Warblers, wrens, and similar species use their narrow forceps-like bills to forage for individual insects on foliage or the surface of tree

Species that feed on fish, such as this Double-crested Cormorant, have a distinctive hook at the tip of their upper bill. The feature is also present in seabirds such as pelicans.

bark, a shape ideal for accurately aiming at their targets. Flickers and other woodpeckers have bills adapted to chiseling openings into tree bark, a tough job requiring structural strength as well as an appropriate shape for cutting into wood.

Bills of insectivores that target larger insects and other invertebrates are generally wider at the base and more robust; American Robins are one example. Robins and related species have an extended diet that includes foliage, buds, seeds, nuts, and fruits in certain seasons; the shape of their bills reflects an ability to securely grab larger insects as well as larger berries and seeds.

The bills of some species that feed on fish are hooked at the end, giving them an advantage in holding slippery prey. Raptors also have hooked bills, an adaptation that is effective in dismembering prey after capture.

Vegetarian waterfowl like Mallards and Pintails can identify food in dark or murky water by touch. Bills of shorebirds are soft and flexible around the edges, with sensory organs that function much like those in human fingers. Recent studies show that this kind of pressure-sensitive capability matches that of star-nosed moles, which forage in the dark and rely on their snouts to identify food.

The bills of different family groups of waterfowl vary according to what kinds of food they forage for. Pintails have narrow bills and

Nostrils (nares) are found in all birds, but their size, shape, and position vary from species to species. In some birds, such as doves, the operculum covers the nostrils. From top to bottom: Ferruginous Hawk; Mourning Dove; Canvasback. *(Photos, top to bottom, by Bill Florence, JaredwellS007, Harold Stiver)*

feed primarily on seeds; shovelers have broader bills, effective at foraging for aquatic insects and other invertebrates; mergansers have serrated bills for catching fish; geese have shorter, narrower, hard-edged bills with minimal lamellae to pull, prune, and cut plant material on land and underwater.

Nostrils: Almost all birds found in North America have nostril holes located in the upper bill, closer to the skull than the tip. The scientific term for this feature is nares. Some birds that forage for food underwater, such as cormorants, have nostrils that become permanently sealed in adults; these species breathe only through their mouths.

Nostrils of turkeys, owls, eagles, and falcons are enclosed by a fleshy structure called the cere, with differences in size, shape, color, and texture depending on the species. It is a featherless area at the base of the bill in raptors, an area where feathers would get soiled as they use their bills to rip flesh from their prey.

Although similar in appearance to the cere, the operculum is a different feature present in some species, such as pigeons. Unlike the cere, which is part

Falcons have a protrusion on the upper bill called the tomial tooth (edge highlighted here for emphasis), which fits with corresponding notches on the lower bill. This Peregrine Falcon has just used this feature to feed. *(Photo by Michal Ninger)*

of the upper bill, the operculum is a structure at the base of the bill. In diving seabirds, it prevents water from being inhaled; in land birds, it blocks pollen. Highly visible in pigeons and doves, it closes the nostrils when an adult pigeon has its head in its chick's throat feeding it liquid known as "pigeon's milk."

Some species may also have stiff hairs known as rictal bristles, similar to feathers, on either side of the gape. Flycatchers, woodpeckers, and a few other species share this characteristic. Rictal bristles were traditionally thought to improve the ability of insect-eating birds to capture prey on the wing, but they probably function to deflect insect parts from the bird's eyes as it catches its prey. Crows, however, have nasal bristles that extend from the forehead over the nostrils to protect the nostrils from food while they feed.

Other structures: The upper bill of some falcons features a pointed protrusion along its outer edges called the tomial tooth, which fits into a notch in the lower bill. This useful tool for grasping and killing prey improves the efficiency with which the bill can sever the spinal cord of a small animal. This bill projection can be distinctive enough in size and shape to identify a particular species. The tomial tooth is part of the bill sheath, not the bony structure of the bill itself, to allow it to regenerate from wear.

Other bird species may have another kind of variation in bill adaptation: a ridge of serrated projections on either edge of the upper and lower bills. These projections provide a tooth-like grip that improves effectiveness in grasping prey. Serrations such as these are found in some woodpeckers and some fish-eating birds, the better to grip their squirming prey. These keratinous serrations sometimes have the appearance of tiny teeth, but they do not have the structure or enamel coating of true teeth like those in mammals, nor are they used to chew.

Ducks and geese have a related adaptation in their bills: rows of bristle-like lamellae that line the edges. Flamingos and most waterfowl have this feature on both upper and lower bills. The shape and size of lamellae vary from species to species and are adapted to different kinds of food sources and feeding behavior. Canada

Bills on some birds, such as the Common Merganser (top left), are serrated along the edges, an adaptation that improves their ability to catch and hold their food. *(Photo by Daniel Bruce Lacy)* The Snow Goose (right) and other goose species have a related adaptation—modified bristles called lamellae that sift food particles from water. Lamellae are common in waterfowl, but differ in size and form from species to species. The Northern Shoveler (bottom left) has thin, hairlike lamellae, an adaptation, along with its wide bill, that allows it to extract tiny edible particles from water and mud. *(Photo by Brian Lasenby)*

Geese have harder, sharper lamellae; Northern Shovelers have very thin, hairlike lamellae, which can filter out food particles as small as diatoms.

Lamellae, which can be somewhat pliable in some species, can function to grip food items, but their main purpose is filtering. Water captured in a bird's mouth during feeding is strained out through these lamellae, which retain edible food pieces. Snow Geese have bills with a slight downward curve along their edges, called a "grinning patch." The lamellae of some waterfowl provide an effective drain site where water inside the bill is concentrated and pushed out through the lamellae.

The upper bill can be marked by a ridge that runs along the center from tip to base in some species. This center line is the culmen or dorsal ridge. More distinctive in some species than others, it provides a standard of measurement for ornithologists: from its attachment point on the skull to its tip, the length is a benchmark for age, sex, and species. The culmen varies in shape and color in different species; it can be a distinctive mark or barely visible.

All waterfowl have another unique feature on their bills: a hardened "nail" at the tip of the upper bill. This addition, more pro-

Some waterfowl, such as this Mallard, have a small hardened extension at the tip of the upper bill. Referred to as a "nail," this feature improves the duck's effectiveness at foraging through mud. *(Photo by TPROduction)*

nounced on some species than others, is an advantage when sifting through soft soil or mud.

Nestlings in many bird species have another special feature: the tissue lining the upper and lower bills may be brightly colored, some with markings such as dark spots or bands, all of which help guide their parents when they deliver food. When flashed, these features may also trigger parents' feeding behavior.

TONGUE

After its bill, a bird's tongue may be its most essential eating tool. Birds' tongues have often been portrayed as less complex than those of humans and other mammals, but this portrayal doesn't take into account how much more a bird must accomplish in food selection and manipulation without the use of hands and fingers.

Bird tongues vary widely in size, shape, and dexterity, a range that is among the most varied in the animal kingdom (see the Bird Tongues sidebar). These variations and the range of functionality reflect what birds eat—tiny seeds require different handling than live fish do—and what has to be done to ingest the food before it enters the digestive system. The tongues of various bird species can trap, clamp, flip, sort, extract, and position food for swallowing, as well as hold and channel fluids such as nectar and sap.

In all birds, the central structure in tongues is a bone. More accurately, it is a complex arrangement of bones, cartilage, ligaments, muscles, and tendons formally known as the hyoid apparatus, with a hyoid bone at the center. Humans have this bone, as do all vertebrates, but its shape, size, and specific location vary according to the type of animal and its function. In birds, it is a thin Y- or U-shaped bone suspended by muscles and connective tissue, part of the support for and function of the tongue. In the human body, it is the only bone that does not connect directly to any other bone.

The hyoid apparatus is the primary mechanism for moving the tongue, responsible for providing internal support and extending the capabilities of this fleshy appendage. In humans, the hyoid and its position near the larynx are important for speech; many scientists believe our voice developed primarily because of the hyoid bone.

BIRD TONGUES

Tongues perform the same functions for birds as they do for mammals—and more. Lacking paws or hands, birds have adapted to perform some of the functions of hands and fingers with their tongues, using them in conjunction with their bills to manipulate food.

A Herring Gull tongue (top left) has a backward-pointing structure to help pull material toward its esophagus. *(Photo by Barry Paterson)*

In songbirds, like the Eastern Bluebird (top right), the tip of the tongue functions to help manipulate insect prey. *(Photo by Bonnie Taylor Barry)*

A hummingbird tongue, like that on the Anna's Hummingbird (bottom left), probes flowers to capture nectar. *(Photo by Jennifer Bosvert)*

The Canada Goose (bottom right), like other waterfowl, grabs grass and other vegetation by grasping it between the tongue and the edge of the bill. *(Photo by Sandra Standbridge)*

In some reptiles, a modification of the hyoid created the ability to capture prey. In all animals, the hyoid provides assistance in swallowing, as well as vocalizations in mammals.

Tongues of bird species vary, relating to their diet and method of feeding, and their hyoid bones vary in size and shape accordingly. If you can observe the tongue in a living bird, what you see is typically just the fleshy tissue attached to the hyoid bone underneath. The bigger the tongue, the bigger the hyoid bone.

Because muscles produce force only by contracting, the tongue cannot be pushed out of the bill but must be pulled, a function that the hyoid apparatus provides for all birds. A linked series of muscles pull on the thin, flexible arms of the hyoid bone, extending it forward, and a parallel set pulls in the opposite direction to retract it.

Geniohyoid muscles propel the tongue out of the bill by contracting between their two attachment sites: the farthest end of the hyoid bone's arm and the underside of the lower bill. As the geniohyoid muscles contract, the arms are pulled away from their termination points and down, around, and forward. This action pushes forward the narrow stem of the Y, most of which consists of the tongue.

A different set of muscles, also attached around the arms of the hyoid bone, contract to pull the tongue back into the bill. One study concluded that the muscles that extend the tongue have a combined length of at least three times the length of the tongue itself (see the Extreme Extension of Bird Tongues sidebar). This is necessary because muscle fibers in all animals can contract to only half of their resting length at most; actions that require more length than this are generated by successively overlapping bundles of muscle fibers.

After a bird flicks its tongue forward, it can use it to capture food and bring it into its mouth, then position the food for swallowing. Generally, diets that involve the most manipulation of food in the bill, such as severing, crushing, or hulling, are linked to species with more-complex tongues. Studies document the dexterity with which birds' tongues can flip or rotate seeds or insects. Birds that ingest large food items (think pelicans that swallow fish whole) have the least complex tongues.

EXTREME EXTENSION OF BIRD TONGUES

Woodpecker and hummingbird tongues are unique for the distance they can extend beyond the tip of their bills, an adaptation that reflects how they acquire their food. To manage this extreme extension, these birds rely on the hyoid apparatus at its maximum capability. These birds feature hyoid bones with the greatest relative length in the animal kingdom, structures that allow their tongues to extend as far as the length of their elongated bills and beyond. To gain maximum extension, the arms of these hyoid bones are thin, flexible, and very long. In both of these bird types the hyoid arms curl back, around, and over the skull, terminating near the nostrils. In some species, they extend well into the nostrils.

Hummingbirds and woodpeckers do not hatch with fully developed tongues. The unique length of the tongue in these birds grows as nestlings mature into adults.

The hyoid also provides important support for the behavior woodpeckers are well known for: hammering holes into trees. The elastic horns of the hyoid, which curl back and around the back of the skull, add a cushioning effect for the shock produced by this hammering.

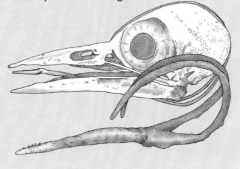

In woodpeckers, the tongue locates and adheres to insects, the targeted food source. To accomplish this, the tip of a woodpecker tongue features a variety of barbs, bristles, and sticky saliva, which are very effective at working like a spear to ensnare prey. Pileated Woodpeckers have relatively short tongues with backward-facing barbs near the tip; flicker tongues have flatter tips.

The tip of a hummingbird tongue is divided into two side-by-side halves with edges lined with flexible petal-like fringes. The fringes curl around a source of nectar, trapping the fluid until the tongue is withdrawn into the bill. As the tongue flicks out again, the edges of the bill squeeze out the liquid so it can be swallowed. This Buff-bellied Hummingbird is likely cleaning its tongue. *(Photo by Norman Bateman)*

Hummingbird tongues are similar to those of woodpeckers in their engineering, but they are designed for a different food source: plant nectar. Correspondingly, the tip of the hummingbird tongue forks into two thin halves with rows of tiny fringes along the edges. These fringes are smallest at the end, gradually increasing in size toward the back of the fork. When the tongue is inserted into a source of liquid, the fringes unfurl, then close around the fluid, trapping it as the tongue is withdrawn. As the bird retracts its tongue, its upper and lower bills press together, squeezing the trapped nectar out and toward the back of the bird's mouth.

Hummingbird tongues can flick in and out as quickly as fifteen times a second; for many natural nectar sources, the bird takes only a second or two to remove all of the nectar. This extraction method has only recently been discovered; for more than one hundred years, observers believed that the tongues of these tiny flying animals pulled in liquid through capillary action.

Because raptors feed on animals, the shape or function of their tongues are not specialized for feeding. Raptors of different sizes typically dismantle large animals piece by piece, principally using the bill and talons, and swallow small animals whole. But some raptor species such as vultures have spine-like papillae (hairs or bristles) at the back or edges of their tongues, which aid in grasping and removing tissue from carcasses.

These papillae on the tongue's surface, which help the tongue to hold food and move it back into the throat, vary in size and shape in different birds. In some waterfowl, such as mergansers, papillae are more like spines, providing a more effective tool for holding slippery live fish. Geese forage for plant material by grasping it with the serrated edges of their bills, and the tough papillae on their tongues act as reinforcements for pulling and tearing off vegetation.

Pelicans catch and swallow fish whole with little assistance from their tongues, which are not much larger than toothpicks. But unlike other birds that swallow their food whole, the pelican also ingests up to 12 quarts (11 liters) of water along with its prey, which it holds in its pouch, or gular sac. Its tongue allows the water to drain out of the pouch before the pelican swallows its catch.

The largest group of birds, the passerines (which includes songbirds), eat a wide variety of items, some of them specializing in seeds and grains, fruit, nectar, insects, and even larger animals, while others take a wide variety of prey. Despite the range of food types, most members of this group share a basic tongue shape: a very narrow triangle, with the narrow end pointing forward, and it does not extend beyond the bill when in use. Typically, the surface of passerine tongues has small barbs facing backward, which draw food deeper into the bill and then the throat. Some passerine tongues have a split at the tip, and many species have feather-like fringes at the tip as well—both features that help in sensing, tasting, and selecting food. Birds with a split at the tip of their tongue mostly

The pouch on pelicans expands considerably to hold its catch, which initially includes water. (Photo by Nancy Bauer)

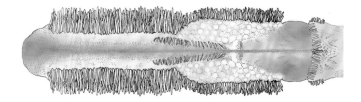

Waterfowl that feed on plants in the water rely on fringes on the edges of their tongue to filter small organic matter. This fringe is not hair but papillae, thin strands of tissue that act like a sieve or comb. Different species have different amounts and arrangements of these papillae, relating to their dependence on filter feeding. The Northern Shoveler is a duck with one of the greatest filtering adaptations, as depicted here. (Illustration adapted from Leon Gardner in *Proceedings of the United States National Museum* 67, 1925)

A small hardened plate at the tip of the tongue of most geese and ducks helps them grasp vegetation. Called a lingual nail, it is barely visible on the end of the tongue of this Canada Goose. (*Photo by Ray Hennessy*)

feed on nectar. The split, along with fringes, allow the tongue to curl and form a brush-like sponge that holds fluid.

Many waterfowl have additional fringes across the surface of their tongues, which play a significant role in filter feeding, extracting bits of plant or animal food from water and mud. In a species such as the Northern Shoveler, this fringe forms a noticeable band along the sides of the tongue, with exceptionally longer and denser fringe. A waterfowl draws water into its bill, then closes its bill and creates a slight vacuum by depressing its tongue, forcing the water back out through the filtering fringe. Mallards and teals use a different system to push material through the fringe: swinging their heads from side to side while their bills are under the surface, continuously flushing food particles through the bristles.

In some bird species, zones in the surface of the tongue are hardened with keratin to improve handling of plant material. Geese, ducks, and a few other species have this adaptation, creating a specialized feature called a lingual nail, which gives them more pulling power.

SENSORY PHYSIOLOGY

Birds, like other animals, have anatomical features that enable them to see, hear, smell, taste, and touch. These sensory organs play a role in how birds eat and correspond to variations in how they find their food sources, differentiate between edible and inedible material, and respond to threats and opportunities in various habitats.

VISION

The superior vision of birds is directly involved in most of the critical areas that define their lives: mating, migrating, competing, self-defense—and, of course, feeding. The types of food that birds depend on to survive, and their ability to find it, are linked to the anatomy of their eyes as well as the behavior dependent on their vision.

All birds, even those that rely on other senses to find food, share essential characteristics with those of all other vertebrates, including humans. Variations in how much and how well birds can see are closely linked to the behavior associated with their diets. Of course, vision is also a critical defense against predators.

Shape is one key characteristic that sets bird eyes apart from those of mammals and many other animals. In most mammals, including humans, eyes are spherical or nearly so, but various bird species have eyes that range from flattened to tubular in shape (see the Bird Eye Shapes sidebar). This variation reduces the volume and weight of eyes relative to a bird's size; eyes and brain compete for space in a bird's skull, and weight is a general adaptation that impacts flight. The most common shape among all birds is flattened; tubular eyes are most common in owls and a few other raptors. Despite an

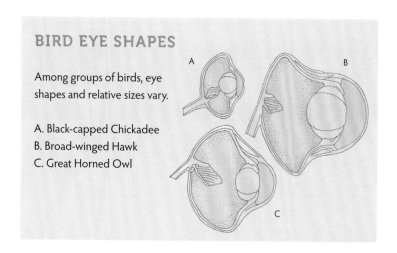

BIRD EYE SHAPES

Among groups of birds, eye shapes and relative sizes vary.

A. Black-capped Chickadee
B. Broad-winged Hawk
C. Great Horned Owl

evolutionary trend toward saving weight for flying, bird eyes are relatively heavy; in most birds they outweigh their brains.

For all bird species, eyes are large in proportion to their heads. The eyes, in fact, are the largest organs in a bird's head, larger than the brain. This is not surprising, because at least in general, eye size is directly related to quality of vision: the bigger, the better. This crowds the available space, and the result is eyes that must sit closer together inside the skull than in most other animals. In some birds, the eyes are so close together they are separated by only a thin layer of bone.

Ostrich eyes, at the extreme in size, are about the largest of any animal that lives on land, at an average of 2 inches (5 centimeters) in diameter; for comparison, elephant eyes are about 1.5 inches (3.8 centimeters) in diameter, human eyes about 1 inch (2.5 centimeters) across. The eyes of eagles and large owls are about the same size as human eyes; raptor eyes are the largest among North American birds. Also, raptor species generally have eyes that are about one and a half to more than two times larger than the eyes of birds of similar size that do not hunt live animals. As a rule, the faster a species of raptor flies, the greater the resolution power of its vision.

Larger eyes are also linked to activity during lower available light. Birds that are most active at dawn or just after generally have larger eyes than species that forage in full sunlight. Owls, as nocturnal

Birds typically use only one eye to get a close look at an object, as this American Robin demonstrates while searching for earthworms.

hunters, are the extreme of this equation, with eyes that are among the largest in proportion to head size among all birds.

Fields of view: The placement of a species's eyes in the skull is an initial clue to its diet. All birds have binocular vision, the better to focus, judge distances, and adjust reaction times. But most species use their eyes one at a time for close up, monocular vision. Most perching birds (passerines), for instance, spend much of their time focusing up close, their normal span for feeding. To use their most acute vision, they examine their food with only one eye.

Similar to the way most humans have a dominant hand, some birds' dependence on a single eye for much of their vision has generated apparent visual "handedness," more formally called laterality, in some species. Ornithologists have discovered that some species repeatedly favor one eye over the other when involved in certain activities, such as foraging or approaching other birds. Peregrine Falcons, for example, mostly use their right eye once they have fixed on a target. Pigeons are also known to favor their right eye when homing. In some laboratory experiments with birds, right eyes outperformed left eyes.

FIELDS OF VIEW

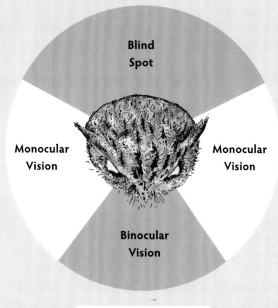

Blind Spot

Monocular Vision

Monocular Vision

Binocular Vision

Horizontal Field of View

Vertical Field of View

PARTS OF A BIRD'S EYE

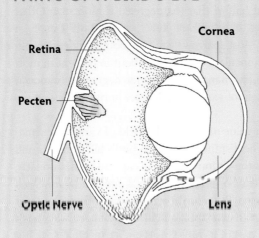

Retina

Cornea

Pecten

Optic Nerve

Lens

The main parts of a bird's eye are relatively familiar, like those of other vertebrates, with one main exception. Located at the back of a bird's eye is a small structure called the pecten, a dark projection from the surface of the retina.

Birds' Eye Movability table). The advantage is a loss of weight, the ever-present factor attached to flight efficiency.

The American Goldfinch can move its eyes 66 degrees in the horizontal plane. Pigeons have been measured moving their eyes up to 20 degrees, but typically they move their eyes no more than 2–5 degrees whether the bird is on the ground or flying. In owls these eye muscles are barely functional. The Great Horned Owl has less than 2 degrees of eye movement; Barn Owls about the same, at 3 percent. Eye movements in the Cooper's Hawk are limited to about 8 degrees and in American Kestrels it's even less, about 1 degree. Head movements make up for any restrictions in eye movements, supporting the essential functions of vision.

Some of the eye muscles in birds contract to alter the shape of the lens (see the Parts of a Bird's Eye sidebar), changing its focus. To compensate for a relative lack of eye movability, birds have very mobile necks. Much of the mobility comes from the number of cervical vertebrae, from thirteen to twenty-five depending on the species (most mammals, including humans, have only seven). Owls have fourteen cervical vertebrae, which give them the equivalent of up to 270 degrees of eye movement; humans are limited to about 180 degrees.

Parts of the eye: All color is detected by the photoreceptors called cones that are located in the retina of the eyes. Human eyes have three types of cones that combine to yield a full spectrum: red, green, and blue. Birds are even better equipped, with four types of cones: red, green, blue, and ultraviolet. Other animals, including most insects, fish, amphibians, and reptiles, also have this UV-detection capability.

Photoreceptors called rods detect light but not color. The number and density of rods determine how well an animal can see in reduced light. Most perching birds, which are mostly active in daylight, have many more cones than rods, with the opposite true in owls, whose retinas are about 90 percent rods.

Light receptors in the eye are at their densest in the center of the retina, a zone called the fovea. In bird eyes, foveas have slightly more

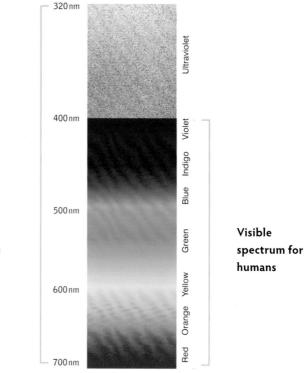

320 nm

400 nm

500 nm

600 nm

700 nm

Ultraviolet

Violet

Indigo

Blue

Green

Yellow

Orange

Red

Visible spectrum for some birds

Visible spectrum for humans

(Adapted from graphic by solar22/Shutterstock)

than 600 cones per square inch (400,000 per square millimeter), which is more than twice as many as humans have. Raptors can have more than 1,500 per square inch (about 1 million per square millimeter). This foveal density determines image detail and explains how hawks can spot prey from much farther away than other birds can.

Most animals have eyes with a single fovea. Some bird species, however, have vision enhanced by a second fovea, a noted feature in bird groups such as kingfishers, swallows, hummingbirds, and hawks. In these birds, a temporal fovea provides enhanced binocular vision to the front and a lateral fovea enhances monocular vision to the sides.

Bird eyes have a feature not found in the eyes of other animals, though some reptile eyes have a similar formation: a dark structure called the pecten projecting from the surface of the retina. It is composed of thin folds of tissue and its function is debated; the leading concepts suggest that the high density of blood vessels found in these structures provide nutrition (in the blood) to retinas.

In order to keep their eyes functioning at peak efficiency, birds have specialized eyelids. In addition to an upper and a lower outer lid, birds have a movable lid called the nictitating membrane, which wipes across the cornea from the inner corner of the eye to the outer, at right angles to the eyelids. This third lid provides important protection for the cornea as a shield against potential damage from intrusions. This membrane's type of redundant protection is also found in most reptiles, fish, amphibians, some species of shark, and a few mammals. The nictitating membrane also cleans the lens as it moves and helps distribute moisture from glands around the eye.

This immature Cooper's Hawk demonstrates its third eyelid, the nictitating membrane, which helps protect bird eyes and keeps them clean. *(Photo by Stacey Ann Alberts)*

This membrane is usually translucent, allowing birds to maintain continual visual surveillance, an asset when tracking food sources or watching out for predators. In a few types of birds, such as owls, this membrane is opaque. In some diving birds, such as cormorants and loons, the nictitating membrane is relatively clear in a circular zone at the center; when underwater and closed, the membrane allows these birds an unobstructed view of their prey.

Visual acuity: An aspect of avian eyes that is important for feeding is their ability to perceive motion. Motion detection in animal eyes is determined by the flicker fusion rate, measured in hertz (Hz) or cycles per second, the frequency at which motion is perceived as steady. Human eyes operate at about 60 Hz (the same rate at which high-definition television is broadcast); this is also referred to as sixty frames per second. In comparison, early movies were shot at sixteen frames per second, which resulted in visible flickering. Birds detect motion at about 100 Hz, and some species may average more than 130 Hz, which gives them a decided edge in the ability to identify and react to food on the move, such as dragonflies and mayflies.

Birds such as eagles and owls have definitively better eyesight than humans. It is likely that all birds have better vision than we do, but studies show that, among birds, some species have a range of visual capabilities. In a comparison of Carolina Chickadees, Tufted Titmice, and White-breasted Nuthatches, nuthatches had the most visual acuity and chickadees the least, and chickadees and titmice had wider binocular fields of vision than nuthatches. Differences in these measures of visual capability relate to differing foraging strategies: nuthatches seek food on tree trunks and larger branches; chickadees focus on twigs and smaller limbs; titmice utilize both of these as well as hunt on the ground.

Avian eyesight has also been influenced, along with variations in foraging activity and type of favored habitats, by dangers from specific predators. Open habitats such as fields and meadows benefit eyes with photoreceptors that are more effective at scanning the sky, where raptors are a major threat. In closed habitats such as forests and thickets, eyes that excel at motion detection on the

The external ear opening in this American Robin nestling is visible before its feathers grow in and cover it. *(Photo by Anne Schwartz)*

ground are of greater value, such as the Dark-eyed Junco's and the Wood Thrush's.

HEARING

To animals, including birds, the sound of the environment around them provides essential cues for action, from mating to territorial defense to escape from predators. Most birds do not depend on hearing as a primary tool for feeding, but it can be an important asset. Most ornithologists believe it is the second most important sense after vision.

Parts of the ear: Avian ears have three components: the outer ear, the middle ear, and the inner ear, which are roughly comparable to ears in mammals, including humans. But bird ears are more closely related to ears in reptiles than other animal groups.

Unlike mammals, birds (as well as reptiles, amphibians, and fish) lack the visible outer structure that provides the distinctive external form of mammalian ears. Bird ears, hidden behind a layer of specialized feathers, are openings in the skull, below and slightly behind the eyes. Ear openings vary in shape, from round to narrow slits, with varied patterns.

The feathers that cover the ear openings differ in size and shape from flight feathers. They protect the ear opening without

BIRDS' EARDRUMS

Owls have the largest ratio of the size of their eardrums to the size of their foot plates, a relationship that represents a key factor in detecting sound. Grebes and songbirds have the smallest ratio, generally between 20:1 and 30:1.

SPECIES	SIZE OF EARDRUM (IN SQUARE CENTIMETERS)	RATIO OF EARDRUM SIZE TO FOOT PLATE SIZE
Long-eared Owl	0.480	40:1
Ring-necked Pheasant	0.368	28:1
Mallard	0.285	26:1
Common Blackbird	0.160	22:1
Domestic Chicken	0.291	22:1
House Sparrow	0.091	22:1

restricting airflow during flight and allow the transmission of sound during flight. In some diving seabirds, these feathers, and the muscles that control a flap under them, close over the ear opening while the bird is submerged, keeping water out of the middle ear.

The muscles that control this flap form a ring that also helps funnel sound into the middle ear. The size and shape of this muscular funnel varies, typically reflecting preferred habitats and activities. Most birds, including some seabirds and raptors that rely primarily on sight for hunting, have outer ears with little or no such funneling, whereas some species of owls rely entirely on sound for hunting and have well-developed funnels.

Some owl species, particularly Barn Owls, also have a pattern of outer ear

With the exception of the Snowy Owl, all North American owl species, including this Barn Owl, have distinctive feather patterns around their eyes, called a facial ruff. These dish-shaped structures funnel sound to the external ear openings, located behind and just below the eyes. *(Photo by A. S. Floro)*

PARTS OF A BIRD'S EAR

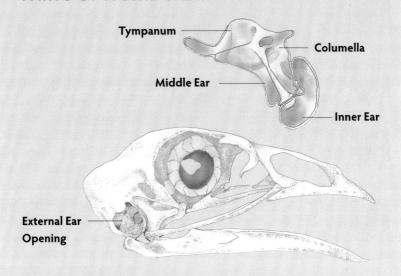

The skull of the turkey illustrated here shows the placement of the external ear opening and location of the middle and inner ear, as enlarged on the right. The middle and inner components of the bird ear function the same as that in mammals, but with a different type of mechanism: a central bone called the columella transmits vibrations created by sound from the eardrum (tympanum) to the fluid-filled inner ear.

feathers that form an additional large, shallow funnel that helps condense and channel sound. This feature, called a facial disc or ruff (in conjunction with specialized components of the middle and inner ear), provides these owls with the most sensitive hearing among all twenty-three orders of birds. These dish-shaped antennae are visibly oriented around their eyes, but they actually funnel sound to their ears, which are located just below and behind their eyes.

A bird's ear opening contains the tympanic membrane that covers the middle ear. One of the biggest differences between bird and mammal ears is in the engineering of the middle ear. In

LIMITS OF BIRDS' HEARING

SPECIES	HIGH-FREQUENCY LIMIT (IN KHZ)	LOW-FREQUENCY LIMIT (IN KHZ)
Barn Owl	12.00	0.32
American Robin	8.73	0.34
Northern Bobwhite	8.70	2.13
Field Sparrow	8.65	0.32
Dark-eyed Junco	8.25	0.68
Red-winged Blackbird	8.20	0.33
Rock Pigeon	7.50	0.05
European Starling	6.43	0.23
Blue Jay	6.31	0.28
House Finch	6.00	0.44
Western Meadowlark	5.55	0.37
American Kestrel	5.25	0.36
Wild Turkey	5.25	0.29
Mallard	5.22	0.32
American Crow	4.57	0.47
Great Horned Owl	4.15	0.03
Domestic Chicken	4.10	0.20

Barn Owls have the highest threshold of hearing of all North American birds.

humans and other mammals, this structure has three tiny bones, the incus (anvil), the malleus (hammer), and the stapes (stirrup), but birds have only one bone, the columella. The size and shape of the columella vary among species; generally speaking, the larger the columella, the more sensitive the hearing.

As with mammals, the middle ear in birds contains a group of specialized hairlike sensory cilia that generate signals from physical vibrations. The bone in the middle ear, along with other characteristics of the middle and inner ear (where the cochlea is

HEARING AND NOISE RANGES

VERTEBRATES	HEARING RANGE (IN HZ)	SOUND GENERATORS	COMMON NOISE RANGE (IN HZ)
cats	55–7700	light rain	13–2500
dogs	64–4400	mosquito	17–2000
humans	20–4000	dog whistle	23–5400
birds	10–4000	hand clapping	200
porpoises	75–1500	middle C in music scale	2048
elephants	17–1100	air conditioner	6000
goldfish	20–300		

located), contribute to the range of sounds that birds can detect (see the Birds' Eardrums sidebar).

One of the most critical factors influencing hearing ability in birds is the development of the sound-detecting components of their brains. Specialized cells in the nervous system called ganglia (also found in most other animals) fulfill this task; the more ganglia, the better the hearing. Some species of crows have up to 13,400 ganglial cells; Barn Owls have as many as 47,600.

Hearing ability: As a general comparison, the ability of birds to discriminate different frequencies of sound may be only half that of humans. The range of human hearing spans about 20 Hz to about 20,000 Hz, or 20 kiloHertz (kHz), with most of the sounds we hear ranging between 4 kHz and 8 kHz. The normal range of hearing for birds is frequencies between 1 kHz and about 4 kHz. Frequencies correlate to octaves: humans can detect about nine octaves, but birds hear only about five, with variations between species (see the Limits of Birds' Hearing table).

Pigeons are thought to hear best at 1–2 kHz, with an upper limit at 10 kHz. House Sparrows detect sounds between 675 Hz and 11 kHz. Owls have the most sensitive hearing, detecting sounds between 100 Hz and 18 kHz. Birds share a similar range of hearing with their reptilian cousins, crocodiles. No birds are capable of hearing ultrasonic frequencies (over 20 kHz), such as those detectable by dogs (see the Hearing and Noise Ranges table).

At the low end, a few studies report that some birds can detect sounds as low as 2 Hz (frequencies below 20 Hz are known as infrasonic), but 200 Hz is possibly the limit for low frequencies. Some birds also seem to be able to "hear" or at least detect sounds that are at extremely low frequencies, below the threshold of normal hearing. Pigeons, for one, have been tested for such ability in laboratory settings. This kind of sensory input may relate to tactile inputs from vibrations, which all birds can sense, and function as a signal warning of danger, such as the footsteps of predators.

Threshold levels of detection for birds are about the same for sounds from 1 kHz to 4 kHz, but much less sensitive for sounds above and below these frequencies, making them about as sensitive to sound volume as humans. But above 4 kHz, birds' ability to detect sounds drops off as frequencies increase. To detect higher frequencies, the sound source has to be louder. Prolonged exposure to loud sounds damages the sensitive hairlike cilia in the middle ear of birds, just as it does in humans (see the Sound Volume table). As far as ornithologists can determine, however, birds (as well as reptiles, amphibians, and fish) regenerate these cilia and can recover from a loss of hearing. This is especially critical to birds that depend on their hearing to find prey, owls in particular. In one study, Barn

SOUND VOLUME

For reference, a human eardrum bursts at 160 decibels and the human pain threshold is 130 decibels.

SOUND	VOLUME (IN DECIBELS)
large cicadas	120
chain saw from 3 feet away	110
busy traffic from 15 feet away	80
vacuum cleaner from 3 feet away	70
human speech	60
whisper from 3 feet away	20

Plovers, like this American Golden-Plover consuming an aquatic worm, hunt primarily by sight but are capable of using sound to locate prey. *(Photo by Steve Byland)*

Owls were found to retain their hearing as they age, a marked difference compared to humans.

Sound detection: Whatever sensitivity to sound that any bird has, birds have an additional task necessary to have sound make sense: an ability to discriminate critical sound from "noise"—the natural or unnatural buzz from background sources such as wind, other animals, and vehicle traffic. Birds as well as other animals must be able to mask this background sound in order to pay attention to important sounds such as mating calls, predator cries, and potential prey activity. This masking capability is complicated by distance. A bird benefits if it can tell how far away it is from the source of threatening, nonthreatening, and beneficial sounds.

Most bird species that hunt animals for food use sight as the primary sense for location and capture. Most owls use sound cues, but some other kinds of birds use a combination of sight and sound. Robins, for instance, are well known for their preference for earthworms, at least at certain times of the year. When worms emerge on the surface of the soil, typically early in the day, robins are able to find them by sight alone, but when worms are beneath the surface, sound provides birds the cues they need. Robins use a head-cocking posture to pinpoint the sound source, much like the head posture used to visually focus with one eye. The sounds that robins detect must be faint—the rustling of soil particles as worms move through the earth.

In one controlled study, mealworms were offered to captive robins after every potential sensory input was blocked except for hearing. The birds had no problem detecting and capturing the mealworms. By comparison, when white noise was added to tests where other sensory inputs were included, their success rate at finding this prey was reduced. Magpies in Australia were also tested for this ability, with the same outcome. Plovers are also believed to use their hearing to locate prey under sandy surfaces.

Woodpeckers are also capable of detecting insect larvae by listening for them moving or chewing beneath an outer layer of tree bark, though this may not be their primary clue. Most adult boring insects leave telltale holes in the bark that mark their entry or exit locations during the egg-laying phase. Birds use these holes as visual markers. They can also cling to the surface of tree trunks and detect hollow spaces under the bark by tapping with their bills. Hollow wood sounds different from solid wood, potential evidence of adult insects or their larvae.

Owls rely on their hearing when hunting, even though they also have superior eyesight. Various experiments have concluded that night-hunting owls often combine vision with

This Acorn Woodpecker can detect insects (typically beetle adults and larvae) beneath a tree's bark by tapping on the surface with its bill and listening for sounds of movement. Woodpeckers also use their bills to drum on solid objects, especially tree trunks, as a territorial and mating call and are noted for their ability to excavate nest cavities. *(Photo by Robin Keefe)*

Even with its exceptional night vision, this Barred Owl can detect, locate, and capture prey using only its hearing. The large circular feather ruffs around its eyes function as funnels for sound, concentrating it at the ear openings. *(Photo by James Pintar)*

hearing to hunt, but that in complete darkness, they are able to identify and pinpoint the location of prey with hearing alone. Tests have proven that not only does sound allow them to accurately target their prey, they can also adjust their direction in flight to track its movement. Other elements can also be involved as well; owls respond most often to prey sounds that they recognize, such as the frequency and pattern of noise associated with a small rodent scurrying along the surface of the ground. Owls typically do not respond to sounds they are unfamiliar with because experience is an important part of their foraging success.

Not only do prey sounds have characteristics that allow owls to identify what they are hunting, but the owls are also equipped with remarkable abilities in detecting faint sounds. Studies show that, in comparisons with humans at the same distance, owls can detect sounds that are inaudible to humans, at least within the range of frequencies at which humans hear best.

Sound detection in the dark is only part of the task for owls. An owl must also be able to orient where the sound is coming from in order to fly accurately to its source—a potential meal. This performance is possible because of tiny differences in the times that sound is detected by each of their two ears; their brain processes this discrepancy to compute distance and direction.

Some owls have ears with an additional structural accommodation that could make this binaural effect even more effective: the height of their ear openings are asymmetrical between one side and the other. Not all owl species have this characteristic, and the height variation from one side to the other is not always the same in the species that do. It is most pronounced in Barn Owls, whose ear openings are higher on the left side. North American owls with asymmetrical ear openings that are higher on the right include Spotted Owls, Barred Owls, and Great Gray Owls. Great Horned Owls do not have this asymmetry, but it doesn't seem to detract from their hunting skill in the dark.

Echolocation: Some animals emit a vocal signal and find objects through reflected sounds. Bats are well known for their ability to use echolocation to capture flying insects; most use ultrasonic frequencies above 20 kHz. At least sixteen species of birds also have the ability to echolocate, but because there are no birds that can hear in the ultrasonic range, these hunters must rely on lower frequencies. They typically emit vocal "clicks" in a variety of patterns.

Echolocating birds include species in two groups—oilbirds and swiftlets—neither of which are present in North America. Oilbirds, primarily fruit eaters, are thought to use echolocation mostly for direction inside the caves where they nest, but when flying at night, they might possibly use this ability to locate ripe fruit. Swiftlets are insect eaters that mostly feed during daylight. The sounds they emit are most likely ineffective at targeting the small insects they feed on but are thought to help them find their nests inside caves.

Vocalizations: Birds, especially songbirds, are recognized for their distinctive and often tuneful songs, which are associated with attracting mates and defending territory, and calls that identify their family and give warnings.

Passerines are subdivided into two major groups, oscines and suboscines. Oscines are songbirds, species with a vocal organ called the syrinx that generates the vocalizations that characterize the group. About 80 percent of all passerines are oscines. Suboscines produce vocalizations as well, but these sounds are typically less complicated than those of the true songbirds. The only examples of suboscines in North America are members of the family Tyrannidae, which includes flycatchers, kingbirds, pewees, and phoebes.

Some birds are also known to use calls to communicate about food. Adult chickens may use specific calls, or modify specific calls, to indicate the presence of food, the availability of preferred food items, the presence of unpalatable food, and food availability for chicks. A few studies have reported that in the wild, the males of some bird species may use specific calls to indicate the availability of food, as has been shown in American Crows, or as a lure for prospective mates.

Birds known to use food calls include Black-capped Chickadees, Carolina Chickadees, House Sparrows, Cliff Swallows, and ravens, but the practice may be more widespread. In general, the evidence indicates that food calling exists in some bird species, but not much research has been done to determine how it works. Do birds that live

American Coots are typically found in groups swimming or foraging on land during the nonbreeding season, but mating pairs defend their territory while nesting. When in flocks, they are noisy communicators, with calls that establish and maintain the "pecking order" and provide early warnings of danger. The calls are also an effective means for individual birds to locate a flock, indicating the availability of food, although vision might be more effective in daylight. *(Photo by Bob Pool)*

in flocks use food calls more than birds that are solitary? Can one species of bird identify the food calls of another species? With some birds, including American Crows, visual clues are usually also part of a food alert system, and sight may be the primary signal.

Why would a bird open a food source to competition by emitting food calls? One theory is that by having more birds together in a group, the risk to an individual from predation is reduced. Another concept is that this kind of communication provides a two-way benefit: food calls are cooperative behavior with rewards for all participants despite the risk.

Cliff Swallows use food calls, which researchers dub "squeak calls," when they forage for insect swarms; the benefit is that by attracting more foragers, it's easier to track a moving mass of insects. While these swallows are in or near their communal nesting sites, though, their food calls are rare. They are not used consistently while foraging but seem to be most common early in nesting seasons when weather has a negative effect on individual foraging success.

Nestlings of most birds use vocalizations that are certainly associated with food. Although a wide range of species-specific calls are

Parents and nestlings use both visual and auditory signals to communicate about food. This Yellow Warbler feeds caterpillars to its young. *(Photo by James Pintar)*

involved, the message is universal: "feed me!" Parents are generally and instinctively motivated to keep their young fed, but the insistent calls of young birds serve as an additional incentive.

A well-documented problem with food-begging calls from nestlings, however, is predation. Such calls can attract a variety of flying and climbing predators. Some species of birds, including the Eastern Phoebe and Red-winged Blackbird, have developed a response to this threat. Phoebe nestlings do not vocalize for food unless they recognize food calls coming from their parents that indicate they are nearby and available to defend the nest. Blackbird nestlings are quiet until they detect the physical presence of their parents (such as vibrations from landing).

In general, research so far indicates that species with nests that are more vulnerable to predation have nestlings that are less likely to have loud or repetitive food calls. Nest predation may be responsible for up to 80 percent or more of all nestling mortality, suggesting the value of moderation when it comes to nestling vocalization. In a variety of studies, begging sounds from nestlings always increased the rate that nests were targeted by predators. Nest predators such as predatory birds, snakes, and mammals locate and prey on nests using cues other than sound, but at least for predatory birds, sound seems to be a major factor, if not the only influence.

SMELL

Birds have long been thought to have little or no sense of smell. John James Audubon promoted this concept in the early 1820s after running a simple field test with Turkey Vultures. He observed that they flocked to a dummy deer carcass, attracted by sight only, but did not detect a reeking carcass of a hog when it was obscured by brush.

Laughing Gulls gather in flocks as they forage for food. Some gulls, albatross, and petrels, among other seabirds, use smell to locate sources of food. *(Photo by Gerald Marella)*

His experiment was notable for its concept, and the published results influenced generations of bird lovers and ornithologists to believe that birds could not smell. This notion was never universally accepted, however, even during Audubon's life. In the mid-1900s, scientists found that Turkey Vultures actually relied solely on smell to locate prey. Not only odor but also a specific chemical compound emitted by decomposing animal flesh, ethyl mercaptan, identified their preferred food—namely, dead meat.

One of the key findings about the avian sense of smell relates to seabirds. Dimethyl sulfide is a gas produced by phytoplankton, a prime food source for krill, themselves a major food target of different birds—albatross and petrels among them—as well as fish and marine mammals. Bernice Wenzel, one of the pioneering modern researchers into olfactory capabilities in seabirds, concluded in an *Audubon Magazine* article by Nancy Averett that they "have their own map, an odor landscape, in the air above the water."

BIRDS' OLFACTORY BULBS

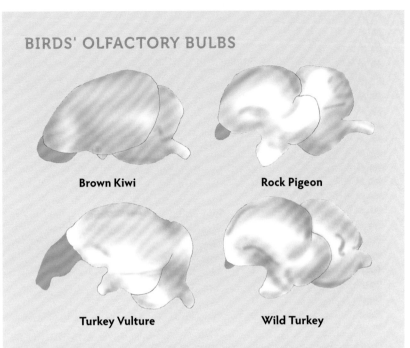

Brown Kiwi

Rock Pigeon

Turkey Vulture

Wild Turkey

One of the factors that influences how well birds can detect smells is the olfactory bulb and its size relative to the brain's. The range of brains depicted here represents both ends of the spectrum, with the Turkey Vulture having one of the largest olfactory bulbs among all birds—worldwide, not just in North America—and the Wild Turkey one of the smallest.

Birds sense odors using roughly the same anatomy as mammals: an olfactory system that combines nasal cavities with a specialized part of the brain, the olfactory bulb. Scent that is inhaled into nasal cavities is detected by neurons in the lining of the nasal structure, and signals are sent directly to the olfactory bulb through the olfactory nerve.

There is an olfactory bulb in every bird species, but the size varies considerably, with seabirds having the largest measured so far, up to 37 percent of the total mass of their brains. At the other end of the spectrum, the olfactory bulb in some songbird brains is as small as 3 percent of the total brain mass. In humans, the bulb is only about o.oı percent of the brain's total volume, but because we have large brains, the bulb's actual size is relatively large.

Turkey Vultures may be the most highly endowed in this capacity among birds, having the largest known avian olfactory bulbs; the Northern Fulmar has the largest among seabirds. In general, waterbirds tend to have larger olfactory organs relative to brain size, along with ratites, ducks, pigeons, rails, songbirds, cormorants, and crows. Parrots have the smallest.

Although an animal's sense of smell is generally linked to the actual and relative size of olfactory bulbs, there may be other factors involved as well, such as the number of neurons within the bulb and the ability of other parts of a brain to process odor-related information, which is likely linked to the number of olfactory receptor genes. Domestic cows are champions in the latter category, with more than 2,000 such genes, compared to 400 in humans. The number in domestic chickens varies from 280 to 550; in penguins, the number is a mere 29. The Kakapos, a flightless parrot native to New Zealand, might have the most advanced sense of smell in the bird world, as suggested by this measure: it has 667 olfactory genes.

The degree to which birds rely on scent to find and target food sources is related in part to their lifestyles. Some birds that feed at night, in conditions with limited visibility—fog, low clouds, dense vegetation—or while foraging over a wide area are more likely to rely on smell than those feeding in other conditions. This does not include owls, noted nighttime hunters, which rely on sound and sight. Other factors that influence a bird's dependence on smell include where it seeks food, its nesting strategy, its social communications, and its overall diet. Some ornithologists theorize that olfaction also plays an important role in migration, including being an essential factor for homing pigeons.

Even when odors do play a role in locating food, vision is still significant. Various projects have determined that odor alone can lead some birds directly to a food source, from up to 20 miles (32 kilometers) away in the case of the Black-footed Albatross and more than 15 miles (24 kilometers) for some petrels. Terrestrial birds that may use scent to find food at least some of the time include crows, ravens, magpies, jays, hummingbirds, pigeons, and chickadees.

A variety of species have been tested in laboratory conditions to determine the threshold of their response to specific odor cues, but there is not much evidence from field studies to suggest how actively most birds use smell while feeding. The outcomes of such studies are mostly theoretical, suggesting for example that insect-eating birds are likely to have less response to smells than fruit-eating species. With or without input from smell, birds are primarily visual foragers.

When smell is not an active tool for locating food, some birds use smell in reverse, to avoid potentially dangerous food sources. Plant-eating species, for example, are thought to detect sulfurous odors and volatile emanations of fatty acids, both associated with the body waste of carnivores. One report from European farmers observed that geese were rarely seen foraging in fields where cabbage had been planted in a previous season. The reason, according to scientists, is that unharvested cabbages emit compounds such as hydrogen sulfide and methyl sulfides as they decay, and the birds use these as signals to avoid potential toxins associated with rotting vegetables.

Though geese are known to be selective about which plants they eat, they will eat some plants known to be either toxic or unpalatable to other birds and animals. As part of their foraging, most geese regularly ingest soil, which is known to bind to the alkaloids associated with some plant toxicity. This remediation process is referred to as geophagy.

Other than food, smell has a proven role in other aspects of bird activity. It assists some colony-dwelling birds in locating their mates or nests, helps some birds find mates, and guides birds to locate plants useful in deterring insect pests. European Starlings, for one, are known to collect leaves of aromatic plants to add to their nests, including yarrow, milfoil, and hogweed, which are thought to repel mites, lice, and other parasites. No decline in parasite numbers has been measured from this usage, but in comparison to nests without these plants, both nestlings and parents had healthier outcomes. It is not clear, however, if these birds select such plants by smell, taste, or vision.

TASTE

If birds detect food primarily through vision, why would taste be important? The ability to select food based on taste allows all animals, not just birds, to assess risk, especially the presence of toxins, and the value of nutritional content.

Taste is sensed by taste buds, and in mammals, taste buds are typically distinctive structures that line the tongue. In humans, many of these can be seen with the naked eye from simple observation in a mirror. When it comes to taste, bird tongues are less capable than human tongues and those of many other animal groups.

Canada Geese make some grazing decisions based on taste. Bluegrass is their favorite grass because it has a better nutritional profile than other grasses (which they will also eat), although this grass in its modern form is not native to North America.

Early ornithologists believed that bird tongues did not have taste receptors and therefore birds could not taste food, though this has since been proven untrue. The avian tongue has comparatively fewer taste buds, but they are present and well used. Humans have about 10,000 taste buds, pigs about 15,000, and catfish up to 100,000. For birds, the number varies widely by species (see the Avian Taste Buds table). Most songbirds have 50 or fewer taste buds.

AVIAN TASTE BUDS

SPECIES	NUMBER OF TASTE BUDS
Eurasian Bullfinch	46
Rock Pigeon	50–75
European Starling	200
Mallard	375
domestic chicken	375–767

Bird taste buds are not visible because they are located within surface tissue and linked to the surface by "taste canals" or pores. Birds' taste buds sense food through these pores, transported primarily by saliva; birds produce saliva at a higher rate than mammals as a consequence.

Avian taste buds are found throughout the inside of their bills, roughly concentrated near the back of the tongue and the upper surface of the pharyngeal floor. In a few species, especially Mallards, taste buds are also found near the tip of both the upper and lower bills. On average, only 5 percent of a bird's taste buds are found on the tongue. By comparison, about 80 percent of the taste buds in a rat are on its tongue. In birds, 70 percent of these receptors are on the palate and 25 percent are on the lower bill and pharyngeal floor. In practice, this distribution provides a last line of defense before a food is swallowed.

Chickens are one bird type that has been studied more extensively than others because of their importance in commercial agriculture as well as their wide accessibility as specimens. Their sense of taste is no exception: chickens have long been one of the primary models for investigation and measurement of avian taste capabilities.

Most of the taste buds in birds are located in the palate and inside the upper bill. About 5 percent of the taste buds are on the tongue, but most of these are located at the back. When birds reject an object because of its taste, it is usually after the object is already in its mouth, and rejecting it is the last action before swallowing. *(Photo by MadeK)*

In early eras, chickens were originally thought to lack taste buds altogether; subsequent studies found 24 taste buds. In recent years, research has added to the total: various breeds have from 240 to 360 taste buds, with the number typically higher in breeds raised as broilers than for those bred for egg laying. The number keeps climbing, however. Several of the most recent studies report up to 767 taste buds in some chickens. In mammals, taste bud cells have a life cycle of seven to fourteen days; in chickens, it is only three to four days.

Taste buds in birds are grouped into three categories based on general shape and structure, and these categories generally correspond to birds' habitat and diet. Type I taste buds are typical of songbirds; Type II are common in ducks and shorebirds; Type III are found only in parrots.

Five essential factors define taste: sweet, sour, bitter, salty, and umami. The latter is tied to foods rich in protein or amino acids, a sensory category well appreciated in fine dining by humans. Felines do not have the ability to taste sweetness, which is attributed to their carnivorous diet. Over a long period of time, the lack of sweet in their diet influenced the decline of functionality in the gene known to control this taste quality. The same result happened independently in other animals that either do not have sweet as part of their normal diet and/or swallow their food whole, bypassing a dependence on taste. These animals include sea lions, dolphins, and spotted hyenas, among others. Laboratory studies of birds show that most species have general responses to standard chemical compounds used to designate concepts such as sweet, sour, salty, and bitter. Chickens exhibit reactions to threshold amounts of these standards in direct relation to how many taste buds they have: the more taste buds, the more sensitive they are to taste.

Specific genes are directly associated with the kinds of tastes animals can detect. Gene T1R2, for example, corresponds to the ability to detect sweetness, but it is not active in felines. As a result, lions, tigers, and domestic cats do not detect sweetness. Birds, with a few exceptions, have very few of the T1R2-type genes and also do not detect natural sugars. Domestic pigeons have only one of these

The caterpillars of the monarch butterfly share toxins with their parents, making them unpalatable to birds.

genes; the average among all birds studied is four. Hummingbirds are a notable exception, but not because they have the T1R2 gene. Their attraction to and dependence on naturally sweet liquids is attributed to remapping of two other genes associated with taste reception linked to the umami flavor.

Within the world of birds, penguins have the least ability to taste; no penguin species has genes or taste buds that detect sweet, bitter, or umami tastes, three out of the five taste categories. Two penguin species, Adelie and Emperor, are capable of detecting sour and salty tastes.

An additional taste-like sense in animals is the ability to detect capsaicin, the active ingredient in hot peppers. The "hotness" we detect from peppers is not a true "taste," but a burning reaction triggered by a receptor known as TRPV1 (also known as the capsaicin receptor), which can also respond the same way on other parts of the body, particularly the skin, when these body parts are exposed. All mammals have the TRPV1 receptor, as do birds, but unlike humans, birds are immune to its effects. Pepper plants profit because birds help disperse their seeds widely, while the capsaicin defends against mammals that have much less dispersal range.

For most animals, natural toxins are most often expressed with a bitter taste, and birds are well endowed with both the specific genes and specialized taste buds to identify these potentially deadly threats. For example, monarch butterflies and their caterpillars share a toxin, and once most birds encounter these insects, they learn by visual identification not to ingest them. One notable exception is the Black-headed Grosbeak, which can tolerate the toxin, although these birds will limit their ingestion to reduce the potential harm.

The most important genes related to sensitivity to bitterness are known as Tas2r genes. The number tends to correspond with diet; the more Tas2r genes, the larger the proportion of plants or insects that are tolerated, with insects acquiring toxicity from the plants they consume. A few bird species have none of these genes, most have at least several, and a few have a lot (see the Birds' Ability to Taste Bitterness table). There are twelve in the Bar-tailed Trogon and sixteen in the White-throated Sparrow.

TOUCH

Animals have a range of sensory capabilities relating to touch. Our human hands provide a primary tool for a tactile interface with the world, but birds are also well equipped for this kind of physical perception. Alone or in conjunction with sight, hearing, smell, and taste, their bills, tongues, skin, and even feet can be used to find and identify food by touch.

Bills are the most important source of tactile information for birds that make use of touch. The specific designation for a zone of enhanced touch in the bill is called the bill-tip organ, an area with a high density of specialized cells called Herbst and Grandry corpuscles. These cells, known as mechanosensors, are found in pits

BIRDS' ABILITY TO TASTE BITTERNESS

SPECIES	NUMBER OF TAS2R GENES
Red-throated Loon	0
Barn Owl	2
Peregrine Falcon	2
Killdeer	3
Downy Woodpecker	4
Anna's Hummingbird	6
American Crow	7
White-throated Sparrow	16

Ducks and other waterfowl that forage for food in silt and debris rely on touch and taste to evaluate the quality of edible food sources. The evidence of this dabbling can be seen on the bottom of bodies of water such as the one pictured here.

within both the inner and outer surface of bills, though the placement and concentration varies by species. In general, birds associated with aquatic habitats have more of these sensory pits, and larger areas of the bill tip are involved. Higher concentrations of these sensors are also found nearest the outer edge of bills.

Scientists believe that the touch-sensing ability of duck and shorebird bills is greater than the tactile senses of species such as mice, which rely on their whiskers for touch detection in the dark. Dabbling ducks and shorebirds that probe for food require the ability to find food sources without visual cues: like owls, they are hunting in the dark. With initial contact from touch-sensitive bills, they are also able to selectively screen for worms, crustaceans, or plant material in water or mud that is typically too murky for vision. Between touch and taste, these avians are effective feeders.

Dabbling ducks have bills with the highest density of tissue specialized for tactile sensing. Ducks and geese, which rely on dabbling to find food, make more extensive use of the sensitive mechanoreceptors. In these waterbirds, Herbst and Grandry corpuscles are not only located on the tips of bills but are also concentrated on the inner surfaces as well as the outer. They can be as dense as 970 per square inch (150 per square millimeter).

The mechanosensors in Mallard bills are sensitive enough to tell the difference between edible and inedible objects of the same size and shape. A well-publicized experiment reported on the ability of Mallards to differentiate between dried peas and plastic fake peas under a covering of sand, using only their bills. The dried peas won every time.

HERBST AND GRANDRY CORPUSCLES

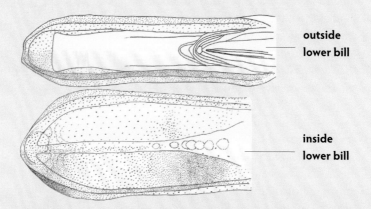

outside
lower bill

inside
lower bill

In this schematic of an upper mandible, the vertical rods represent the relative number of Herbst (orange) and Grandry (green) corpuscles located at various sites of a Mallard's bill. The greatest number of rods are located toward the front and sides of the bill, generating the greatest sensitivity to touch.

For the probing activity of shorebirds, pressure sensitivity is involved. As the bill is pushed down and into a substrate, it displaces water, which generates back pressure in the presence of an object. The tip of the bill provides the initial feedback from this pressure, which may or may not represent a source of food. Small rocks, for example, or other inedible material are often intermixed with the desired prey a bird seeks, and water is an effective medium to transmit signals that are identified as either a food target or something to ignore.

The Red Knot, a shorebird known for its foraging in this manner, was the focus of a research project that determined that the sensitivity of bill tips was closely linked to the presence of water. Foraging in dry sand was much less productive, if productive at all, compared to probing in wet sand. When a bird can detect something in this way, before actually touching the object, it is referred to as "remote touch." In order to take advantage of the sensory information detected by their bills, birds that depend on this ability also have brains with a much larger fraction of total volume dedicated to processing this kind of input than birds that are primarily visual foragers.

Some bird species are more dependent on touch than others. Sandpipers and curlews, for example, have highly developed sensory organs at the tips of their bills. Just like fingertips in humans, their bills are used to probe in sand or mud, and their bills' sensory organs "feel" the vibrations made by worms and other invertebrates. In combination with the bird's sense of smell and visual clues, its bill is a sensitive tool that successfully delivers information.

Some seed-eating land birds, including finches, quail, and chickens, also have mechanoreceptors, but they are typically concentrated more on the inside of their bills and are limited to Herbst corpuscles. Grandry corpuscles are found only in waterfowl. Seedeaters benefit from tactile feedback because it improves their ability to manipulate seed husks.

Woodpeckers, on the other hand, benefit from these receptors as remote detectors on the tip of their tongues, though the receptors likely also provide useful input from the signature pecking that is

The bills of dabbling ducks, like this male and female Mallard pair, are equipped with sensory cells similar to those in human fingertips. Mallards are able to use this touch-sensitive ability to detect edible food items hidden within the muck on the bottom. *(Photo by Anne Richard)*

Earthworms comprise as much as 60 percent of the diet of the American Woodcock, which finds its prey in organic litter using its long bill and a well- developed sense of touch at the tip. *(Photo by Dalton Rasmussen)*

part of these birds' foraging activity. Since woodpeckers can extend their tongues deeply into insect holes or the bird's own exploratory fissures, their ability to find prey by touch is an effective advantage.

Herbst corpuscles are also found in the tongues of ducks and geese. Inside their bills, the function of these cells is to help birds manage food that has already been selected rather than identify it in the first place. The tongue's mechanoreceptors provide pertinent information about where food items are inside the bills, assisting in positioning them before they are swallowed.

Herbst corpuscles are not unique to bills, but are scattered throughout bird bodies, including the skin. They have a primary role in detecting vibrations and changes in pressure, a function that supports movement. In mammals such as cats, these corpuscles are the functional center at the root of vibration-sensing bristles and whiskers.

DIGESTIVE ORGANS AND PROCESSES

Birds developed and thrived primarily because of their ability to fly. Flying provided an effective means to escape from predators and to access a wide range of food sources. In order to extract necessary nutrition, the basic components of birds' digestive organs have developed in accordance with the type of food being ingested, from the most generalized diets to the most specific.

With high metabolisms, most birds digest food fairly quickly, at least compared to mammals (see the Digestion Time Ranges sidebar). Shrikes process small animal prey in as little as three hours. The fastest digestion—and the most rapid metabolism—is that of hummingbirds, whose main diet is nectar and insects. These tiny fliers can process food in minutes. Songbirds that ingest berries can complete a digestive cycle in less than thirty minutes.

SALIVARY GLANDS AND ESOPHAGUS: SWALLOWING FOOD

Food intake begins at the bill, a characteristic shared among all birds. As discussed in the Bill section earlier in this chapter, bills represent a wide spectrum of size, shape, and function, which correspond to the diet of a particular species. All birds share one important limitation in their diet: their food has to be ingested without the aid of teeth.

For most birds, this limitation is resolved with food choices that are limited by size. Seeds, berries, plant material, sap, and insects generally pose no size issues for the birds that feed on them and, in most cases, can be swallowed whole. Birds that feed on amphibians, fish, reptiles, mammals, and other birds have two approaches to this potential problem: they either select prey small enough to be swallowed whole or use their bills and claws to dismember it into bite-size pieces.

Seabirds, which often feed on the water, have adapted another technique: flexible jaws and throats that can expand to accommodate the length and width of their catch, enlarging the concept of "bite-size." Seabirds and raptors share an additional hurdle when hunting: they must be able to fly away with the added weight of their prey. Young birds learn this by trial and error; when adults capture something too large to ingest or too heavy to move, they either abandon it or, in the case of some raptors, dismember it on the ground.

Salivary glands: Saliva is the lubrication birds use to help them swallow their food. Salivary glands are located in the oral cavity.

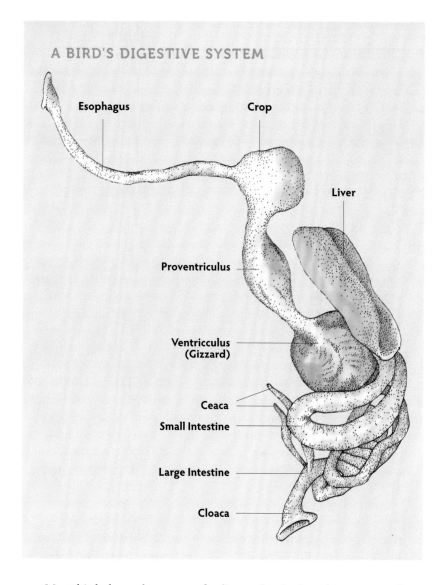

Esophagus

Crop

Liver

Proventriculus

Ventricculus
(Gizzard)

Ceaca

Small Intestine

Large Intestine

Cloaca

Most birds have three sets of salivary glands, but the amount of saliva produced varies according to diet. Salivary glands in birds that eat mostly seeds and grain are more developed than in birds with other primary diets. Raptors and seabirds are at the other end of the spectrum, with the least developed glands.

DIGESTION TIME RANGES

Almost all research studies that tracked digestion times reported average times using controlled circumstances, including the type of food. In the wild, as in the laboratory, the time of complete digestion (see the table below) is likely to vary depending on how much food is already ingested by a bird, the type of food introduced to the system, and the mixture of various kinds of food in the same digestive cycle.

SPECIES	DIGESTION TIME
Rufous Hummingbird	15 minutes
American Robin	22 minutes
House Wren	33 minutes
Cedar Waxwing	42 minutes
Chipping Sparrow	62 minutes
Song Sparrow	82 minutes
House Sparrow	85 minutes
Eastern Towhee	92 minutes
House Finch	92 minutes
Field Sparrow	101 minutes
Ring-necked Pheasant	5 hours

Chimney swifts are noted for the large amount of saliva they produce, using it as an adhesive for securing nest materials to surfaces. In some birds, such as woodpeckers, saliva also serves a secondary purpose: it forms a sticky film on their tongues that improves their ability to snag insects.

Esophagus: A bird's esophagus is relatively straight and narrow when food is not being ingested. In many species this passageway is elastic and capable of expanding to accommodate food that is many times larger than the esophagus's resting diameter. Thin muscles lining the esophagus contract rhythmically to carry food down, a process called peristalsis; mucus secreted from glands along the tube lubricate the process. Swallowing is a simpler maneuver for birds than other animals, especially mammals, because a bird's esophagus does not have sphincter-like mechanisms on either end to close its openings.

A Blue Jay swallows a hazelnut. This object is on the large size of what this bird typically consumes, and the shell is too hard for it to break open, but its digestive system is capable of making up for the lack of teeth. *(Photo by Mike Truchon)*

Birds that eat other animals whole instinctively swallow their prey headfirst. Birds that feed on fish follow this practice, usually flipping or manipulating the fish to swallow it headfirst. This is an important part of ingestion, since it reduces the chance that scales (which overlap from front to back on fish) and fins (which point or fold toward the tail) will catch on or scrape the interior of the esophagus. If the fish is large enough, its head might be in the process of being digested while the tail is still jutting out of the bird's mouth.

More so than most other birds, owl throats are able to expand considerably to accommodate prey, which is often swallowed whole. The expansion of their esophagus is possible because it has long folds along its length.

American Crows have an expandable zone at the beginning of the esophagus where they hold food meant for caching. A similar feature of Pinyon Jays is important because they rely heavily on their capacity to carry pine nuts to cache sites. Clark's Nutcrackers also carry and cache pine nuts, using a slightly different anatomical characteristic, a sublingual pouch that sits under their tongue.

CROPS: STORING FOOD

Most birds have a distinct compartment in the esophagus called the crop. The crop is typically about halfway down the esophagus, and in many birds, including passerines, its position is visible as a bulge in the neck when it's full. Some birds have a pair of crops, one on each side, which can produce two bulges. In some species, the crop may not be present at all, occur in a rudimentary form (very small or very narrow), or exist as a well-formed, rounded extension. Birds that do not have crops include owls, coots, cormorants, gulls, and some insectivores; the food these birds ingest passes directly from mouth to stomach.

The crop is a holding compartment before food enters the stomach. At the least, it is a simple chamber that regulates the flow of food into the stomach and stores food for later digestion. Pigeons, for example, have complex crops with multiple lobes, a feature associated with

Aquatic vegetation, which can be an essential part of the diet of Canada Geese and other waterbirds, especially during migration, is easily swallowed. Some types of water plants also benefit from this predation, as the birds that consume them help spread their seeds.

seed-eating species. Seedeaters and omnivores often have larger crops than meat- and fish-eating species.

The pelican's expandable pouch is not a crop but a gular sac that is part of the lower bill used for catching fish (see the Bill section earlier in this chapter). Owls do not have crops, or "true crops," but hold their animal prey in a widened section of their esophagus. Most—perhaps all—diurnal raptors have crops, and vultures are endowed with especially large ones.

The length of time food is stored in a bird's crop varies. It can pass through in minutes or remain for several hours or longer, depending on how much food is already in the rest of the digestive system and the availability of additional food. When diurnal birds first begin feeding in the morning, most of their food intake bypasses the crop and goes directly to the stomach. Studies on domestic chickens report that the amount of food stored in the crop varies by feeding frequency: when more food is available, less food stays in the crop. In general, the more food that is available to be swallowed, the less time already ingested food spends in the crop. Caged chickens with a continual supply of food store little in their crops and those that are free

BIRD CROPS

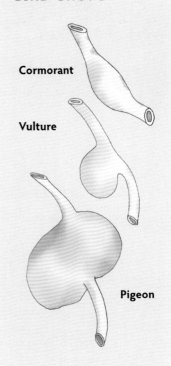

Cormorant

Vulture

Pigeon

Most birds have crops, but not all crops are the same. At the least, some species have almost nothing except a slight widening of the esophagus (top), a characteristic of many fish-eating seabirds. Many passerines have a single simple pouch-like extension (middle) where food is stored temporarily. Birds such as the Rock Pigeon have large crops (bottom), sometimes as two symmetrical structures.

In order to reduce the risk of harm from struggling animal prey, birds usually stun or kill their catch before swallowing it. This Great Blue Heron (top) instinctively maneuvers its catch to swallow it headfirst, a procedure that helps in the swallowing process: fins and scales are less likely to get snagged as the fish passes down the esophagus. *(Photo by James P. Mock)* The Red-tailed Hawk (bottom) has captured a large gopher snake and swallowed it headfirst, a precaution that keeps the snake from striking the bird while it is in the hawk's grasp.

range store more. Food passes out of the crop through the contraction of the muscles that encase it and is pushed back into the esophagus; its next stop is the stomach.

Predigestion: Depending on the type of food and the speed at which it passes through the crop, the digestive environment inside the crop can include fermentation through the action of probiotic microbes. This predigestion process can provide an important supplement to the digestive stages that follow and has also been shown to help birds suppress the effects of potentially dangerous bacteria.

Crop milk: For some bird species, crops provide a function other than storage. Pigeons, flamingos, and a few other species produce a nutrition-rich fluid in their crops called crop milk, which is regurgitated to feed their young. Crop milk varies by species; in general, it is 50–60 percent protein in the form of undigested solids, 33–45 percent fat, and 3–5 percent carbohydrates. Pigeon crops also secrete a compound called Pigeon Milk Growth Factor (PMGF), which adds an important nutritive boost for nestlings.

STOMACH: BREAKING DOWN FOOD

The stomach has two distinct components. First in line is the proventriculus, which has similar functions as the stomach in humans; next is the gizzard, or ventriculus, also sometimes referred to as the ventriculus gastric mill. All birds have gizzards, but this organ is also part of the digestive system in earthworms, crocodiles, alligators, and some fish.

Proventriculus: Among species, the largest proventriculus is found in raptors and aquatic birds that feed primarily on fish. The raptor proventriculus has well-developed folds along its length, allowing it to expand to accommodate the animal bodies that pass into it, but these folds are not found in seed- and fruit-eating birds.

The proventriculus produces gastric juices from glands to soften and begin the decomposition of ingested food. Gastric juices, enzymes that break down tissues and other components of food, vary in composition and capability according to bird species and diet. The main digestive enzymes in gastric juices are hydrochloric acid and pepsin. These vary in acidity and volume in relation to the

HAWK STOMACH

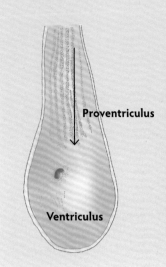

Proventriculus

Ventriculus

Unlike seed-eating birds, raptors have little use for a traditional avian gizzard, because digestive juices do most of the work for their two stomachs. This graphic of a hawk stomach indicates the longitudinal folds that guide food down through the proventriculus and into the relatively smooth interior of the ventriculus (gizzard), with almost no separation between the two. The hole is the exit to the small intestine. (Adapted from Langlois, 2003)

type of food being ingested, from seeds and berries to meat, even bones. These fluids can be measured with the pH scale of relative acidity and alkalinity; pH 7 is neutral, representative of pure water. Alkaline numbers are greater than pH 7: baking soda is pH 9 and soapy water pH 12. Acidic numbers are less than pH 7: milk is pH 6, orange juice is pH 3. Gastric acid in humans is normally about pH 1.

Birds generally produce digestive juices that are less acidic than those in humans, but the acidity varies by species and the particular stage of digestion. Raptors tend to have more-acidic gastric juices than seedeaters: Bald Eagles have been measured as high as pH 1.3 to 1.5, Red-tailed Hawks at pH 1.8 to 2.8, and Peregrine Falcons at pH 1.8 to 3.5. Compared to these, pigeons, chickens, and turkeys measure about pH 4.8.

Acidity can also spike in other parts of the digestive system, where fermentation from bacteria and the presence of other digestive fluids (bile, for example, secreted into the small intestines) can also be high. Vision, smell, and taste operate in conjunction with the production of gastric juices, just as in mammals. When birds sense the presence of food, the proventriculus initiates the flow, preparing the digestive system for action.

Gizzard: From the proventriculus, food moves to the second stomach compartment, the ventriculus (gizzard), through contractions of the muscles that surround it. Birds have a high rate of metabolism compared to mammals and need to quickly extract nutrition and energy from food, but lack the teeth that mammals use to reduce food to particles small enough to digest quickly. The gizzard replaces some of the pulverizing action of teeth with a grinding action produced by the contraction of muscles that encase it.

The overall shape, size, and strength of the gizzard varies by species and diet. The internal surface of a gizzard is marked by ridges and folds, which also vary in relation to species and diet. Seeds require more grinding than other food sources, and birds with the largest gizzards are those that eat the most seeds, including chickens, turkeys, pigeons, and finches. The gizzards of these birds feature harder internal ridges, and in some cases—pigeons, for example—tough protrusions function much like molars in mammals.

Gizzards in raptors are not well developed because there is little or no mechanical action involved in the deconstruction of their food; digestive juices are sufficient. Some birds, especially those that feed primarily on fruit, have small, weak gizzards.

Seed-eating birds ingest grit to assist the grinding action of the gizzard; churned along with food, grit makes the gizzard more effective. Grit is also found, usually to a lesser degree, in the gizzards of insectivores, omnivores, and frugivores, but rarely if ever in carnivores. Grit can be sand or small particles of stone or shell (for more on grit, see "How Do Birds Get Grit?" in the Feeding Behavior of Birds chapter). An added nutritional benefit can come from minerals, especially calcium, that are present in rocky grit material.

The grit inside a gizzard assists in the digestive process, but it is the crushing strength of the gizzard itself that supplies the pressure. A test conducted on unshelled hickory nuts and pecans determined up to 336 pounds (151 kilograms) of force was required to break them open (maximum was associated with the hickory). When captive turkeys were fed these whole nuts, pieces of the shells that passed out of their digestive systems averaged about 1 inch (2.5 centimeters) in length.

BIRD GIZZARD

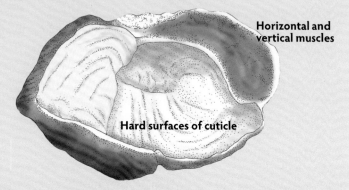

Horizontal and vertical muscles

Hard surfaces of cuticle

Birds with diets that include seeds and nuts have gizzards adapted to replace the grinding action provided by teeth in other vertebrates. The gizzard is covered with bands of strong muscles that run both longitudinally and at right angles, providing the churning power needed for breaking down edible material. Folds of tough tissue line the interior, usually faced with a cuticle, an abrasive surface layer that works with ingested grit to grate and pulverize food.

In some bird species, the gizzard develops a projecting layer called the cuticle that aids in reducing the size of food masses. Produced from a complex of carbohydrates and protein, the abrasive cuticle is asymmetrical, with the thickest part opposite the largest, most muscular inner section of the gizzard. The cuticle, along with grit held in the inner folds of the gizzard, is a hard element that provides rasping surfaces needed to rend food into bits.

Gizzards also function as screens for indigestible fragments of animal prey, such as feathers, fur, bones, claws, and beaks. Instead of passing on through the intestines and potentially causing blockage or harm, these fragments are compressed by the gizzard into pellets and regurgitated.

Owls are noted for this stage of digestion, but it is also common in other raptors, gulls, and shorebirds. Grebes regurgitate indigestible food, but they produce pellets in the digestive passage just after the gizzard. Their diet of primarily seafood includes crabs, shrimp, beetles, and other aquatic insects, which have indigestible exoskeletons. The bits that accumulate from the grinding of these elements are condensed within a screen-like mass of feathers, which these birds swallow just for this purpose.

Some birds may rely on a mix of methods to remove inedible parts of ingested foods. After ingesting fruit, for example, American Robins are known to regurgitate large seeds or pits but defecate seeds from smaller fruit such as mulberries. Cedar Waxwings eat fruit in a range of sizes but void all seeds. Studies show that there are similar rates of germination no matter how seeds are voided—the most important function of the bird in this process is for its digestion to remove the pulp, which helps trigger the growing cycle.

The stomach's digestive process is not just one-way. Muscular contractions pass food back and forth between the proventriculus and the gizzard, adding exposure to the digestive enzymes between grinding sessions in the gizzard. There may also be further exchanges between the gizzard and the initial part of the intestine, the duodenum, which secretes additional enzymes. In any case, normal functions of birds allow some digestive juices to pass into the gizzard, adding to its effectiveness.

INTESTINES AND RELATED ORGANS: EXTRACTING NUTRIENTS

Intestines form the final component of the digestive system. All birds have a small and large intestine designed for only liquids and semiliquids. The intestines are where most nutrition and energy is extracted from food, just as in other animals, but the length and function of the intestines vary among birds according to the specifics of their diets.

Small intestine: In mammals, the total length of the intestine is four or five times the body's height, meaning the intestine can be 20 feet or more (6 meters) long. Relative to body size, bird intestines are much shorter than those in mammals. The length roughly corresponds to the general diet: the longest intestines are associated with birds that eat seeds, plants, and fish, while the shortest are in those that eat fruit,

The Spruce Grouse's diet consists mostly of conifer needles, which require more time than most other vegetation to digest. As a result, these birds can have small intestines that are up to 28 percent longer than other birds of the same type. *(Photo by Frank Fichtmueller)*

insects, and meat. In birds, the length varies from only a few inches in hummingbirds to 8 or 9 feet (2.4–2.7 meters) in ospreys.

Birds with longer intestines include the Spruce Grouse, which feeds mostly on conifer needles that require a longer digestion period in order to extract nutrition. The Spruce Grouse's small intestine is roughly 28 percent longer than those of birds of the same size but whose diets are richer in nutrition and easier to digest. Birds of the same species but linked to different habitats with varying food sources can have small intestines of different length too.

In some birds, including the House Wren and House Sparrow, the small intestine may be longer in females than males; in European Starlings, the reverse is true. North American birds with the longest small intestine relative to body length include Bald Eagles, Broad-winged Hawks, Cooper's Hawks, Least Bitterns, and Ospreys; all these species have diets focused on mammals, birds, fish, or reptiles and amphibians. North American species with small intestines with the smallest relative length include American Robins, Hairy Wood-peckers, House Wrens, and White-breasted Nuthatches, with diets that favor either insects or a combination of insects and seeds.

Researchers note that in conditions that trigger birds to ingest more, such as cold weather, the intestines in some species grow longer (up to 22 percent longer in House Wrens), providing more surface area to absorb nutrients from their meals. This characteristic is shared with the Eastern Towhee, Rock Ptarmigan, and Spruce Grouse. Many birds also grow more intestines in order to quickly put on weight when they're preparing to migrate. The longer the intestines, the better they can process a surge of food. Birds are able to temporarily grow up to 22 percent more intestines for this purpose.

House Wrens have evolved to be less efficient at absorbing natural sugars from their diet, which is not surprising, as sugars are not a significant component of the insect food they ingest. Birds with mixed diets, such as American Robins, ingest more carbohydrates and have developed digestive systems that absorb more sugars.

Liver and gall bladder: Just as with mammals, birds' livers produce bile that assists in processing food while it is in the small intestine. The main function of bile is to break down fats and oils and to help fat-soluble vitamins (A, D, E, and K), as well as vitamins B1 and B2, be absorbed into the bloodstream. Bile produced by the liver passes into the gall bladder, where it is stored before passing into the small intestine.

The liver also produces glucose, the primary fuel animals need to function. The liver (in conjunction with secretions from the pancreas) maintains a continual level of glucose in the blood. This organ also functions as a detoxifier, converting harmful compounds, including pesticides, carcinogens, and by-products of metabolism such as ammonia, into water-soluble wastes that are passed on to the kidneys.

Livers in birds with primary diets of fish and insects are larger than those of birds that eat mostly seeds and meat. In proportion to body size, bird livers are larger than those in mammals.

Pancreas: The role of the pancreas is to produce insulin as well as enzymes to help in processing food in the small intestine. These enzymes are primarily involved in the digestion of proteins and fats to allow them to be absorbed into the bloodstream and lymph system. This takes place in the tissue lining the wall of the small intestine. The insulin produced by the pancreas regulates metabolism by controlling the amount of sugars in the blood.

Large intestine: The large intestine is the final link in the digestive system: its lining absorbs both water and electrolytes. Unlike mammals, in birds the large intestine is relatively short and straight.

Birds that eat plant leaves have the most complicated task in extracting nutrition from their food, and the large intestines of these birds have an additional feature to break down and isolate essential nutrients. Caeca are small paired sacs that are part of the lower end of the large intestine. These sacs can ferment partially digested leaves, producing nutrients using bacteria.

The final section of the large intestine is a storage zone for fecal material. Several folds in the lining of the large intestine hold the fecal material before it is ejected.

Many birds prefer to eat fruits and berries, but hard pits and seeds pose a problem for digestion. Depending on the size of the pit or seed, it can pass through the digestive system and end up in the bird's droppings. Or in the case of the chokecherry seed seen here, it can also be regurgitated.

CLOACA: ELIMINATING WASTE

The cloaca is a single compartment where the large intestine discharges fecal matter and the bladder excretes urine. Thus, birds defecate a mostly liquid mix of feces and urine through the vent. The urine is actually uric acid, a concentrated, nitrogen-heavy compound distilled from urea that is also the main compound in mammal urine, including humans'. It appears as the white part of bird poop and varies in liquid consistency from chalky to watery; the darker bits are the feces.

Plant eaters, such as geese and pheasants, produce tubular droppings that contain leftover bits of the vegetation they have consumed. Birds that feed on seeds, berries, and other fruit typically produce irregularly shaped droppings that also contain remnants of their meals. Although some insect eaters produce pellets, bits of insect bodies often end up in their droppings. Woodpecker droppings often include bits of bark and wood fiber ingested along with their intended meals.

Many birds vary their diet during the same day as well as season to season, creating inconsistency in their droppings. But there may be patterns that provide intriguing clues, sometimes enough to determine identification of the species leaving this evidence behind.

Wild Turkeys produce two kinds of droppings: adult males generate long, cylindrical tubes roughly 0.5 inch (1.3 centimeters) in diameter and up to 3 inches (7.6 centimeters) long, while adult females leave behind groups of small condensed clumps, each less than 0.5 inch in diameter.

Canada Geese may defecate every twenty minutes—or even more often, according to some observations—especially when foraging in parks, where large expanses of grass provide ample food and unrestricted grazing. These aquatic birds also defecate in the water while they are swimming. In a single day, one goose can produce as much as 1.5 pounds (0.6 kilogram) of feces, and since these are flocking

Seeds from berries and fruit, if not regurgitated, pass through a bird's digestive system and are deposited in its droppings, helping to disperse the seeds. The chiltepin pepper, reputedly the "grandmother" of all hot peppers, is native to Mexico and ranges as far north as Arizona. The seeds must be eaten by birds to germinate, marking a unique benefit for both being bird food and becoming bird poop.

birds, the evidence of their group foraging can leave behind a considerable mess.

Many birds habitually employ projectile defecation, which effectively avoids fouling their nests. Nesting songbirds are recognized for their cleanliness, discarding or carrying away the fecal sacs expelled by their young; other nestlings, such as Barn Swallows, defecate directly over the edge of their nests.

Almost all perching birds defecate just before they begin flying, an instinctive reaction that reduces the weight they carry. But they are not restricted to such timing. Birds defecate when they need to, including in the air.

Birds that eat animals whole—raptors, herons, and cormorants, for example—often void only white liquid, the uric acid component, producing stains aptly called whitewash. Whitewash is a dead giveaway for the habitual roosts of owls, eagles, and hawks; hawk fans call it "hawk chalk." Eagles and hawks typically produce a spray or splash that fans out under their roosts, while falcons generally drop theirs in rivulets. Whitewash from some eagles and hawks may also contain streaks of black or green, which are by-products of the digestive process, mainly bile.

Avid hawk watchers use the term "slicing" to refer to defecation in a single stream. Falconers use a different term—the objects of their interest are said to "mute." Owls generally have smaller streams, but as they favor the same perches over time, the whitewash tends to overlap and build up. Cormorants and other waterbirds that roost in colonies produce large volumes of whitewash that tends to blanket larger zones of tree trunks, boulders, and sides of cliffs.

Pathogens are present in bird droppings but are rarely considered a problem unless the birds in question are present in large numbers, such as Canada Geese, pigeons, or starlings. Although pathogens have been identified in various field tests, there is little evidence of these being transmitted to people or pets or resulting in any harmful outcomes.

Among the potential toxic agents are waterborne parasites such as *Cryptosporidium*, *Giardia*, and toxoplasmosis; bacteria including *Campylobacter*, *Chlamydia* (transmittable to humans as psitticosis),

E. coli, Listeria, Pasteurella multocida (linked to avian cholera), and *Salmonella* (present in some geese droppings); avian influenza, a virus; and *Histoplasma*, a fungus.

PELLETS: CASTING WASTE

Raptors digest their prey—including insects, amphibians, reptiles, fish, other birds, and mammals—whole but cannot break down some components of these animals. Exoskeletons, fur, feathers, scales, bones, teeth, bills, and claws are part of this nondigestible menu. Most of this waste is ejected through the mouth as compressed pellets.

The process of pellet-forming begins in the second part of a bird's stomach, the ventriculus (gizzard), after food has been exposed to digestive juices in the proventriculus. Strong muscular contractions squeeze fluids out of the food mass, applying pressure for up to six hours. The same muscular contractions that help food move down the esophagus now work in reverse, generating a cycle of antiperistaltic waves to push the newly formed pellet back up into the esophagus.

Finally, the bird drops the pellet out of its mouth—a movement called casting. The ejection process is aided by lubrication from mucus that lines the esophagus; fresh pellets found under roosts are damp from this fluid. The formation of a pellet leaves most of the outer surface of the prey animal—fur or feathers—on the outer surface of the pellet.

Owls are particularly noted for casting pellets, a consequence of the relatively low level of acidity in their digestive juices, the lowest among raptors. The typical pellet cycle from ingestion to casting ranges from ten to thirteen hours, depending on the owl species and the size of the prey, but it can span as little as six hours. The contents of one feeding session will end up in a single pellet, but if an owl consumes more than one small animal during a nighttime feeding session, the remains will be combined in a single pellet. Casting usually occurs just before an owl begins a new hunt, but in captivity, owls have been observed casting pellets when they see new live prey. The remains of as many as six voles have been found in a single

This Northern Saw-whet Owl is in the process of casting a pellet from its last meal. *(Photo by Jim Cumming)*

Owl pellets generally conform to a look that links to individual species but, depending on the prey animal, may vary in size, shape, and color. A. Snowy Owl; B. Eastern Screech-Owl; C. Barn Owl; D. Short-eared Owl; E. Long-eared Owl; F. Great Gray Owl; G. Great Horned Owl; H. Northern Saw-whet Owl

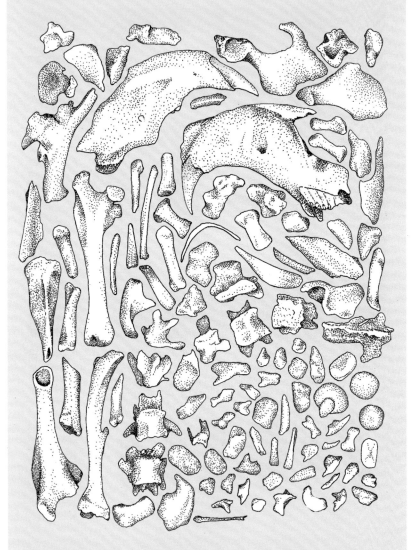

A single pellet often contains a complete skeleton if the bird's meal was a small rodent. The pellet contents illustrated here are of a pocket gopher, a meal for a Great Horned Owl.

pellet from a Barn Owl. Piles of pellets are a confirming sign of an owl's feeding site.

In general, all owl pellets are longer than they are wide, and the width is more likely than the length to reflect the species of owl it came from. However, pellets are not really an accurate way to identify an owl species because as its diet varies, the size of its pellets vary with the size of the prey.

Birds that produce pellets include cormorants, crows and other corvids, dippers, flycatchers, grebes, gulls, herons, kingfishers, phoebes, sandpipers, swallows, swifts, and thrushes. Pellet sizes vary considerably, with the smallest coming from phoebes—roughly the diameter of a BB—less than 0.2 inch (0.5 centimeter). At the other extreme, the largest pellets—those of Great Horned Owls—can be up to 4.5 inches (11 centimeters) long.

Large raptors such as Bald Eagles and Red-tailed Hawks may produce pellets, but their prey is generally large and not usually swallowed whole, so they produce pellets only when they consume smaller prey or ingest inedible parts such as feathers or fur. Hawks typically eat their prey by stripping off bits, not by swallowing them whole, and they often leave the bones behind. In any case, these birds have acidic enough digestive juices to dissolve bones and do not regularly produce pellets. If hawks do produce pellets, it takes twenty to twenty-four hours. Ospreys may cast pellets when their diets are primarily fish, but the pellets are small and infrequently produced.

Other nonedible materials also end up in pellets, including shells of snails, mussels, other small mollusks, and nuts. Pellets can also contain plastic, wire, fishhooks, and shotgun pellets or rifle bullets, among other elements of human activity.

FEEDING BEHAVIOR OF BIRDS

Birds are one of the most successful colonizers on earth, at home on every continent and in almost every ecosystem. In order to survive throughout this extensive range, they have adapted to find and benefit from almost every type of natural food, both flora and fauna. Birds are active feeders on prey in all biomes but are particularly successful in forests. Not surprisingly, with forests being their most productive zone, that is also where birds have their highest population densities and species diversity.

Some birds are herbivores, feeding mostly on flora, and some are carnivores, feeding mostly on fauna. Others are omnivores, with a mixed diet. Within these categories, there are specialists with a narrow dietary range and generalists with wider, more varied diets (see the Prevalence of Bird Diet Types table).

A bird species is considered a specialist if its preferred food source—insects, nectar, or seeds, for example—makes up half or more of its diet (see the Contents of Bird Diet Types table). It is extremely rare for any species, however, to have a diet that is exclusively focused on a single food category. Hummingbirds have a primary diet of nectar but also feed on insects, especially during the

PREVALENCE OF BIRD DIET TYPES

DIET TYPE	PERCENT OF TOTAL BIRD POPULATION	NUMBER OF SPECIES WORLDWIDE
insectivores	55	5,409
omnivores	12	1,159
frugivores	12	1,141
granivores	8	824
nectarivores	6	542
carnivores	3	280
herbivores	2	189
piscivores	2	233
scavengers	0.3	33

CONTENTS OF BIRD DIET TYPES

TYPE OF DIET	FOOD CONTENT
avivore	birds
carnivore	animals
crustaceavore	crustaceans
frugivore	fruit, berries
granivore	seeds
herbivore	plants
insectivore	arthropods
molluscivore	mollusks
nectarivore	plant nectar
omnivore	mixed diet
piscivore	fish
vermivore	worms

nesting season, as do American Goldfinches, which shift from seeds to insects when feeding their young.

According to a theory regarding evolutionary pressures, specialist feeders are considered more "fit" at the task of identifying and acquiring food. They can outcompete generalists if both are competing for the food the specialists prefer, but the specialists lose out to generalists in terms of survival if their preferred food is scarce or not available.

Ornithologists also sometimes classify bird guilds by an additional characteristic relating to the predominant location of their feeding. For insectivores, for example, the choices include terrestrial (on or near the ground), aerial (while prey is in the air), and arboreal (on or in trees). Subsequent chapters provide details on the primary bird diets, while this chapter's focus is on when and how much birds eat, as well as other feeding behaviors.

WHEN BIRDS EAT

Birds are a class of animals that maintain a constant internal temperature, which requires an almost continual intake of food or the conversion of stored food to generate energy. Most birds slow their

WHAT BIRDS GET OUT OF THEIR FOOD

FOOD TYPE	ENERGY CONTENT (IN KILOJOULES PER GRAM OF DRY WEIGHT)	AVAILABLE WATER
dicotyledonous crop leaves	89	11%
soil invertebrates	85	19%
fruit	84	12%
forbs	82	18%
aquatic plants	81	15%
caterpillars	79	22%
aquatic invertebrates	77	20%
grasses	76	18%
arthropods	71	22%
fish	71	21%
carrion (bird and mammal)	69	23%
small mammals	69	22%
nuts	66	5%
tree leaves	51	21%
cereal seeds	13	17%
weed seeds	12	21%

metabolism while resting or sleeping, in order to reduce their energy needs and to have less of a drain on energy reserves, which are usually in short supply (see the What Birds Get Out of Their Food table). Some birds store undigested food in their crop as an energy reserve. Ingested food that is still being digested can also bolster energy requirements during rest periods. Stored fat is typically not a major feature of bird physiology except during migration.

Hummingbirds, among the smallest birds, have the highest metabolism of all bird species. They must forage frequently to obtain the high-energy nectar they depend on. However, that doesn't mean they spend all their time eating. Even when feeding their young, adult hummingbirds spend much of their time in rest breaks to save energy. For hummingbirds, energy expenditure is mostly related to the energy cost of flight, and there is a critical trade-off between how much energy they get from nectar and how much energy it takes to acquire it. Backyard hummingbird feeders with perches provide a helpful assist.

The more nectar hummingbirds ingest, the more weight they have to carry, which requires even more energy for flight. A study of Anna's Hummingbirds reported that adults may spend up to 14 percent of daylight hours foraging (for flowers as well as insects), but only as much as 8 percent if their territory has high densities of appropriate flowers. In a study of male Calliope Hummingbirds, less than 15 percent of total waking time was spent feeding and sometimes as little as 10 percent. In these cases, the severe dietary need of hummingbirds is balanced against the energy costs of flying, especially hovering. Hummingbirds apparently gain a lot of benefit from resting between feeding excursions. For similar information on other species, see the Amount of Time Birds Forage and Feed sidebar.

DAY OR NIGHT?

Most birds are diurnal, active during daylight hours, and require food soon after they wake. It's no surprise that the most active feeding periods for diurnal birds is early morning. Birds also tend to feed more heavily at the end of the day, just before their period of nighttime dormancy begins, to provide necessary energy while

A White-eared Hummingbird takes a rest from a nectar feeder in Tucson, Arizona. Preening is an important activity that helps fill the time between feeder visits.

AMOUNT OF TIME BIRDS FORAGE AND FEED

Within a species, there are individual differences, and foraging and feeding time is affected by the abundance and quality of food available, the season, the weather, the presence of predators, and interference from human activity. Some results of this study were limited to male or female, a single season, or limited range.

SPECIES	PERCENT OF TIME SPENT FORAGING AND FEEDING
Pileated Woodpecker	58 (foraging on dead wood) to 36 (foraging on live wood)
Yellow-bellied Sapsucker	47–32 (fall and winter)
Gadwall	35–75 (surface, subsurface, and land feeding combined)
Trumpeter Swan	30–45 (winter and spring)
Ring-necked Duck	30–44
Sandhill Crane	20–85
Mallard	20–38
Ring-billed Gull	17
Golden-cheeked Warbler	3–5

they rest. Owls and other nocturnal birds are often most active at the beginning of their waking period as well.

Morning is also a profitable period for feeding because cooler temperatures and higher humidity combine to improve success when foraging. Some birds' potential prey—small mammals and amphibians—are often more active in the morning as they warm from the rising sun.

Dawn represents opportunity for birds as emerging light enables them to use their major food-finding sense, vision. Some prey animals favor a relationship with the dark in response to the threat represented by daylight, but many of these creatures are often still active in the transitional hours between total darkness and full sunlight; earthworms, for one, favor periods with the highest humidity, which often are during dusk and dawn. It is not only robins that follow the mantra "the early bird gets the worm."

For insect eaters, however, morning is not always the prime time for feeding. Grasshoppers, butterflies, and other flying insects become more active during the heat of the day because they require sunlight and warmth to reverse the torpor induced by the chill of night.

NESTING

House Wrens are typical insect eaters. Their priority targets include beetles, caterpillars, grasshoppers, and spiders, and they are active hunters in multiple zones, including on the ground, in low-lying vegetation such as shrubbery, and up in trees. When they are feeding nestlings, their hunting activity is at its peak, with captive prey brought to a nest as often as every three minutes. One study reported a single wren could capture more than 1.5 ounces (44 grams)

An Eastern Bluebird feeds its chick. Bird activity increases during migration, mating, and nesting, activities that require greater amounts of energy. The beginning and ends of daylight periods are always the most active times, since most birds have relatively little in the way of energy reserves. The nighttime rest period uses energy that must be replenished in the morning, and at the end of the day energy must be stockpiled until feeding is resumed on the following day. *(Photo by Steve Byland)*

of insects per day, more than four times its body weight, for itself as well as its nestlings.

SEASONAL PATTERNS

Seasonal changes affect birds' feeding behavior by altering what kinds and quantities of food are available. Small perching birds that do not migrate spend more time foraging in winter than summer. Not only are there fewer hours of daylight in this season, but colder temperatures require increased energy expenditure to maintain their internal temperature. In the winter, some birds can spend up to 90 percent of daylight hours foraging, compared to as little as 20 percent during the summer.

In general, small birds have faster metabolisms per unit of body mass than do large birds, compelling them to eat more often, but overall they eat less food per unit of mass than do large birds. This general principle is also influenced by factors such as local weather. Cold weather, for example, requires birds to eat more in order to sustain their body temperature, and extreme heat requires extra energy for cooling.

Hummingbirds can lower their metabolism to an extreme extent in response to cold by relying on a process called torpor. During a short period, usually limited to the hours of nighttime, they slow their metabolism by as much as 95 percent, which gives them a corresponding drop in the amount of energy they need to expend and, thus, food they need to eat to maintain their internal temperature.

MIGRATING

Birds that migrate require periods of intense feeding to prepare for and support lengthy flights. Migratory birds may shift diets from seeds to fruit or insects, for example, to build up fat reserves. During migratory flights, they may selectively focus on high-energy food sources wherever they stop.

HOW MUCH IS ENOUGH?

If you "ate like a bird," how much would you be eating? When flocks of pigeons, sparrows, or crows crowd together to feast on an

HOW MUCH BIRDS EAT

Amounts in this chart are averaged for normal weather, though birds consume more food when temperatures drop, in order to gain the calories required for the sped-up metabolism they need to generate heat.

SPECIES	DAILY FOOD INTAKE (IN PERCENT OF BODY WEIGHT)
domestic chicken	3%
Common Raven	4%
Rock Pigeon	5–6%
Northern Bobwhite	9%
Blue Jay	10%
Canada Goose	10%
Mourning Dove	11%
Cooper's Hawk	12%
Common Goldeneye	20%
Bald Eagle	up to 33%
chickadees	35%
Belted Kingfisher	50%
hummingbirds	100%

abundant food source, it seems as if they have insatiable appetites, but all birds have a limit. Most of the time, birds find enough to eat in their preferred environments (see the How Much Birds Eat sidebar). They eat to survive—but at times they may also eat to take advantage of abundance.

Some birds—the California Gull, for example—are noted for apparent bouts of overeating. When a food source is abundant, as with periodic outbreaks of Mormon crickets in the West, these gulls are known to regurgitate partially digested food in order to continue feeding, an avian form of binge eating. During peak seasons of seed or fruit production, birds quickly take advantage and eat as much

Lesser Goldfinches at a backyard bird feeder

as possible. A similar reaction occurs during population peaks of insects, such as the emergence of periodic cicadas. During these events, millions of cicadas hatch over a period of weeks, quickly leading to a drop-off in interest by the birds that normally eat them. Once the birds are satiated, feeding on these insects may not resume for several weeks. Population booms of shellfish or spawning fish generate the same response in seabirds.

When a population explosion of insects does produce a massive feeding opportunity, birds are unlikely to make much of a dent. For most birds, when presented with generous amounts of food, they slow down, become more selective, and eventually quit feeding. The greatest effect on population numbers of such prey animals is at the beginning of a growth cycle and near its end, not at its peak.

Birds that cache food are less likely to lose interest in times of abundance. Though most birds do not store food, those with a diet primarily of seeds are most likely to exhibit caching behavior. Clark's Nutcrackers cache pine nuts, Black-capped Chickadees cache various seeds, and the aptly named Acorn Woodpeckers cache acorns. Some carnivorous birds are also hoarders, at least some of the time. American Kestrels, Northern Shrikes, Snowy Owls, and Sparrowhawks are among those that save prey.

When most people think of birds eating, the context is usually backyard bird feeders. Those who have been tasked with keeping feeders full recognize that despite the small size of seed-eating birds, they can consume a lot of seed. Studies of feeder use show that satiation is not a typical reaction, however. Most of the time, birds use feeders as a supplementary source, cycling between these and natural resources that are within the same foraging zone. Despite some negatives associated with feeders, there is an overall benefit as reported by a study from Project FeederWatch, which examined the health of ninety-eight bird species that are common visitors to feeders.

EATING IN FLOCKS

One of the more common observations about birds in cities is that they are frequently seen eating in flocks. In an urban environment, this is regular behavior for Rock Pigeons and House Sparrows—and, if bodies of water are present, ducks and geese. This flocking activity is not a peculiarity forced on birds by the unnatural environment of a city, but an innate characteristic of many species.

Flocking behavior is well established in the evolution of birds. Fossilized remains of birds from millions of years ago have been

Rock Pigeons, an introduced species, have a poor reputation in North American cities because of the effects of their group behavior. Feeding in flocks is a natural behavior for these birds, even when the food is provided by pigeon lovers. *(Photo by Bob Saget)*

found grouped together in feeding situations. In the natural environment, flocks improve survival for individual birds against attacks by predators, as well as enhance access to food by sharing in the discovery of food sources. If not already in a flock, an individual bird benefits from the sight of a group feeding, a sign that food is available. Conversely, bird flocks can also attract predators, especially raptors.

Although some bird species dwell in colonies and are active in groups at least most of the time, flocks can also form spontaneously in response to a bounty of food. These group feeding events can involve multiple individuals of the same species or individuals from varied species that share the same diets.

Sparrows, pigeons, ducks, and geese are well-known group feeders, as are domestic chickens and Wild Turkeys. Waterbirds known for group feeding include gulls, pelicans, petrels, and terns, which band together in same-species associations as well as in mixed flocks, particularly when feeding on schooling fish. Scavengers such as Black Vultures are also seen together at massed feeding events, although not all carrion eaters are as social as this species.

Feeding advantages can trigger flocking in otherwise solitary birds, at least during some seasons. Juncos demonstrate flocking behavior at some times of the year, benefiting from multiple birds locating sources of seeds. Northern Shovelers sometimes swim as a group in tight circles to create a funneling effect, which brings food items into range. Most extreme among group feeding behaviors is active cooperation in hunting, when two or more birds work together to flush or drive prey toward capture. Harris's Hawks, the only North American raptors to live in extended family groups, gang up in hunting to improve their capture rate.

DO BIRDS DRINK WATER?

The role of water in physiology is key for all life-forms. Birds require a regular supply of water because of their rapid metabolisms. Thus, access to water is a primary need of birds.

All birds need water, but not all of them drink water. Other than drinking water directly, birds also obtain water from the foods they

The structure of many plants creates holding zones for rainwater that is then accessible to birds, as illustrated by this common teasel (an invasive plant species able to support some insects and birds).

eat. For many species, most or all of the water they need comes from the food they eat. Fruits and nectar are mostly water, and all animal tissue, including that of insects, includes some water. Rainfall generates pockets of water that collect in junctions of stems and branches of trees and other plants. Dew that has collected overnight on foliage, flowers, and fruit also provides a common source of water for birds.

In general, bird bodies contain from 60 to 70 percent water, regardless of a bird's size (that's not much different from humans, whose adult bodies contain from 68 to 72 percent water). Bird anatomy and physiology is designed to reduce the loss of water through conservation and reuse. The bigger the bird, the smaller the percentage of water lost through evaporation. The issue is more acute for small birds, which suffer more because of the effect of this ratio. At the same temperature, wrens, finches, and sparrows can lose 20 to 35 percent of their body mass in water per day, while doves, cardinals, and mockingbirds lose 5 percent or less.

HOW BIRDS DRINK WATER

All pigeons and doves drink water using suction created when a bird pulls back its tongue within its bill, generating a low-pressure zone toward the front that draws water inward. Most birds, however, immerse their bill in water, and once water enters the bill, the bird tilts up its head and allows water to flow into its esophagus.

Some birds drink while flying, a technique common in swallows as they flit near the surface of lakes and rivers while foraging for insects. They dip their lower bill into the water during a low pass over the surface. Other birds known to drink on the wing are swifts and terns.

Aquatic birds drink water—even those, like pelicans, that normally ingest water as they swallow their food. Most seabirds that are active in saltwater environments have modified nasal glands that remove excess salt from their blood. Ospreys in most locations feed almost exclusively on fish, from which they extract all the water they need, with occasional exceptions in hot weather.

Most birds, such as this House Finch, drink water by immersing their bill, then tipping back their head to let the water flow into and down their esophagus.

Sap and nectar feeders, including hummingbirds, may not need to drink water because of the water content already in their diet. Hummingbirds, however, typically nest and forage near water sources and will drink water, sometimes while bathing. Sage-grouse species drink water when it is available, but some researchers believe they are capable of surviving on only the water content of the vegetation in their diet. Roadrunners are also able to survive without direct access to water because their diet—mostly animal prey—is one-half to two-thirds water by weight. Their bodies also recycle more water than other terrestrial birds by extracting salts through their nasal glands, a process similar to that of seabirds. They do drink water from natural sources when it is available.

BIRD BATHS

In urban environments, the widespread use of bird baths and other artificial water supplies provide ready access to water. Birds are not harmed by the chlorine or other additives found in typical municipal water supplies, with the exception of swimming pools that may be overchlorinated. Bird baths are also prone to fostering bacterial growth from droppings and spoiled bird food. These contaminants can create unhealthy conditions that sicken or kill avian visitors. The best practice for bird bath maintenance is to change the water daily and, if necessary, scrub with a mild bleach solution, then rinse thoroughly.

GETTING ENOUGH CALCIUM

All birds need sources of nutrition beyond what supplies energy, including a range of micronutrients that support growth, immune response, and reproduction. Calcium is one of the most important of these supplementary elements, because it's required for producing eggs and supporting bone growth and strength. It takes birds ten to fifteen times more calcium to produce eggs than it takes mammals to produce embryos. In a few species of birds, one clutch of eggs requires more calcium than that of the mother's entire skeleton.

Various studies, some using chickens, show that birds alter their diets to increase calcium intake during the egg production cycle.

Without an adequate supply of calcium, birds may delay egg laying, lay fewer eggs, or lay eggs that are not strong enough to protect developing chicks. While producing eggs, birds do supply some of their calcium needs from their own skeletons, but it is not more than a few percent of the total required, and most of this calcium comes during the final day before an egg is laid. A British study determined that 60 percent of an egg's calcium is deposited in the last eight hours.

Other studies point to another facet of the calcium quest for birds: domestic chickens as well as wild birds most actively seek sources of calcium during the first hours when eggshells are being formed and during late afternoon and early evening (for caged chickens, grit is supplied along with their feed).

On the hunt for calcium, birds may search for broken eggshells (including their own), snails and snail shells, seashells, small animal bones, and even raptor pellets, which contain the skeletons of small vertebrates. Snails are one of the most common calcium sources for passerines in forest habitats, but snails in some areas of the world may be under threat due to the acidification of soil from pollution. Snail populations are shrinking in part because acidification neutralizes calcium, and with weakened shells, these gastropods cannot thrive.

Snail shells, such as that of this Florida apple snail, are sought by birds seeking the calcium they contain. *(Photo by Ryan Hagerty, USFWS)*

Studies of chickens have shown that when calcium is added to a test food source, they detect and prefer that food even when there is no visible evidence of the additive. The birds appear to detect calcium by taste. Related tests have also shown that with a lack of calcium in their diet, birds increased their pecking activity by selecting small items that were

Bare ground provides an open foraging area for birds like this Red-winged Blackbird searching for calcium. Light-colored grit is a visual target birds use to find appropriate sources to ingest.

Birds often do not get enough calcium from their normal diets and may turn to alternatives to acquire this essential mineral. This House Sparrow has discovered that the mortar used in brick buildings is a good source. Over time, exposure to the elements leaches calcium from mortar into the soil, boosting the calcium content of insects and plants in the vicinity. *(Photo by M. G. White)*

white or light in color, a natural color characteristic of calcium-rich materials such as bones and snail shells. This indicates that birds also use vision, along with taste, to seek this mineral.

Soil is often a good source of calcium, and birds gain a significant calcium boost if they have a worm-heavy diet, since earthworms acquire calcium from dirt. Feeding worms to chicks also provides them with an important calcium boost. Other living sources of food, such as wood lice, millipedes, sawfly larvae, spiders, and caterpillars, also have elevated levels of calcium if their local habitat includes calcium-rich soil. Backyards typically have enough accessible calcium for songbirds and other avian visitors, especially if there are patches of bare ground or gravel paths.

Some plant sources can provide calcium, not surprising considering that much of the calcium in plant-feeding arthropods comes from the plants they feed on—but neither greenery nor seeds themselves are a significant direct source of calcium for birds. Plants growing near brick walls may absorb calcium from the residue of mortar leaching into the soil.

HOW DO BIRDS GET GRIT?

Grit assists the grinding action of the ventriculus (gizzard) to prepare food for further digestion and extraction of nutrients (see "Digestive Organs and Processes" in The Anatomy and Physiology of How Birds Eat chapter). Variations in diet influence the type and quantity of grit that birds select. Willow Ptarmigans, which forage on twigs and tree buds, ingest more than twice as much grit as seed-eating birds; birds with diets consisting primarily of seeds utilize grit more than those with diets of insects, fruit, or animals.

The amount of grit and its size usually varies from season to season to reflect changes in a bird's diet, such as a shift from seeds to insects or an increase in feeding to prepare for migration. Small songbirds, such as House Sparrows, generally select particles averaging about 0.02 inch (0.5 millimeter) in diameter, with a range of 0.001 to 0.05 inch (0.2 to 1.4 millimeters) in diameter.

In a comparison of multiple North American species, the most grit per gizzard was reported in American Tree Sparrows, House

Caged domestic chickens and turkeys do not have access to natural sources of grit, so commercial grit is supplied as part of their regular diets. Wild birds that visit backyard bird feeders are unlikely to need any additional grit but may benefit from access to calcium, which is a standard part of most commercial grit products. During the breeding and nesting seasons, extra calcium is especially important, and it may also be supplied through specialized feeder mixes for this purpose.

Sparrows, and Ring-necked Pheasants. How much grit can a songbird hold? House Sparrow grit counts vary considerably from bird to bird, with an average of 580 particles and a high of more than 3,200. The lowest counts were for Barn Swallows, Cedar Waxwings, Common Yellowthroats, Dickcissels, Eastern Kingbirds, Northern Orioles, and Yellow-rumped Warblers (averages at the low end range from a few pieces to less than ten per gizzard). This list is necessarily incomplete, as most species have not yet been investigated for grit usage and grit found in gizzards may be accidentally ingested.

Another investigation of House Sparrows showed that throughout a year, their gizzards contained 66 percent grit and 34 percent food, as measured by weight. Research with domestic chickens reinforces these results. Commercial chicken farms routinely provide grit for their birds as a necessary part of their diet, as do owners of backyard coops.

TOXIC GRIT

Birds' natural instinct to select and ingest grit has become an issue in recent decades as agricultural suppliers have turned to granulated pesticides to improve the effectiveness of the chemicals. These small particles are toxic to birds but are also increasingly ingested because they are visually appealing: granulated pesticides look just like grit to birds. This poses a considerable threat to the animals that ingest the particles, as well as to those animals that ingest the insects already dosed with the pesticides.

A similar threat involves lead, the principal component of pellets used in shotgun shells. Ducks foraging for food at the bottom of lakes and ponds ingest expended lead shot in a quest to acquire grit. The mortality from lead poisoning in ducks and geese is estimated at 2 to 3 percent of the total population, with up to two million deaths annually. See "Lead Poisoning" in the Calamities and Solutions chapter for details on this topic.

BIRD DIETS: INSECTS

Insectivorous birds represent the largest proportion of all bird species, both worldwide and in North America, and the majority of birds eat insects. Some eat only insects; others eat insects and other animals in addition to seeds or other plant material. Nestlings of the majority of North American birds are primarily fed insects by their parents, even though as adults their diets may be primarily seeds or other nonanimal content.

Birds that are described as insectivorous do not eat insects exclusively. As a general rule, birds are considered insectivores if their adult diet consists of 70 percent or more of insects or other arthropods. In North America, there are about 140 insectivorous bird species, but as many as 220 species can be considered insectivorous if the minimum percentage of insects consumed regularly is less than 70 percent.

The most important insectivorous families are the Corvidae (crows, jays, magpies), Picidae (woodpeckers), Sturnidae (starlings), and Emberizidae—subfamilies Emberizini, Parulini, and Icterini (buntings, warblers, sparrows). Many smaller raptors, such as Burrowing Owls, also prey on arthropods.

Robins and other omnivorous birds rely primarily on insects during the nesting seasons but switch priorities before and during

HOW MANY INSECTS DO BIRDS EAT?

ECOSYSTEM	BIRD CONSUMPTION OF ARTHROPODS WORLDWIDE PER YEAR
temperate forests	234 billion pounds
farm fields	62 billion pounds
deserts	11 billion pounds
grasslands	11 billion pounds

Western Meadowlark with a grasshopper

migration as well as in the winter. For the energy-intensive activity of migration, fruit typically dominates, up to 90 percent of all food ingested. In cold-weather seasons, this switch is more about availability, as insects are not as plentiful then in comparison to fruit, although eggs, larvae, and pupae may be available.

Some bird species include insects in their diets only during part of the insects' life cycles. Birds may target insects at any stage—egg, larva, pupa, adult—or specialize in a single stage. This is not an accident, since the range and availability of insects make them close to a universal food source. The estimated combined size of

INSECT CALORIE COMPARISON

TYPE OF INSECT	CALORIES PER GRAM
weevil	5.7
caterpillar	3.7
grasshopper	1.5

this worldwide resource is 10 quintillion (that is, a 10 followed by eighteen zeroes) individual animals, an immense number.

Estimates of the insects that birds consume worldwide are between 440 million and 550 million tons (400–500 million metric tons) every year (see the How Many Insects Do Birds Eat? table). This covers a wide variety of insects—butterflies, beetles, grasshoppers, and so on—in addition to other arthropods such as spiders, mites, and centipedes. Bats and other mammals, frogs, lizards, and predatory insects are also important predators of arthropods, but no other predator group matches birds for overall consumption of insects.

A robust model of abundance, insects are not only the major source of food for birds, but their viability represents a touchstone for the survival of birds. This is an increasingly urgent topic, as various reports from around the world indicate that the populations of many insect species are in decline or threatened, likely a consequence of multiple causes including warming temperatures, increased use of insecticides, and pollution. At the same time, the population of many species of insectivorous birds worldwide are also in decline. The connection is definitive, and the consequences are worrisome.

NUTRITIONAL VALUE OF INSECTS

Insects are a primary source of food for birds because of their availability and high nutritive content. Although there are some differences in the species and food value of insects found in different habitats and geographical zones, the general nutritional value of specific types of insects is about the same. The nutritional value of insects is also usually greater than that found in plant sources, including seeds.

But even among insects of the same species, nutritional value can vary dramatically, a function of season, phase of life, and the quality of food that an insect has access to. Birds that eat insects adjust to this variability by choosing insects within a group that are larger, for example, or by switching to different species. Among the specific characteristics known to influence a bird's selection is the concentration of amino acids, fatty acids, and protein. During nesting season, birds typically more actively target insects, not only because this type of food may be more available than seeds or nectar early in growing seasons but also because parent birds must find the highest-quality food sources for their young (see the Insect Calorie Comparison table).

Fat content in insects ranges from 10 to 60 percent. The content of insect fats includes triacylglycerols, phospholipids, oleic and lin-olenic acids, and similar compounds. Insects are also rich in pro-tein, especially digestible forms of protein. Beetles' protein content consists of up to 60 percent of their mass. Beetles also have one of the highest calcium contents among insects. Caterpillars, a major food source for at least 310 bird species in North America, are espe-cially rich in nutrition, containing more than 50 percent protein and among the highest amounts of fats. Insects also provide minerals, vitamins, and amino acids, essential elements in bird diets. From a nutritional perspective, insects generally provide more energy than plant sources, especially fruit. Ounce per ounce, berries and other fruit yield less than half the energy of insects.

Birds have the ability to identify and select food that provides them with the nutrition they need. This is especially true of birds that are omnivorous. Yellow-rumped Warblers were tested for the ability to choose between food sources that provide more or less of the specific unsaturated fatty acids found in certain insect baits. In low-temperature conditions, the birds not only preferred the unsaturated selections but ate more than the less-fatty options. A similar experiment with Wood Thrushes and American Robins duplicated this result. Researchers noted that the food selection was likely based on a combination of smell and taste, reinforcing the concept that birds are able to actively detect the components in food

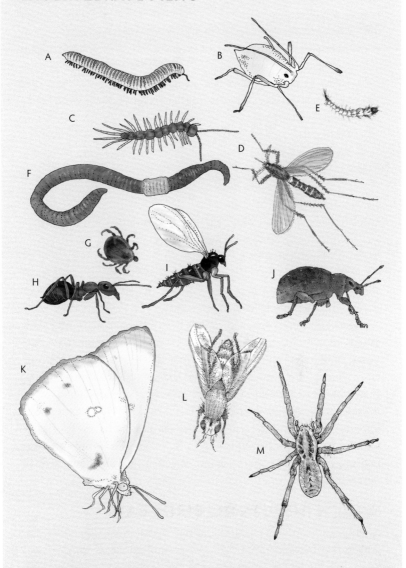

A. Millipede; B. Leaf hopper; C. Centipede; D. Mosquito; E. Mosquito larva;
F. Earthworm; G. Tick; H. Fire Ant; I. Gnat; J. Weevil; K. Clouded sulphur butterfly;
L .Marsh fly; M. Wolf spider

INSECTS IN TREES

The list below shows food sources for insect-eating birds in trees, in order of the greatest effect by birds on insect density.

1. Dermaptera: earwigs
2. Opiliones: harvesters or daddy longlegs
3. Hemiptera: stinkbugs and other true bugs, cicadas, aphids, and related
4. Neuroptera: lacewings
5. Lepidoptera: butterflies, moths
6. Psocoptera: bark lice
7. Coleoptera: beetles
8. Blattodea: termites and related
9. Araneae: spiders
10. Hymenoptera: bees, wasps, ants, and sawflies
11. Diptera: mosquitoes, gnats, and related

that are important to their diets. Memory as well as learning from parents also play a role in such selectivity.

Insects and some other arthropods have a conspicuous outer shell that is mostly indigestible to birds. Insect exoskeletons are composed of chitin, a stiff natural polymer. There is a little protein in chitin and minor amounts of other nutrients, but for most birds, this material is discarded as part of an ejected pellet or passed out in droppings. American Robins and Northern Bobwhites digest about 10 percent of the chitin from their animal prey, and a few species of seabirds are known to absorb up to 85 percent. Chickens are also able to assimilate this material, but in general, it contributes little to bird nutrition.

WHICH INSECTS DO BIRDS EAT?

Among all taxonomic classes of animal phyla, insects represent the largest number and variety. Almost 1.5 million insect species have been identified, with estimates of millions more yet unnamed. This represents about 75 percent of the total number of known species of all animals. Insects are an essential part of almost every ecosystem:

CATERPILLAR MENU

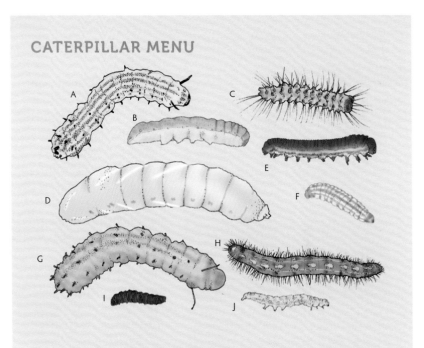

A. Green-striped mapleworm; B. Cabbage moth; C. Fall webworm; D. Big poplar hawk moth; E. Sawfly larva; F. Sunflower moth larva; G. Pink-striped oakworm; H. Green cloverworm; I. Tomato pinworm; J. Forest tentworm

pollinating plants, decomposing dead plants and animals, and providing a source of food for many other animal groups, including birds. Forests are where 75 percent of all bird consumption of insects and other arthropods occurs.

Insects are also available in enough numbers locally to provide ample food for birds. Various studies in North American habitats estimate there are from 124 million to 425 million individual insects per acre in undeveloped areas, representing more than 90,000 known species. In the United States, beetles are the most varied in terms of species, with 23,700 species; there are also at least 19,600 different species of flies. Worldwide, the weight of insects is estimated to average about 400 pounds per acre (180 kilograms per 0.4 hectare). This proliferation is what makes such a food source so critical to the health of bird populations.

PLANT-EATING INSECTS

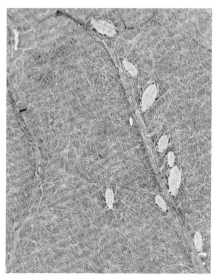

Thistles, both native and invasive species, are widespread throughout North America and an important source of seeds for birds. More than a hundred species of aphids also feed on thistles, providing an additional food target for birds. This variety is the thistle oleaster aphid.

Insects that feed on plants are the major source of food for birds in North America. More than 90 percent of these insects are specialists, adapted to select and feed on one or a few native and nonnative plants. In individual ecosystems, there can be a very large number of plant species, which provide food for great numbers of species of insects (see the Invertebrate Menu illustration), as well as of large numbers of individual insects. These great quantities reflect the established complexity of nature.

Trees, the signature living structures in forests, provide an important habitat for many insects and other arthropods (see the Insects in Trees sidebar). For insectivorous birds that nest in grasslands, the majority of their prey are butterfly and moth larvae and grasshoppers (see the Caterpillar Menu illustration). Adult birds select and eat these insects at all stages of their metamorphosis, but generally choose the soft-bodied larvae when feeding their nestlings.

Aphids: One of the major banes of gardeners, both indoors and out, as well as farmers, aphids are soft-bodied insects that feed on plant sap and are most often found in colonies. There are about 5,000 species worldwide and about 1,350 in North America. Typically smaller than ⅛ inch (3 millimeters) long, adult aphids fly from plant to plant to lay eggs.

An untreated plant, like this sowthistle (left), is a natural host to many different kinds of insects, including both pests (plant predators such as these aphids and lacewings) and benefactors (insect predators, like the ladybird beetle at right) that can keep pests in check. Both pests and predators are food for insectivorous birds.

Among the many aphid species, some are specialists, attracted to only certain plants as hosts: rose aphids, woolly apple aphids, and sunflower aphids represent a few of these. The most common aphid in North American gardens is a generalist (despite the limitations suggested by its name), the green peach aphid, which is known to infest up to 500 plant varieties.

Natural predators of aphids include ladybird beetles, lacewings, and hoverflies. Small insect-eating birds target these insect predators as well as the aphids themselves. The American Goldfinch, despite many sources declaring that it mostly eats seeds, may be one of the most prolific aphid eaters according to other sources.

Other birds that eat aphids include chickadees, sparrows, warblers, and woodpeckers. One recent study in Europe found that Eurasian Tree Sparrows, with aphids as part of their diet, can end up increasing local aphid populations that feed on a cereal crop because the birds also eat some of the aphids' main predators, especially hoverflies and ladybug beetles (up to 77 percent of food fed to nestlings).

A Common Tern consumes an insect, part of a wide-ranging diet that mostly consists of small fish but also includes crustaceans and insects. *(Photo by R. Lavka)*

Beetles: Insects and other arthropods are a part of the diet of many waterbirds. Laughing Gulls, for one, feed on both water-based and terrestrial animals, including insects. Among their preferred terrestrial food sources are beetles and ants, quite different fare from the mollusks, crabs, and fish they seek in the water. Common around coastal urban areas, these birds also are attracted to garbage dumps, as much for the leftover human food as the insects they attract. In one study of these gulls near New York City, 93 percent of the ingested food identified was insects, mostly beetles. These included a wide range of beetle families, especially scarab beetles (the most prevalent), weevils, and stag beetles. Given the urban locations and widespread availability of garbage dumps, it was also not surprising to find that these gulls fed on an invasive pest: Japanese beetles, which have now spread through the Midwest and into the Rocky Mountains. (Other insects found in this local diet: grasshoppers, moths, stinkbugs, wasps, ants, and crane flies.)

Threats: One of the major situations now facing developed countries is an overwhelming reliance on agricultural monocultures, which replaces highly diverse and localized plant communities with crops that are singularly uniform across large surface areas. Over time, this trend has greatly reduced the availability of native food sources for native insects while providing huge feeding opportunities for invasive insect species.

For bird species that have adapted to find and feed on certain insect species, a negative cascading effect follows. Multiple investigations in recent years in North America, Europe, and other continents confirm the outcome: most species of insectivorous birds are now declining or have even disappeared from some areas.

AQUATIC INSECTS

The primary prey for many birds in riparian forests is aquatic insects, which includes insects that are found in the water only during some life stages (mayflies, for example). Unlike terrestrial-breeding insects, aquatic insect populations tend to expand earlier, in the spring, and remain available as food throughout the winter in most geographical ranges. Insect-eating birds that favor riparian zones may vary their diet through the year, concentrating on aquatic insects in the winter and spring.

One North American bird, the American Dipper, is a year-round resident through much of its range, which includes very high elevations subject to severe winter weather. Dippers, unlike most other waterbirds, do not have webbed feet and forage for prey on the bottom of shallow streams by walking along the bottom. They rely on open water to search for aquatic insects and other prey; thus, they move to lower elevations when streams freeze in winter.

Geese and ducks, although often described as plant eaters, consume arthropods as well. Insects on terrestrial vegetation are often ingested by Mallards, along with plant matter, and on and near the water they frequently select caddisflies, dragonflies, and insect larvae, as well as mussels and other crustaceans. Wood Ducks, though primarily vegetarian, feed on beetles, caterpillars, dragonflies, and isopods such as wood lice, as well as slugs and snails. Snowy Egrets will snap up both aquatic and terrestrial insects, although they typically hunt for larger prey, including crayfish, fish, and worms—just about anything small enough to strike at.

Purple Martins are communal nesters that congregate in birdhouses such as this one in Bay City State Park, Michigan. East of the Rocky Mountains, the survival of these birds is supported by this kind of artificial structure, replacing natural nesting sites that have been lost to development. The Purple Martin Conservation Association (see Resources) provides information and plans to back this effort. *(Photo by V. F. Greene)*

While in the air, Purple Martins consume large quantities of insects, ranging from mosquitoes to dragonflies—the latter is shown in this photo. *(Photo by Agnieszka Bacal)*

BITING INSECTS

Many insectivorous birds are known to eat insects that are barely large enough for humans to see, including species of gnats and midges. Swallows have no problem spotting and ingesting these flying insects, but it takes a lot of them to provide adequate nutrition.

Mosquitoes: The highly visible activity of some birds eating unwelcome insects has long been a factor in their attractiveness to humans. This is particularly true with the Purple Martin and mosquitoes. A familiar colony-dwelling bird, this martin species is comfortable in urban environments and is widely supported by homemade structures designed to house them. Martins are active aerial hunters, chasing insects above lawns and gardens as well as more-natural environments. Their prey includes flies, stinging insects, gnats, and mosquitoes.

Mosquitoes were once thought to be the main target for hungry martins, with the myth that a single adult Purple Martin could eat up to 2,000 mosquitoes a day being widely believed. This figure has turned out to be erroneous, though the myth endures. The few

Eyespots on butterfly wings, such as this common buckeye butterfly common throughout the South, are adaptations that startle, confuse, or divert the attention of birds and other predators. *(Photo by Elliotte Rusty Harold)*

detailed projects that have studied martin diets in North America report that mosquitoes make up less than 3 percent of their total insect consumption. More accurately, as a group Purple Martins in North America are estimated to consume up to 262 billion insects every year, making them an important factor in the complex ecological systems that affect both natural and urban environments.

WHY DO BIRDS AVOID SOME INSECTS?

Not all insects are appetizing to birds. Over time, insects hunted by birds evolve strategies to avoid being eaten.

Camouflage: Among these strategies is camouflage in the form of protective shapes and colorings. One of the most studied examples of this reaction is in butterflies. The wide variations in butterfly wing color and pattern are adaptations that provide camouflage for avoiding predation yet also allow species to recognize one another for mating. In general, butterflies and moths that do not feature bright, distinctive colors and patterns have colors and patterns that mimic plant foliage, branches, or tree bark, to help them avoid detection.

Eyespots: One form of warning coloration, eyespots are unique patterns on butterfly wings that can startle predators, confuse them, or divert attention to less vulnerable body parts. A research project has also indicated that such eyespots may be effective because of their ability to mimic the sparkle in corneas, where reflections include ultraviolet light.

Monarch butterflies are associated with milkweed plants, which are essential for their survival, but they may occasionally sip nectar from other plants, such as this coneflower. *(Photo by Annette Shaff)*

Unpleasant taste or odor: Birds learn to reject some insects that have unpleasant tastes or odors and avoid the same species when encountered thereafter. Scientists who have studied this effect define four levels of reactions from birds in such circumstances: nondestructive tasting, destructive tasting, post-ingestion rejection, and visual identification.

Butterflies are the best known example, especially the monarch, which feeds on milkweed plants, a source of potent chemicals called cardenolides. Most birds (and other animals) quickly learn to leave monarchs alone because of toxicity associated with these compounds. But not all birds. Female monarchs have up to 30 percent more cardenolides than males, and the birds that target them can tell the sexes apart, selecting more males than females when feeding. Black-headed Grosbeaks, for one, have developed some tolerance for the poison the monarchs contain and will often gather to feast on these butterflies during monarch migrations. A few other species are known to feed on monarchs occasionally, including some bluebirds, Steller's Jays, and Townsend's Warblers.

A few butterfly species mimic the coloration of monarchs as a copycat strategy, including the viceroy butterfly; the queen butterfly is also distasteful to birds. Other flying insects that repel predation by birds due to being distasteful include several species of the grapeleaf skeletonizer moth, the oleander moth, the zebra butterfly, and the gulf fritillary butterfly. As caterpillars, these species feed on plants with natural toxins, passing these toxins as well as an unpleasant taste to their adult forms. The ladybug beetle, a welcome visitor in gardens because it feeds on aphids, is also avoided by most birds because of its toxicity.

INSECT PREDATION OF PLANTS

Trees, shrubs, and other plants would not survive if all of their leaves were eaten by insects. Plenty of insect species depend on this source of food, and they are capable of stripping trees and other plants bare if left unchecked. In North and Central America, as well as Europe, research has concluded that birds reduce populations of insects that feed on trees by about half, with a similar effect on the percentage of leaf damage. What insects target, however, represents a more varied picture, with consequences that influence how insect-eating birds feed.

In general, plants grow by concentrating nutrients at zones where growth is most active, especially buds, new leaves, branch tips, and treetops. Grasses, herbs, trees, and other plants have growth-nourishing compounds that are most abundant where the growth occurs. Not surprisingly, plant-eating insects are concentrated in such growth zones. Studies of leaf damage on trees show that insects are more active on young trees than old trees because they select foliage that has the highest nutritive value.

Plants may produce repellents that are triggered when predation is detected. Insects such as the Japanese beetle detect such compounds, but they interpret them as signals that other beetles have found a food source. These beetles, an invasive pest in North America, are usually not repelled as intended because the target plants have been isolated by their predation and have not developed compounds that target this species.

Gypsy moths (top) are an invasive insect native to Asia and parts of Europe. *(Photo by Bugwood.org)* They produce caterpillars (bottom) that feed on more than 500 species of trees and shrubs in North America. Birds feed on gypsy moth eggs, caterpillars, pupae, and adults, playing a role in limiting the destruction by these pests. *(Top photo by John H. Ghent, USDA Forest Service)*

INSECT INFESTATIONS

Many insects have multiple breeding cycles in a year, giving them the opportunity to quickly respond when their preferred food supplies are abundant. On the other hand, most insectivorous birds have a single breeding cycle, limiting their ability to keep up with the availability of their prey. The lag between the availability of prey and the predators' response is often at least a year and sometimes several years. These out-of-phase cycles are a normal part of predator-prey relationships in most of the animal kingdom, affecting wolves and moose for one example, and foxes and rabbits, to name another.

Infestations of insects can have profound impacts on local and regional forests. Native insects that are well known for their destructive capabilities include the mountain pine beetle, spruce beetle, spruce budworm, southern pine beetle, and tussock moth. Infestations also come from pests invading from other continents, such as the gypsy moth, emerald ash borer, and Japanese beetle.

In 2011, 6.6 million acres (2.7 million hectares) of trees were killed by insects and diseases, a peak that was nearly repeated in 2015: 6 million acres (2.4 million hectares). This acreage does not include trees that were defoliated but survived. A single tree that is defoliated by insects or disease provides a source of shelter and food for other insects and animals, including birds. When the damage is widespread, however, the impact can last for years, even decades.

Changes in climate are having an effect on forest health, impacting trees themselves and altering the natural barrier that temperature presents to the spread of some insect pests. The history of forests in North America, as shown in tree ring studies and other evidence, indicates that insects are well equipped to take advantage of changes in the climate. In general, during long periods of warmer and wetter weather, insects with diets dependent on tree foliage thrive, and in colder cycles they suffer.

Emerald ash borer: Several studies have focused on the benefit woodpeckers may provide in controlling one of the current insect epidemics, the spread of the emerald ash borer. This nonnative beetle is a natural target for woodpeckers. But there is an unexpected consequence.

Woodpeckers and other insect-eating birds have evolved to be very effective at finding their food. These birds routinely select trees that have the most beetles, typically at the heart of an infestation, not those at the fringes of an outbreak, where there are fewer insects per tree. The trees the woodpeckers select are likely already doomed, which limits the effect of any insect culling by woodpeckers, while those trees that would most benefit from woodpecker feeding are left alone, which unintentionally helps the infestation to spread.

Spruce budworm: As the numbers of insects rises before an infestation becomes severe, birds play a more critical role than during its peak. Various studies show that as birds take advantage of an increase in a local food supply, their rates of reproduction and success in raising chicks increase but over time are not enough to keep up with an insect population explosion. One example is the spruce budworm. Researchers believe that, in normal conditions, predation by birds is an important factor in controlling the spread of these pests and preventing infestations. But if circumstances favor rapid growth for these insects, such as from weather patterns that are ideal for feeding and reproduction or from a lack of predators, the birds have less and less effect.

One of the natural forces that prevents insects from being killed off entirely is irregular peaks in their population cycles. In some forests in New England, for example, insectivorous birds may experience summers with low populations of target insects, limiting the reproductive success of the birds. As the bird populations shrinks, the insect populations grow, eventually overtaking their predators' populations.

Grasshoppers: Other examples support the concept that birds are best at reducing insect numbers that are at low to medium densities. In grasslands, for example, birds reduce grasshopper densities from 30 to 50 percent as long as there are only one to four of these insects in about 10 square feet (1 square meter). As grasshoppers increase in numbers, the birds feeding on them initially

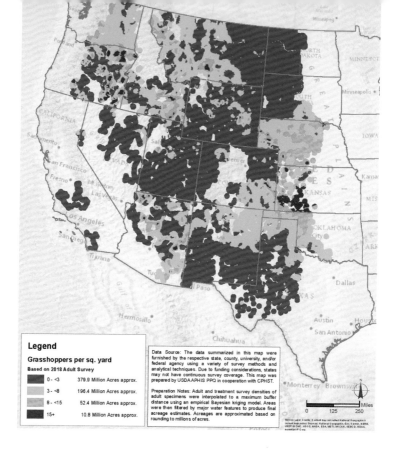

Legend

Grasshoppers per sq. yard

Based on 2018 Adult Survey

▨	0 - <3	379.9 Million Acres approx.
▨	3 - <8	196.4 Million Acres approx.
▨	8 - <15	52.4 Million Acres approx.
■	15+	10.8 Million Acres approx.

Data Source: The data summarized in this map were furnished by the respective state, county, university, and/or federal agency using a variety of survey methods and analytical techniques. Due to funding considerations, states may not have continuous survey coverage. This map was prepared by USDA-APHIS-PPQ in cooperation with CPHST.

Preparation Notes: Adult and treatment survey densities of adult specimens were interpolated to a maximum buffer distance using an empirical Bayesian kriging model. Areas were then filtered by major water features to produce final acreage estimates. Acreages are approximated based on rounding to millions of acres.

Occasionally, drought and other seasonal weather conditions alter the population balance between grasshoppers and their predators, resulting in huge numbers of grasshoppers that overwhelm the appetites of predators, leading to devastation of natural vegetation and agricultural crops. Various agencies monitor these outbreaks and publish reports that help prepare for the onslaught. This 2019 Rangeland Grasshopper Hazard. Map shows the density of grasshoppers per square yard for the western United States. *(Map by USDA-APHIS-PPQ, Cheyenne, Wyoming, Jan. 31, 2019)*

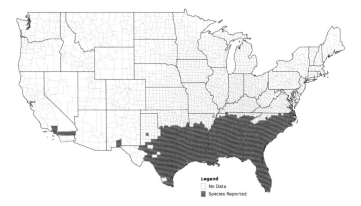

Legend
☐ No Data
■ Species Reported

Northern Flickers (top), like other woodpeckers, are at home in trees, climbing trunks and branches in search of insect prey, but they are also voracious predators of ants, seeking them out on the ground, even using their strong bills to excavate anthills in search of ant larvae; this makes them a welcome element in the fight against invasive fire ants. *(Photo by Steve Byland)* The map (bottom) indicates the spread of these pests as of mid-2019. *(Map by Early Detection and Distribution Mapping System, Center for Invasive Species and Ecosystem Health, University of Georgia, 2019)* benefit. In western North American grasslands, birds that are common predators of grasshoppers include the Grasshopper Sparrow, Horned Lark, Vesper Sparrow, and Western Meadowlark.

In typical years, there are usually enough birds to compensate for the available grasshoppers, but the ratio can get lopsided in a hurry. Following a wet winter or spring, for example, grasshopper populations are likely to expand rapidly in response to a bonanza in plant growth, and they quickly outpace the ability of predators to keep them in check. The overabundance of grasshoppers strips available vegetation bare, and large numbers of the insects migrate to find fresh fodder, spreading an infestation into other areas.

Fire ants: One of the more notorious invasive insects in modern times is the red fire ant, now prevalent across much of the southern states from Florida to Texas, with colonies also now spreading in southern California. Toxic to people, pets, livestock, wildlife, and many agricultural crops, fire ants were initially attacked with the insecticide Mirex. However, Mirex was banned in 1976 because of the harm it caused fish, crabs, other crustaceans, some mammals, and chickens.

The current range of red fire ants is naturally restricted by freezing temperatures. Native to South America, these insects are not able to survive in cold weather. As average temperatures rise across the continent, however, their potential range can expand farther to the north. Some biologists also theorize that this invasive species may eventually crossbreed with native ant species, producing hybrids that can tolerate colder weather. If this happens, fire ants or fire ant hybrids will likely move farther into the Midwest.

Purple Martins are apparently not repelled by fire ants, which they seek out for food. It's estimated that these martins may eat billions of fire ants annually, particularly the airborne mating queens. Barn Swallows, Chimney Swifts, Eastern Kingbirds, Great-tailed Grackles, Northern Rough-winged Swallows, Red-headed Woodpeckers, Scissor-tailed Flycatchers, Tree Swallows, and Western Kingbirds have also been observed feeding on these invasive pests.

Birds, however, have not stemmed the invasion of fire ants and likely will not do so in the future. Meanwhile, a multimillion-dollar industry niche of fire-ant repellent strategies has developed to deal with the problem, from large-scale agricultural applications to those for individual homes. More than a hundred commercial products are marketed as effective against red fire ants, including some that are made from organic or natural compounds. Many of these are sold in granulated form, to be strewn in and around ant mounds. As with other granulated agricultural and gardening products, the granules can attract birds that forage on the ground. Whether or not red fire ant baits and poisons are directly toxic to birds, they are best avoided or used with extreme caution.

BIRDS, INSECTS, AND AGRICULTURE

Farmers and gardeners have a historic dislike of birds, or at least some bird species. Crows eat their corn, starlings eat their wheat, magpies eat their cherries. Yet farm fields are also ripe hunting grounds for insect-eating birds. Crops that are most associated with activity of insectivorous birds (in order of prevalence) are sorghum, soybeans, corn (grain), winter wheat, oats, barley, spring wheat, hay, and durum wheat.

Bird species noted for their activity on multiple crop pests include the Barn Swallow, Common Nighthawk, Dickcissel, Eastern Bluebird, Eastern Kingbird, Eastern Meadowlark, Grasshopper Sparrow, Horned Lark, Killdeer, Mourning Dove, Red-winged Blackbird, Vesper Sparrow, Western Kingbird, and Yellow-headed Blackbird. Birds that are the most common and widespread that prey on crop-damaging insects include the American Crow, blackbirds, Bobolink, Cattle Egret, Common Grackle, Common Raven, gulls, meadowlarks, Northern Flicker, plovers and other shorebirds, and sparrows. These birds represent only the species that have been specifically identified in monitored observations involved in targeted agricultural zones; many more are likely active as well. (See the Birds That Eat Agricultural Insect Pests sidebar.)

Birds that feed on crops or insect pests generally nest near fields. These zones harbor protective territory for bird populations. With bird species that are most associated with agricultural crops, the greatest diversity of species was found, in order of prevalence, in

BIRDS THAT EAT AGRICULTURAL INSECT PESTS

Both native and invasive agricultural pests are targets for many different species of birds, which have found crops ideal habitats for foraging. The birds listed here are noted for their effectiveness in foraging for insects in multiple crops. Some, especially blackbirds, crows, and starlings, however, are also capable of attacking the crops as well. Species well established within habitats adjacent to agricultural fields contribute to the predation, using crops and insect pests to supplement their diets.

American Crow
American Kestrel
American Pipit
American Robin
Black-capped
  Chickadee
Bobolink
Brewer's Blackbird
California Gull
Carolina Chickadee
Common Grackle
Common Raven
Downy Woodpecker
Eastern Bluebird
Eastern Kingbird
Eastern Meadowlark
European Starling

Fox Sparrow
Franklin's Gull
Golden-crowned
  Kinglet
Grasshopper Sparrow
Hairy Woodpecker
Herring Gull
Horned Lark
House Sparrow
Lark Bunting
Lark Sparrow
Northern Flicker
Northern Mockingbird
Pine Siskin
Red-bellied
  Woodpecker
Red-breasted Nuthatch

Red-winged Blackbird
Ruby-crowned Kinglet
Savannah Sparrow
Say's Phoebe
Steller's Jay
Swainson's Hawk
Tree Swallow
Vesper Sparrow
Western Kingbird
Western Meadowlark
White-breasted
  Nuthatch
White-crowned
  Sparrow
Yellow-headed
  Blackbird
Yellow-rumped Warbler

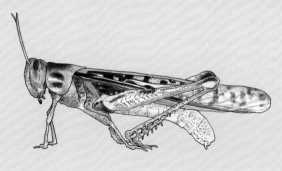

CORN PESTS MENU

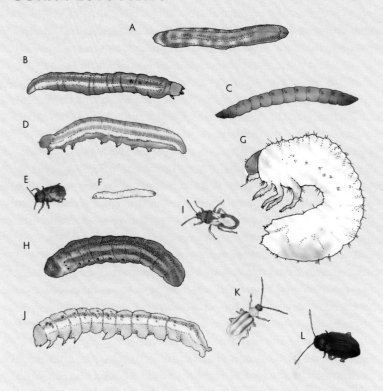

A. Fall armyworm; B. Common stalk borer; C. Wireworm; D. Common armyworm; E. Southern corn leaf beetle; F. Western corn rootworm; G. White grub (June beetle larva); H. Soil cutworm; I. Cinch bug; J. Corn earworm; K. Western corn rootworm beetle; L. Corn flea beetle

Corn is a target for many insect pests throughout its growing cycle. Its seeds,stalks, and cobs attract crawling, burrowing, boring, and flying insects, which face an arsenal of chemical weapons. Birds are natural predators of all of the pests shown here, but they face their own danger from insecticides employed in the battle to save crops. These are some of the most common of the dozens of insect pests of commercial corn grown in North America. Insect-eating birds may prey on any or all of their life-forms: eggs, larvae, pupae, and adults.

floodplain forests, upland forests, shrublands, farmed shelter belts, railroad rights-of-way, former crop fields, natural marshes, tilled row crops, wooded fencerows, pastures, wooded farmland, and restored marshes. This suggests that bird populations in a wide range of habitats contribute to a beneficial goal of agriculture: reducing insect predation.

Some birds, especially blackbirds, crows, and starlings, are capable of attacking the crops as well as insect pests. In recent decades, however, birds have begun to develop a better reputation for their natural ability to target the insect pests that cause economic damage to crops. Multiple studies report the value of insect predation by birds on specific insect pests and in different parts of annual growing cycles. Even crows, renowned for their ability to damage corn, spend as much or more time in corn fields preying on major corn pests, including corn borers and earworms.

European corn borer: Northern Flickers and other common insect-eating birds have quickly adjusted to the presence of one significant uninvited insect pest, the European corn borer. This invasive species was first noticed in Boston in about 1917 and by 1939 emerged as a serious threat in the Corn Belt—Midwest states with a history of commercial corn farming. In a field study in the 1960s, flickers removed 60 to 80 percent of all the borer larvae embedded in cornstalks that were left after harvesting. Flickers and crows are among the few species of North American birds that are motivated to and can identify the entry holes these insects make in cornstalks and then remove the larvae.

Red-winged Blackbirds and other insectivores are not able to target larvae inside cornstalks, but they do target corn fields to feed on the adult moths and eggs that are exposed on the plant. Red-winged Blackbirds in particular have been blamed for considerable damage to corn crops as they seek out the expanding populations of the European corn borer and corn rootworm, among other pests. These and other birds, especially crows, devour corn when they are not foraging for insects.

Research on the threat to crops posed by birds, however, indicates that in the era of the corn rootworm infestation (see the next subheading), it is rootworms and corn borers, as well as other insect pests, that draw birds to fields in the first place. The majority of their feeding is on beetles and grubs. Despite some damage to ripening ears of corn, a net advantage is reported: birds help keep the beetle infestations from expanding out of control.

Unfortunately for farmers and gardeners in the eastern part of North America, the destructive corn borer has branched out and is now also a threat to buckwheat, celery, hops, lima and snap beans, millet, peppers, potatoes, soybeans, and flowers including asters, dahlias, and zinnias. Of little consolation to growers, this pest also has targeted weeds, including cocklebur, dock, jimsonweed, and pigweed.

Scarecrows are the least hazardous of responses traditionally used against crop predation by birds; poison and shotguns are among the

Crops attract birds, singly or in flocks such as this; agricultural activity represents feeding opportunities for both seed-eating and insect-eating birds. During planting, flocks of birds are known to follow seeding equipment, foraging for freshly planted seeds, and, during the growing season, feasting on the seeds of maturing plants, the insects attracted to the plants, or both. These Red-winged Blackbirds are flying out of a field of corn in Massachusetts. *(Photo by Richard Closs)*

most lethal. The corn industry has benefited from the development of genetically modified corn with genes from *Bacillus thuringiensis* (Bt), a naturally occurring soil bacteria toxic to the European corn borer as well as many other insects, including beneficial species. Bt-modified corn generates higher yields without the need for chemical pesticides, and so far this corn has had no measurable negative effects, at least compared to that of the previous generation of agricultural chemicals, on most of the other insects and animal life common in the life cycle of corn plants.

On the negative side, while Bt does not affect many insects, it does affect species such as butterflies and moths, many of them part of the natural food chain for birds. Whatever the real or potential harm to plants, wildlife, and humans, widening exposure to Bt can be expected to unleash one of the most potent tools in evolution's arsenal: adaptation. Sooner or later, if it hasn't happened already, the European corn borer will develop resistance to this natural toxin, a response that will require potentially stronger remedies.

Corn rootworm: This event has already occurred with a closely related version of the original Bt-modified corn, a variation that affects a different pest for corn farmers, the corn rootworm. Corn rootworm beetles cause an estimated $1 billion in damage to corn production around the world every year. A specialized Bt-modified corn was formulated from a natural variation of Bt that was toxic to only a narrow range of insects, including the rootworm.

While this corn strain was initially successful in commercial application, in 2012 reports began appearing about fields of the modified plant that were destroyed by infestations of corn rootworm that had developed resistance to the modified plant. At least for the near future, this direction of control is likely to remain in use because there are multiple variations of Bt-modified corn that can be used to replace those that become ineffective.

BIRD DIETS: PLANTS

Birds that eat primarily plants usually focus on a single part of a plant, such as seeds or nectar, but nuts, fruit, leaves, buds, pollen, and sap are also consumed. Backyard feeders mostly serve plant-eating birds. Feeders usually offer a mix of vegetarian fare that often includes seeds and peanuts, though hummingbird feeders offer nectar, and some feeders are designed to hold suet.

SEEDS

There are more insect-eating bird species than seed-eating birds in the world and in North America, but most people see more of the latter because of backyard bird feeders, which are primarily stocked with seed. Seeds are an abundant resource in most natural bird habitats, from grasses and sedges to forbs, with densities estimated at up to about 2,900 seeds per square foot (31,000 seeds per square meter) in some locations, especially grasslands. With the highest densities comes great diversity, more than six species of seeds per square foot (sixty per square meter), and available production in peak seasons of more than 195 pounds per acre (188 kilograms per hectare).

Seeds in general are a significant source of nutrition to birds, but not all seeds are equal. Most seeds are rich in polyunsaturated fatty acids such as linoleic acid, making them a good source of nutrition, though not as good as insects overall because insects provide more protein. But an estimated 85 percent of seed types provide at least 16 percent or more crude protein, adequate for many birds' metabolic needs.

In nature, birds seek to maximize their dietary input in the most effective way, making the most efficient use of energy and selecting seeds with the most nutritional value. The variables include time of year, demands for feeding nestlings, competition for food sources, availability of food, abundance of food, as well as the size, shape, color, contrast, and taste of seeds. The main components of taste for

NATIVE SEED SAMPLER

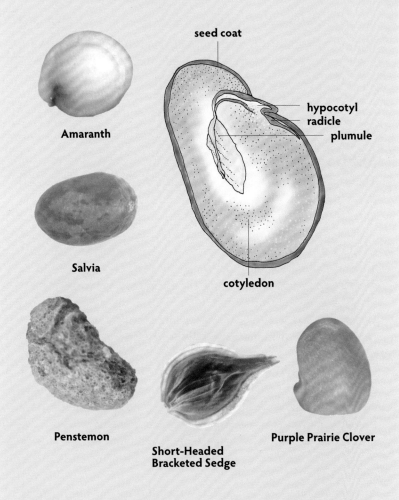

seed coat

hypocotyl
radicle
plumule

Amaranth

Salvia

cotyledon

Penstemon

Short-Headed
Bracketed Sedge

Purple Prairie Clover

Small birds eat tiny seeds. An American Goldfinch has no problem pulling one tiny thistle bract out of the flower head, one at a time, and removing the seed. In the natural diet of birds, there are even more tiny seed varieties, from native as well as invasive species. These greatly magnified seeds are some of the native varieties on the menu for North American birds (see the Grasses Menu illustration).

NUTRITIONAL VALUE OF SEEDS

SEED TYPE	PROTEIN	FAT	MOISTURE
niger	23%	35%	3%
canola	22%	39%	2%
sunflower	18%	39%	2%
amaranth	18%	8%	2%
red millet	14%	4%	5%
wheat	16%	3%	4%
yellow millet	13%	4%	6%
sorghum	11%	3%	5%

seed selections are fat, protein, and carbohydrates; water content is also sometimes a factor (see the Nutritional Value of Seeds table).

All of these variables considered, the most important factor in which seeds birds select may be the speed at which the seed can be consumed. The seeds that are the simplest and quickest to ingest are the ones most likely to be selected first. Weight can influence the choice as well, as heavier seeds can represent more fat content and therefore greater nutritional value, but because smaller seeds have smaller husks, they can be dehusked quicker, increasing a bird's overall intake. Still, seeds benefit birds most when they are selected based on nutritional value. Birds determine this value based on taste, feel, and experience.

If the only object was to ingest the seed and not the husk, birds would always select hulled seeds, such as sunflower kernels provided in some feeders. Yet this is not the case, as many birds select those with husks, perhaps because hulled seeds don't occur in natural environments and birds that cache seeds do so only with unhulled seeds. Black-capped Chickadees, Tufted Titmice, and White-breasted Nuthatches, among other species, often choose hulled seeds when they're provided in bird feeders.

Pigeons, which are large enough to eat many different kinds of seeds, have been measured ingesting some unhusked seeds at sixty to one hundred per minute. Wild Turkeys are also adept at eating this rapidly when they encounter an ample supply of seeds, as they don't waste time removing husks or shells. Smaller birds generally remove the husks from seeds before eating, the common practice with sunflower seeds, millet, and niger (an import from India and Africa), but can do so at a fast pace. The black surface of a niger seed is actually a thin husk.

Bills and tongues are well suited for the task of husking, which takes only a few seconds or less per seed, especially for songbirds such as finches. Most finches and seedeaters have a groove at the outside edge of their upper bill into which a sunflower seed can be maneuvered with their tongue. When they close their bill, the lower bill splits the hull open. Small birds, such as chickadees, may hold an unhulled seed in their bill and pound it against a hard surface to break it open.

GRASSES AND SEDGES

The taxonomic family of grasses occupies between 31 and 43 percent of the earth's surface (depending on how grasslands are defined); the planet's major habitat is grasslands. Worldwide, there are more than 10,000 species of grass, including many of the most important agricultural cereals such as wheat, oats, barley, rice,

Many smaller songbirds, like this House Finch, can readily break through the thin shells of black oil sunflower seeds, using unique features of their bills.

NORTH AMERICAN GRASSES AND SEDGES SAMPLER

Grasses and sedges are widely varied, representing many different species that are found in almost all habitats. This list includes those adopted for yards and ornamental plantings, which dominate nonnative landscapes, but all grasses and sedges provide food for birds and other animals.

Alkali grass	Idaho fescue	Rice grass
Bent grass	Indian grass	River oats
Blue grama	Ivory sedge	Ryegrass
Bluegrass	June grass	Salt grass
Bluestem	Love grass	Sea oats
Bottlebrush grass	Manna grass	Sheep fescue
Bristle grass	Muhly grass	Side oats grama
Bromegrass	Needle grass	Squirrel tail
Broom sedge	Oat grass	Star sedge
Buffalo grass	Orchard grass	St. Augustine grass
Bur sedge	Palm sedge	Switchgrass
Cordgrass	Pennsylvania sedge	Thread-leaf sedge
Creek sedge	Pine grass	Three-awn grass
Drop seed	Plantain sedge	Wheatgrass
Field sedge	Porcupine sedge	Wild rye
Fox sedge	Prairie sand reed	Witchgrass
Galetta grass	Purple top	Wool grass
Hair grass	Red fescue	

millet, sorghum, rye, and corn. More than 1,400 species of grass are found in North America (see the North American Grasses and Sedges Sampler sidebar), including nonnative species introduced deliberately and others that are accidental invaders. The natural grasslands of North America that span the continent were originally one of the dominant habitats.

Dozens of bird species breed in grasslands, including grouse, larks, pheasants, plovers, and sparrows, as well as raptors that depend on these species for food (see the Grasses Menu illustration). Grasses (and sedges) are one of the most important food sources for many birds, including in agriculturally developed zones. Grassland habitats include shortgrass prairie, tallgrass prairie, mixed-grass prairie, desert grassland, southeastern pine savanna, and low-bush barrens. In grasslands, the seeds of grasses and sedges are not only food for birds; the foliage also provides important nesting sites and cover from predators. Birds that depend on grasslands for food and shelter are under increasing pressure as development whittles away at the minimum zones they require. With the range of habitats and food sources they represent to birds, grasslands are a valuable natural resource.

Sedges are a related group of perennials with one distinguishing feature that separates them from grass: their stems usually have edges—three (though some have round stems). There are about 500 species of sedge in North America, the largest family of flowering plants on the continent. Like grasses, various sedges have adaptations for a variety of habitats, from wetlands to deserts, and have conspicuous seed heads that make them a foraging target for birds.

Natural disruptions to grasslands, such as flooding, fires, and drought, are typically local. In the modern era, human-caused disruptions are larger, more frequent, and more severe, from development, agriculture, and overgrazing. Some land that was cleared for grazing or farming as far back as the 1700s, mostly in northeastern US, has reverted to forest as land use has changed.

The biggest negative impact on native grasslands is intensification of agricultural use. Farms increasingly manage land by monoculture, a large-scale single-crop system that replaces smaller fields and

GRASSES MENU

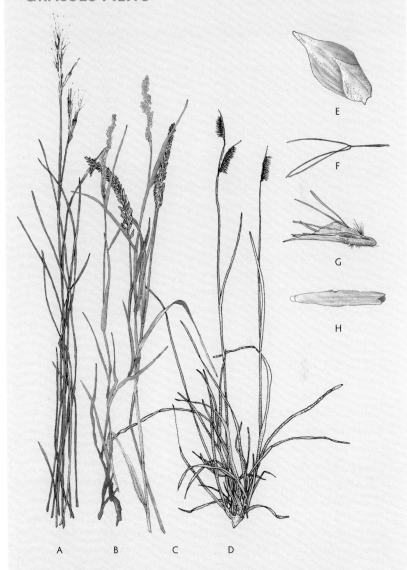

A. Purple three-awn grass; B. Witchgrass; C. Wheatgrass; D. Blue grama grass;
E. Witchgrass seed; F. Purple three-awn grass seed; G. Blue grama grass seed;
H. Bromegrass seed

diverse plantings. Smaller fields provide more fencerows and natural breaks where birds can thrive, both in numbers and species diversity. As fields get larger, the zones that support birds shrink, and as the diversity of crops narrows, vulnerability to disease and pests increases, elevating the risk to both plants and animals.

Ranching on grasslands has also changed, with larger herds and more intensive grazing altering natural support for birds. Native grazers such as buffalo and pronghorn work within a well-established, complex system that maintains species diversity and ecosystem health. Modern ranching can be supportive of grassland birds when managed appropriately, but overgrazing, among other factors, has damaged native habitats and the wildlife within them.

Surveys conducted over recent decades report that there has been a loss of 717 million grassland birds since 1970. Species suffering the greatest losses are Bobolink, Eastern Meadowlark, Field Sparrow, Grasshopper Sparrow, Henslow's Sparrow, and Northern Bobwhite. The loss of grasslands impacts seedeaters by reducing the amount and diversity of seed sources, but has an equally negative impact on insect eaters because of loss of food sources for the insects themselves. The problem is compounded for seed-eating birds because of their dependence on insects during the nesting season.

FORBS

Forbs are broadleaf flowering nonwoody plants, including both annuals and perennials (see the Native North American Forbs Sampler sidebar). Forbs include both sunflowers and thistles, major plant resources in the food chain for birds, as well as asters, balsamroot, goldenrod, and milkweed.

Thistles: There are more than sixty thistle species that are part of the indigenous North American plant population (see the North American Native Thistle Sampler sidebar). Ranging in size and habitat preference, many native thistles still thrive in much of their original ranges.

Like the natural pairing between monarch butterflies and milkweed, field thistles are a host plant for the painted lady butterfly (also known, appropriately, as the thistle butterfly). The thistle

NATIVE NORTH AMERICAN FORBS SAMPLER

Aster
Balsamroot
Bee plant
Biscuit root
Black-eyed Susan
Blanketflower
Blazing star
Camas
Clover wooley
Daisy
Dusty maiden
Evening primrose
Flax
Fleabane
Geranium
Gilia
Globe mallow

Goldeneye
Hawks beard
Joe-pye weed
Lily
Lupine
Mariposa
Milk vetch
Milkweed
Mocroseris
Pea vine
Penstemon
Phacelia
Phlox
Prairie clover
Prairie smoke
Prince's plume
Scurf pea

Small burnet
Starflower
Sunflower
Sweet clover
Sweet vetch
Thistle
Trefoil
Vetch
Violet
Wallflower
Wild onion
Wyethia
Yampah
Yarrow
Yucca

long-horned bee relies solely on this species for pollen. The flowers of all native thistles attract pollinators, and both generalist and specialist insects also benefit from thistles, including aphids, butterflies, grasshoppers, lacewings, moths, sucking bugs, and weevils. Birds benefit from these herbivorous insects attracted to these plants.

However, some native thistles are increasingly threatened by the increasing spread of alien varieties and the vigorous attempts to control them. The most conspicuous thistles are not native to North America but are alien invaders. Originally, seeds from European thistles hitchhiked here hidden in loads of wheat and other grains. These include the bull thistle, musk thistle, and Canada thistle (which, despite the name, did not originate in Canada).

Most thistle plants that we see are scattered along roadsides, in empty lots, and strewn throughout farmers' fields where they are widely regarded as a noxious weed, mostly with good reason. In at least one state, all thistles are considered invasive and targeted for eradication, complicating efforts to protect the natives.

In North America, these species have mostly outcompeted native species because the few native thistle predators (native insects are less attracted to nonnative thistles, and few mammalian herbivores eat thistles due to their prickles) aren't sufficient to deter their spread. There are exceptions, however, including a few native insects that have successfully attacked bull thistles in Nebraska.

Native and invasive thistle plants are an important source of food for American Goldfinches and other seed-eating species. Individually, thistle seeds are tiny, but these small birds are capable of plucking them one at a time from the seed heads. Inset: Enlarged seed of the native tall thistle, about 0.2 inch (5 millimeter) long.

One of the strongest ways to fight back against the alien thistle invasion is to plant native thistles in American backyards. Gardeners can plant native species as part of bird-friendly gardens. Thistle feeders are one of the most popular options for backyards in North America. They are popular with bird-watchers because they draw birds such as finches, goldfinches, juncos, and redpolls.

However, there are no commercial suppliers of thistle

NORTH AMERICAN NATIVE THISTLE SAMPLER

This list illustrates the variety to be found among more than sixty species of thistles.

Arizona thistle	Fringed thistle	Tall thistle
Bicolor thistle	Graygreen thistle	Texas thistle
Brewer's swamp thistle	Hill's thistle	Snowy thistle
California thistle	Long-style thistle	Soft thistle
Carolina thistle	Mountain thistle	Swamp thistle
Clustered thistle	New Mexico thistle	Undulating thistle
Cobwebby thistle	Nuttall's thistle	Venus thistle
Eaton's thistle	Pasture thistle	Virginia thistle
Edible thistle	Peregrine thistle	Wavy-leaf thistle
Elk thistle	Pitcher's thistle	Western thistle
Field thistle	Platte thistle	Wyoming thistle
Flodman's thistle	Sandhill thistle	Yellow thistle

seeds for bird feeders because there is no agricultural production of these plants. Gardeners can find sources of native thistle seeds online and grow them. As part of pollinator-friendly gardens, native thistles attract butterflies, bees, and birds, and the seeds are already part of birds' natural diet. Thistle feeders are not usually stocked with thistle seeds but with niger seeds, which come from a plant not native to North America and traditionally supplied from overseas sources (see "Feeder Food" in the How to Support Birds chapter).

Sunflowers: All sunflowers are part of the genus *Helianthus*, which is a type of composite. There are about seventy species of native sunflowers in North America, most of them perennials (see the North American Native Sunflower Sampler sidebar). Most thrive in open habitats, with a few that have adapted to dense shade. Canada hosts thirteen of these original species, and some are also native to northern Mexico.

Indigenous tribes made use of sunflowers for at least a few thousand years, and some developed hybrid varieties that greatly

More than sixty thistle species are native to North America and have well-established connections to pollinators. Because of the threat of invasive thistle species, all thistle varieties are sometimes targeted as noxious agricultural weeds. The photo is of a musk thistle, an invasive species.

increased the size and oil content of seeds. Following the arrival of European explorers and settlers, sunflowers were introduced on the other side of the Atlantic by the early 1500s and quickly spread eastward. Some modern hybrids that were developed in eastern Europe were brought back to North America by the late 1800s.

North American birds have depended on this staple plant for much longer than humans. Birds with a preference for sunflower

Thistles, native as well as invasive species, are a critical food source, providing seeds for finches and other birds as well as nectar for hummingbirds; the insects attracted to thistles also provide food for birds and animals. At left, an introduced honeybee feeds on a Texas thistle. *(Photo by Jungle Explorer)* At right, a female American Goldfinch feeds on a nonnative bull thistle. *(Photo by Nan Bauer)*

seeds in their native habitats include blackbirds, bobolinks, buntings, chickadees, cowbirds, crows, doves, finches, grackles, larks, longspurs, meadowlarks, nuthatches, pheasants, quail, sparrows, titmice, and turkeys.

As with other widespread native plants, sunflowers are hosts to a variety of insects that provide food for insectivorous birds. More than 150 plant-eating insect species are associated with sunflowers, both specialists (insects feeding on only specific species of sunflower) and generalists. The plants attract aphids, bees, beetles (including weevils), butterflies, cutworms (moth larvae), grasshoppers, midges, moths, wasps, and wireworms (beetle larvae), which at various times of the sunflower growing cycle feed on shoots, roots, stems, flowers, nectar, seeds—and each other (for example, ladybird beetles, stinkbugs, and parasitic wasps).

The seeds of native or heritage hybrid sunflowers are typically smaller than those of the major commercial types but are still well fortified with nutrition. The older types generally flower and produce seeds sequentially throughout a growing season, with multiple

NORTH AMERICAN NATIVE SUNFLOWER SAMPLER

Alkali sunflower
Anomalous sunflower
Apache brown-striped
  sunflower
Arizona sunflower
Beach sunflower
California sunflower
Common sunflower
Cusick's sunflower
Deceptive sunflower
Desert sunflower
Divergent sunflower
Downy sunflower
Dune sunflower
Dwarfish sunflower
Eggert's sunflower
Florida sunflower
Giant sunflower
Gray sunflower
Hopi branched
  sunflower

Jerusalem artichoke
Long-leaf sunflower
Maximilian sunflower
Mountain sunflower
Neglected sunflower
Odorous sunflower
Oxeye sunflower
Pale-leaved sunflower
Paradox sunflower
Porter's sunflower
Prairie sunflower
Purple-disk sunflower
Resinous sunflower
Runyon's sunflower
Rydberg's sunflower
Sawtooth sunflower
Schweinitz's sunflower
Scraper sunflower
Serpentine sunflower
Showy sunflower
Silver-leaf sunflower

Slender sunflower
Small-headed
  sunflower
Smith's sunflower
Smooth sunflower
Southeastern
  sunflower
Swamp sunflower
Texas blueweed
  sunflower
Texas sunflower
Thin-leaf sunflower
Tickseed sunflower
Variable-leaf
  sunflower
Western sunflower
White-leaf sunflower
Whorled sunflower
Willow-leaf
  sunflower
Woodland sunflower

heads. Long before retailers routinely stocked sunflower seeds, the plants were widely used in gardens.

Cultivars produced within the agricultural system are more likely to bloom and produce seeds synchronously, with a single main stem and large central head bred to improve the effectiveness of mechanized harvesting. These commercial types are often also attractive to gardeners because of their dramatic size. The commercial market for sunflower seeds has ballooned in the last few decades because of increasing demand for its oil, which is widely used in the food

Sunflowers are native to North America, though most of the varieties familiar to gardeners are hybrids originally developed for agricultural production. Although these hybrids are not harmful to birds, there are sources for seeds of native species that are more authentic residents for eco-friendly gardens.

industry, and seeds, which are increasingly used for human food (mostly snacks).

Birds and squirrels do not discriminate: any sunflower will do. Sunflower seeds have been a staple since the first commercial bird feeders appeared in the market in the early 1900s. Now about 25 percent of all sunflower production is channeled to the birdseed industry. Birds seek sunflowers for the nutrition-rich seeds they produce, but they are not picky about where the seeds are found. Backyard feeders that are well supplied provide a reliable resource, often year-round (see "Feeder Food" in the How to Support Birds chapter). An option to store-bought sunflower seeds for birds is homegrown sunflowers.

Sunflower seed shells contain toxins, natural compounds called sesquiterpene lactones that repel other plants after a seed drops to the ground. This is an asset for sunflowers in the wild but can become a problem in backyards and gardens. In as little as a few weeks, the shells accumulating under a bird feeder will begin to kill grass and other plants. The effect can be prevented, or at least controlled, by keeping the shells from piling up. If they are raked away and tossed

SUNFLOWER MENU

Sunflowers are a common source of seeds used in bird feeders. More than 675 million pounds (340 million kilograms) of these seeds are consumed every year at feeders in the United States. Almost all of these seeds come from a few dozen commercial varieties, bred from native North American plants. In the wild, seed-eating birds rely on a much larger menu of sunflower varieties. About seventy species of *Helianthus* are natives. Commercial sunflower cultivars are higher in oil content and seed size than natives, though both provide a substantial source of food for birds. Sunflower plants—native or commercial—attract a wide range of insects, which in turn attract insect-eating birds. The seeds shown here are from both commercial and wild sunflowers. The two columns on the right are examples of commercial hybrid varieties.

onto a well-managed compost pile, the heat from the compost will neutralize these compounds within a month. At that point, they can be safely used as mulch.

The bioactive compounds in sunflower seed shells are of interest to researchers looking for new approaches to treating diseases such as cancer. These compounds have also been found to be effective as antimicrobial agents. Along with sunflowers, sesquiterpene lactones are found in many other plants in the widespread family of Asteraceae (composites).

During the growing season, birds take ready advantage of agricultural fields where the seeds are concentrated, often to the dismay of the farmers who grow this commodity. Annually, birds feeding on sunflower crops account for millions of dollars in lost revenue. Such

NUTRITIONAL VALUE OF SUNFLOWER SEEDS

The table below shows the contents of black oil sunflower seeds, the preferred type used in bird feed. About 50 percent of the dry weight of these seeds is oil. Sunflower seeds also contain amino acids—alanine, arginine, aspartic acid, glutamic acid, glycine, leucine, and lysine—and other micronutrients.

SUNFLOWER SEED CONTENTS	PERCENTAGE OF TOTAL SEED WEIGHT
dry matter	92.8%
neutral detergent fiber (NDF*)	29.6%
acid detergent fiber (ADF*)	19.5%
crude fiber	17.2%
crude protein	16.6%
potassium	9.1%
phosphorus	6.0%
lignin	6.3%
ash	3.5%
magnesium	3.0%
total sugars	2.7%
starch	1.3%
sodium	0.1%
calcium	2.6 grams per kilogram of dry matter

* This content represents cellulose and other roughage that is mostly undigestible.

Sunflowers are a major crop in the United States and Canada, with annual plantings of about 2 million acres (0.8 million hectares). About three-quarters of the US crop comes from only three states: Minnesota, North Dakota, and South Dakota. Most of the annual crop is referred to as oilseed (black oil seeds) and the remainder is non-oil seed (black-stripe), which are larger and used in the snack and confectionary industry.

loss is mostly blamed on large flocks of blackbirds, doves, sparrows, and crows. One study reported 26 percent of the sunflower fields surveyed had losses of 1 percent or higher. (As a rule of thumb, farmers generally consider a loss above 5 percent to be economically significant.)

The task for commercial growers is not to feed birds but to produce seeds, and with expanding demand, methods have been developed in response to this predation, although they either are not effective or are too costly to use. Antibird tactics include spraying ripening sunflower heads with deterrent chemical compounds and deploying loud noisemakers such as propane cannons. At the extreme, resting colonies of birds are located and killed with potent avicides, which can cause deadly collateral damage to nontargeted songbirds, raptors, and other animals.

Several insects also are now considered major pests of the commercial sunflower plants, such as the sunflower beetle, the sunflower moth, the banded sunflower moth, and the sunflower stem maggot, as well as various species of those insects mentioned earlier. The result is an increasing use of insecticides. Even with the most conscientious growers, however, the use of agricultural chemicals can produce a cascading cycle of bad news, poisoning birds attracted to the seeds or the insects, and passing on the chemicals when treated seeds are harvested and sold for backyard feeders (see "Feeder Food" in the How to Support Birds chapter).

Native sunflowers can hybridize with cultivated varieties, which alters the natives' original qualities, some of which are known to provide natural protections against plant diseases that target commercial crops. Even as commercial sunflower crops flourish, some native sunflowers are facing a problematic future. As of 2019, four native species are threatened, endangered, or candidates for such status. The biggest threat comes from human activity, especially development and farming.

Although black oil sunflower seeds are overwhelmingly the food of choice in North American bird feeders, many bird species do not have the necessary bill strength and leverage to open the hulls of these seeds. These birds either depend on larger birds to leave unhusked seeds behind or they look for feeders stocked with shelled whole or broken seeds. Yet unhulled sunflower seeds are relatively puny compared to larger seeds' and nuts' protective casings.

NUTS

Nut-bearing trees, especially oaks, have evolved to produce seeds in an irregular pattern: many in some years, fewer in others. A peak year for nut production is called a mast year, an event that provides a bumper crop of food for birds as well as many other animals. Because of the highly nutritious nature of nuts and competition for them from insects, birds, and mammals, if trees produced the same-sized crop every year, animal populations that focus on this bounty would soon swell in response, outstripping the tree's ability to have enough uneaten nuts for reproduction. But by occasionally producing a bumper crop, a tree (or trees) can overwhelm the local population of seed predators and increase the chance that some seeds will survive to sprout.

Mast years are observed in conifers as well as nut-bearing hardwoods. The phenomenon is also noted in some perennial plants and includes fruit bearers (fruit is sometimes referred to as "soft mast"). The larger mystery is the scope of such events, which happen in synchrony, sometimes across large distances. How this synchronization is triggered is a matter of speculation, though some theories connect such events to local climate and weather events.

Not surprisingly, cycles in the availability of nuts have an impact on the animals that depend on this food source. The relationship between animals and food is not a balance but an imbalance. An excess of food allows predator populations to expand, while a lack of food forces a decline. One side or the other is always out of step with the other, preserving both over the long term.

In hardwoods, the energy expended in producing a large crop of seeds depletes the ability of trees to maintain chemical defenses against insect predators. Following a mast year, a population boom in tree-dependent insects may result, but this population increase attracts more insect predators, including birds.

In studies of mast years in Maine and in New Brunswick, Canada, populations of red squirrels boomed a year after bumper crops of pinecones, but the bird populations decreased by 50 percent. In this case, more squirrels meant more competition for seeds, with birds at the losing end. In most years, the numbers of squirrels in a local area might have little effect on birds, but mast years change the population dynamics of seedeaters in subsequent seasons.

Mast years vary by species. White oak trees experience a mast event about every other year, red oaks about every five years. Ponderosa pines are also on a cycle of about every five years, and white pines vary, from three to ten years, fluctuating across different parts of their range.

In North America, birds feed on hickory nuts, pecans, hazelnuts, beechnuts, walnuts, and other hard-shelled seeds, whether by foraging for nuts that are already cracked, relying on leftovers from squirrels and other creatures that thrive on this food, or gaining access to

NUT MENU

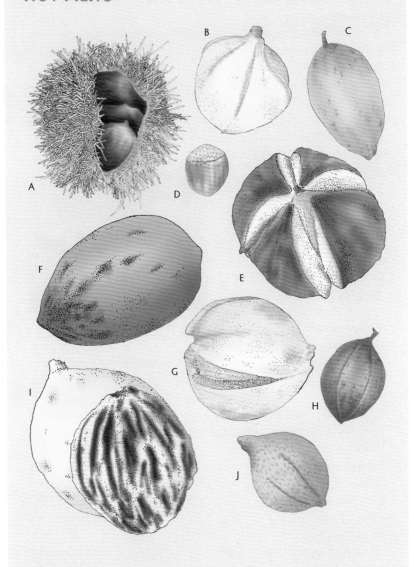

A. American chestnut; B. Bitternut hickory; C. Butternut hickory; D. Hazelnut;
E. Shagbark hickory; F. Pecan; G. Shell-bark hickory; H. Mocker-nut hickory;
I. Black walnut; J. Pignut hickory

the nut meats themselves. (See the Nut Menu illustration as well as the Acorns section below.)

Among birds that are known to forage for and consume hard-shelled nuts are American Crows, Blue Jays, Mallards, Northern Bobwhites, Ring-necked Pheasants, White-breasted Nuthatches, Wild Turkeys, Wood Ducks, and woodpeckers. Most of these birds do not have the bill strength to directly break open nut shells, particularly the nuts of most native hickory trees, but some, including American Crows, Blue Jays, and woodpeckers, can break through by hammering or prying with their bills.

Turkeys follow a more common practice, swallowing nuts shells and all. Whole pecans and hickory nuts are part of their diet in some of their range. The results of one study determined that whole pecans were crushed inside a turkey gizzard in about one hour, while whole hickory nuts required thirty-two hours.

Some birds cache nuts, but this Black-billed Magpie is more likely to crack open the walnut it has found and eat its contents without waiting. *(Photo by Coulanges)*

ACORNS

All oak trees produce acorns. On the North American continent, there are about fifty recognized species of oak, not counting natural hybrids and a few imported species. Unlike most hard-shelled nuts on this continent, acorns are very accessible to birds because of their thinner shells, giving birds a lot of choices. The oak-hickory forest is one of the dominant ecosystems in the eastern region of North America, and acorns are an established natural food source there for birds, insects, and many other animals.

Acorns have a relatively high concentration of tannins, a natural compound plants use to thwart insects. Tannin can be distasteful to some animals and is known to reduce some nutritive value, particularly protein. Acorn Woodpeckers do not seem to be affected, nor

Wild Turkeys are master foragers, with a wide range of acceptable food that includes leaves, seeds, nuts, and invertebrates. When nuts and acorns are in season, turkeys will seek out whatever is available. *(Photo by Nancy Bauer)*

do scrub-jays. There can also be additional dietary value in individual nuts. Various insects, particularly the acorn weevil, target acorns to lay their eggs. Birds that break open acorns with such uninvited guests get a nutritional bonus.

The Acorn Woodpecker is the quintessential avian species when it comes to oak trees. Its name amply identifies its principal food, acorns, which comprise half or more of its overall diet. It also consumes insects and other arthropods, tree sap, nectar, and seeds from other trees and plants. These woodpeckers hammer open acorns to extract the meat but are also well known for caching. They select either immature or mature acorns and jam them individually into holes they drill in trees. These selected cache sites are called granary trees. As part of small colonies, these birds may have one or more granary trees, with each holding up to 50,000 acorns.

Scrub-jays also cache acorns, sometimes in quantities rivaling that of Acorn Woodpeckers. The California Scrub-Jay has a varied diet throughout the year, including beetles, ants, butterflies, caterpillars, grasshoppers, seeds, and fruit, but concentrates on collecting acorns during the fall. From October to February, more than 60 percent of its diet is acorns.

NORTH AMERICAN ACORNS

About ninety species of oak trees are native to North America, providing a rich source of food for wildlife. Birds are attracted to acorns for their nutritional value as well as for the insects that also gravitate to them. Wild Turkeys and geese swallow acorns whole, but smaller birds often break them apart with their bills before ingesting. Some oaks produce acorns up to 2 inches (5 centimeters) long; the smallest are only about 0.5 inch (1.3 centimeters) long.

A. Gambel oak; B. White oak; C. Over-cup oak; D. Chinkapin oak; E. Pin oak; F. Southern live oak; G. Burr oak; H. Water oak; I. Myrtle oak; J. Willow oak; K. Chestnut oak; L. Northern red oak; M. Valley oak; N. Swamp red oak; O. Post oak; P. Black oak; Q. Blackjack oak

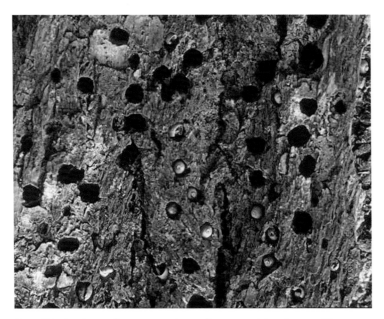

Acorn Woodpeckers gather acorns and carry them to special caches, specific trees used consistently as acorn storehouses. Their drilling skills as woodpeckers produce acorn-sized holes, one per acorn, sometimes numbering in the thousands on a single tree. Other birds and animals, particularly tree squirrels, take advantage of this windfall. *(Photo by Tupper Ansel Blake, USFWS)*

The Florida Scrub-Jay also caches acorns and has a sophisticated selection method to improve the survivability of its stash. This bird detects the amount of tannin in an acorn, which can vary from nut to nut, from tree to tree, and among oak species, and hides those with the highest levels. This jay's cached high-tannin collection may have added protection from insect predation.

Other birds that include acorns in their diet include blackbirds, Blue Jays, clappers, Clark's Nutcrackers, crows, flickers, grackles, Mallards, Northern Pintails, pheasants, pigeons, quail, rails, starlings, Steller's Jays, Wild Turkeys, Wood Ducks, and woodpeckers. Turkeys may swallow acorns whole, but most birds use their bills to break through the shell and extract the seed within. Wild Turkeys in the eastern part of their range depend on acorns for up to 70 percent of their diet in fall months.

CONIFER SEEDS

The seeds protected within cones of many species of conifers are nutritious, tasty, and tough to get to. The nut itself is encased in a thin husk, a relatively weak shell surrounded by the cone itself. Natural fluctuations in cone production affect the bird populations that depend on them. Pinyon pines and other conifers follow a mast-year cycle like that for nut-bearing hardwoods, producing large crops of cones some years and smaller crops in others. On average, pinyon pines experience a mast year about every six to seven years, and in one or more of the in-between years, there may be a complete lack of cones. This mast phenomenon can affect trees across as many as four states: Arizona, Colorado, New Mexico, and Utah.

Birds that depend on pine nuts, at least for part of the year, include different species of chickadees and titmice, corvids (jays, magpies, nutcrackers), crossbills, nuthatches, siskins, woodpeckers, and even Thick-billed Parrots. Many other species will feed on pine nuts for short intervals or as part of general foraging activity.

A few birds, particularly crossbills, are uniquely adapted to pry individual pinecone scales apart to get to the nuts, and they spend a good part of their foraging time doing so. The overlapping tips of their bills are effective tools; the upper bill shape arcs downward (is decurved) and the lower arcs upward (is recurved). Unlike many birds, crossbills are able to push their two bills apart at the tip, creating a prying force that helps to lever cone scales apart.

Crossbills, which do not migrate, depend on conifer nuts throughout the year, including seasons when cones are still immature and have not opened. Their bills are up to the task of not only prying apart mature ones but also cutting into the surface of unopened cones. They remove the pine nut from its husk much like the American Goldfinch removes sunflower shells, by prying the seed open while it's held by the lower bill against a thin groove in the upper bill.

Not only have crossbills adapted to specialize in opening pinecones, different types of crossbills have further specialized in conifers with different kinds of cones. These types have yet to be classified as separate subspecies, so they are all currently

CONIFER CONE SAMPLER

A. Douglas fir; B. Lodgepole pine; C. Blue spruce; D. Ponderosa pine; E. Jack pine; F. Hemlock; G. Pitch pine; H. Shortleaf pine; I. Balsam fir; J. Loblolly pine; K. White spruce; L. Red pine; M. Western red cedar; N. White pine; O. Black spruce; P. Eastern larch; Q. Longleaf pine; R. Englemann spruce recognized as one of two species of crossbills. The ten types are specialized for different cone characteristics, from small to large, including ponderosa pine, lodgepole pine, western hemlock, Engelmann spruce, and Sitka spruce.

White-bark pines are the main source of food for Clark's Nutcrackers, and these birds are the main source of seed distribution for these trees, carrying pine nuts up to 14 miles (22.5 kilometers) from their source. A single nutcracker has been observed carrying up to 150 pine nuts to a cache site, but the average is between 54 and 77 per trip. They do not rely on their crop, but utilize an expandable area at the entrance of the esophagus called a sublingual pouch. A single nutcracker may cache up to 98,000 pine nuts in one year, though the average is less than half this number.

CONIFER CONES

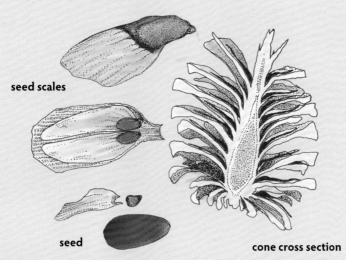

seed scales

seed

cone cross section

Cones are protective cases for conifer nuts, the seeds sequestered inside. When mature, the dried outer scales pull away from the core, exposing the seeds. Most birds are too small to get to the seeds, before or after the cones are ripe, so they depend on the leftovers after larger birds and other animals have had their share.

Pinyon pines in the Southwest are the major source of food for Pinyon Jays, but these trees also attract other jays, chickadees, grosbeaks, nuthatches, and ravens. Pinyon Jays gather in flocks that can number in the hundreds, feasting and caching together. An individual jay can carry up to forty pine nuts in the expandable upper part of its esophagus (a variation on the sublingual pouch of the Clark's Nutcracker, with a similar adaptation in the American Crow), after using its strong bill to remove pine nuts from a pinecone and then breaking open each seed's husk.

Pinyon Jays appear to use seed color to determine ripeness (dark brown hulls are an indication of maturity) but also test unopened seeds in their bills to check for quality, with weight being a deciding factor. A single Pinyon Jay is estimated to collect and cache as many as 2,600 pine nuts in one season. Pinyon Jays will also feed on the cones of other pines and on insects, berries, and seeds of other plants.

FRUIT

Both year-round and migratory birds depend on fruit, with the peak of the avian migratory season, August and September, coinciding with the peak season for ripe fruit. This section focuses on native fruits and berries (see the Native Fruits and Berries Sampler sidebar) rather than those that are commercially available, though of course birds eat some of those as well, cherries being a prime example.

Though the nutritive value of fruit is an important factor for birds and a wide variety of species feed on fruit, few North American birds specialize in this food source. Compared to insects or seeds, most fruit provides little protein or fats though it is often rich in sugars (see the Nutritional Value of Native Fruit table), which can provide valuable energy for migratory birds. Because fruit has less nutritional content than insects, birds have to eat more of it to provide necessary energy.

Fruit not only provides a direct source of food for birds, it also attracts insects that are another food source. For example blueberry plants, when in flower, attract as many as 286 butterfly and moth species in North America.

NATIVE FRUITS AND BERRIES SAMPLER

American beautyberry

American bittersweet (berries)

American crabapple

American cranberry

American holly (berries)

American mistletoe (berries)

American persimmon

American pokeweed (berries)

Arctic raspberry

Bayberry

Beach plum

Bearberry

Bird cherry

Blackberry

Black cohosh (berries)

Black gum (berries)

Black nightshade (berries)

Blueberry

Buckthorn (berries)

Buffalo berry

Bunchberry

Carolina laurel cherry

Chokeberry

Chokecherry

Cloudberry

Common elderberry

Common greenbrier (berries)

Crowberry

Currant

Devil's walking stick (berries)

Dewberry

Farkleberry

Flowering dogwood (berries)

Fox grape

Fringe tree (berries)

Frost grape

Gooseberry

Hackberry

Hawthorn (berries)

High-bush blueberry

Honey berry

Huckleberry

Indian plum

Juniper (berries)

Lingonberry

Madrone (berries)

May apple

Mayhaw

Maypop (berries)

Mountain ash (berries)

Mulberry

Muscadine (grapes)

Nanny berry

Northern bayberry

Oregon grape

Pawpaw

Poison ivy (berries)

Poison oak (berries)

Prickly pear cactus (fruits)

Raspberry

Red baneberry

Red-twig dogwood (berries)

Salal (berries)

Salmonberry

Saltbush (berries)

Sassafras (berries)

Serviceberry (Juneberry)

Snowberry

Spicebush (berries)

Strawberry spinach berry

Sumac (berries)

Thimbleberry

Toyon (berries)

Viburnum (berries)

Virginia creeper (berries)

Wahoo berries

Whortleberry

Wild rose (hips)

Wild strawberry

Winterberry

Wintergreen (berries)

NUTRITIONAL VALUE OF NATIVE FRUIT

FRUIT	PROTEIN	FAT	CARBOHYDRATES
Virginia creeper berries	6%	24%	68%
pokeweed berries	6%	3%	80%
rose hips	6%	2%	88%
bayberry	3%	50%	41%
viburnum berries	3%	41%	50%
winterberry	3%	4%	88%

Many fruits display colors that attract birds. Berries and other fruits ripen in a range of colors, from reds and yellows to blues and blacks. Some studies have shown that mammals are somewhat more likely to feed on fruit that reflect greens, and birds are more likely to feed on those that reflect reds. Color preferences may vary depending on the plant: these studies are inconclusive, but birds seem to prefer purple over green grapes and black over red cherries. Birds can be more attracted to a plant that has fruit in more than one color than those that have fruits with a uniform color. One theory behind this behavior suggests that one of the colors provides a more specific indicator of ripeness when mixed in with fruit of other colors. The visual signal provided by color benefits both bird and plant.

Nonmigratory birds, such as this Tufted Titmouse, rely on fruits and berries for nutrition, especially during the cold winter season when insects aren't widely available. This bird is eating berries from a hawthorn tree. *(Photo by Steven Russell Smith)*

Other factors also influence whether or when birds select certain fruits, including the ratio of seeds to fruit, the fruit's taste, and the time of ripening.

After birds ingest fruit, the time until they either regurgitate or defecate fruit seeds varies. Generally, seeds that are regurgitated spend less time in the digestive system than those that are defecated. The pulp moves through birds' digestive system about twice as fast as ingested insects. Most fruit completes its cycle through a bird's digestive system in about forty minutes. For example, blueberries pass through Hermit Thrushes in about thirty minutes.

Some fruit-eating birds, such as thrushes, robins, and waxwings, usually select smaller fruits and eat them whole. Others, such as tanagers, often select larger fruit and peck off the pulp. Omnivorous birds and even some that are insectivorous often alter their diets

Birds that eat fruit too large to swallow whole use their bills to remove the pulp a piece at a time, like this Bohemian Waxwing feeding on apples. *(Photo by Yury Taranik)*

in the winter when berries and other fruit remains available. Insectivores known for switching to berries include bluebirds, catbirds, chickadees, grouse, mockingbirds, quail, robins, thrashers, thrushes, titmice, waxwings, and woodpeckers.

Birds that ingest fruit require the nutrition, but the plants that bear the fruit that birds eat gain seed dispersal, necessary for the plants' survival. Despite an ingested fruit being bathed in a bird's digestive juices, subjected to grinding in the gizzard, and further exposed to digestive fluids in a bird's intestines, some of its seeds make it through the bird's body, scarred but whole.

Seeds that pass through a bird's digestive system may actually have more successful gemination. A study of chile seeds, for instance, found that there was a profound increase in the germination rate after the chiles were eaten by birds and the seeds passed through their digestive tract, an improvement of 370 percent. The factor at work turned out to be the cleansing activity generated during the digestive process. The chile seeds in bird poop were stripped of their unique odors, chemical signals that, left unaltered, would attract ants. Thus, the seeds were left to sprout rather than being consumed. The same digestive process is known to reduce pathogens that keep some seeds from germinating.

Fruit is a survival mechanism for some plants, which encourage predation in order to spread their seeds. In the eastern deciduous forests of North America, more than 125 species of fruit-bearing trees, shrubs, and vines depend on birds for seed dispersal.

Birds that are key players in seed dispersal include American Crows, bluebirds, bobwhites, cardinals, catbirds, chats, chickadees, finches, flickers, grosbeaks, jays, mockingbirds, orioles, pigeons, sapsuckers, tanagers, thrashers, thrushes such as American Robins, towhees, Tree Swallows, turkeys, vireos, warblers, waxwings, and woodpeckers.

VEGETATION

The insects that feed on plants and tree leaves provide a critical food resource for birds, but birds themselves rarely feed directly on foliage or other parts of plants. Only about 2 percent of the world's bird species are known to eat mostly leaves, but most of these are not found in North America. Plant-based diets are a less efficient way to gain protein, and plant material is in general more complex to digest. Therefore, avian herbivores have to eat more of it and digest it more quickly than other types of food.

A few bird species in North America feed directly on leaves, especially of willow and birch shrubs. These include the Willow Ptarmigan, White-tailed Ptarmigan, and Rock Ptarmigan. They also eat buds, stems, and catkins of the same shrubs (as well as berries). Adults need to eat at least 2 ounces (60 grams) dry weight a day in winter in order to survive. Spruce Grouse, Ruffed Grouse, two species of sage-grouse, and a few other grouse species also have diets heavily dependent on vegetation. The Spruce Grouse mostly feeds on conifer needles, favoring new growth that is found high in trees.

Another leaf-eating species common in North America is the Canada Goose, whose diet is primarily grasses, leaves, stalks, roots, seeds, and other parts of terrestrial and aquatic plants, including algae. Well-established in many urban settings (year-round and as migratory visitors), these large birds can spend up to half or more

This Willow Ptarmigan, in its summer plumage, is foraging for foliage in Alaska. Though primarily an herbivore, the species will also feed on insects. *(Photo by Fran Fichtmueller)*

of their waking hours grazing and will sometimes graze at night. During migrations, they have adapted to also feeding on the seeds of major agricultural crops, including corn, alfalfa, wheat, clover, soybeans, and sorghum. Several studies have confirmed what city park managers might already suspect: Canada Geese prefer bluegrass to most other foliage (it's also a favorite of grizzly bears), although this relates to urban environments. Urban park lovers where there are large populations of Canada Geese recognize the result of their grazing: extensive concentrations of goose droppings.

Although Mallard food is mostly aquatic-based, it does include some terrestrial grasses and sedges, and, like geese, Mallards take advantage of agricultural crops when available, especially corn. Ring-necked Pheasants are primarily seedeaters, at least in the fall and winter months, but will graze on greenery such as grasses and leaves. Even Pine Siskins, which feed primarily on grain, also occasionally graze on greenery, including tree buds and plant stems.

WATER PLANTS

Water and wetlands—both fresh- and saltwater—generate a rich menu of vegetation for birds (see the Aquatic Plant Sampler sidebar). This includes bulrush, cattail, coon tail, cow lily, duckweed, eelgrass, elodea, green algae, hydrilla, musk grass, panic grass, pondweed, spike rush, water lily, water milfoil, water pepper, water shield, wigeon grass, wild celery, wild millet, wild rice, and a variety of forbs. These plants may be foraged for their foliage, roots, stems, buds, bulbs, or flowers (or seeds, discussed earlier in this chapter).

More than forty species of waterfowl have diets dependent on vegetation within wetland habitats. These include the American Black Duck, American Wigeon, Blue-winged Teal, Brant, Cackling Goose, Canvasback, European Wigeon, Gadwall, Greater Scaup, Greater White-fronted Goose, Green-winged Teal, Lesser Scaup, Mallard, Mottled Duck, Northern Pintail, Redhead, Ring-necked Duck, Ross's Goose, Snow Goose, Tundra Swan, and Wood Duck. Shorebirds such as Soras also eat water plants.

Aquatic birds, like many terrestrial species, may vary their diets and include both animal and vegetable sources, sometimes related

AQUATIC PLANT SAMPLER

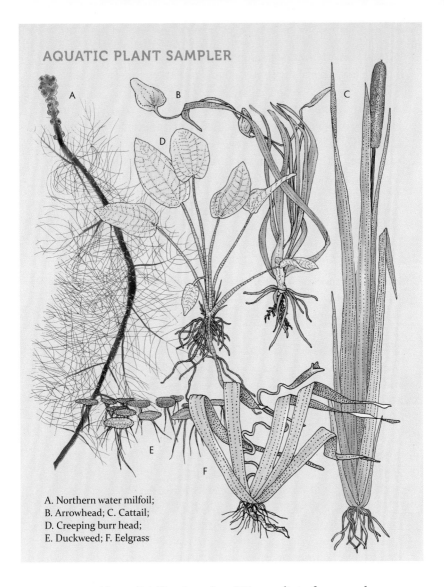

A. Northern water milfoil;
B. Arrowhead; C. Cattail;
D. Creeping burr head;
E. Duckweed; F. Eelgrass

to seasonable availability. American Wigeon diets, for example, may include 90 percent or more plant matter in fall and winter months, but drop to 60 percent or less during other seasons, when they ingest greater amounts of invertebrates and other aquatic animals.

Wood Ducks also have a variable diet but concentrate on plant-based food most of the time. Along with various floating and rooted aquatic plants, they are known to favor acorns, collected on both land and in the water. This species is noted for an esophagus that is much more expandable than in most other birds, a characteristic that allows it to swallow even large acorns, which are broken open in its gizzard.

Similarly, Blue-winged Teal diets are mostly vegetarian, with females adding aquatic invertebrates, such as snails, during the breeding season as an added source of protein. Almost 100 percent of a breeding female's diet can consist of invertebrates, but males also increase their intake of invertebrates before and during migration. Like Mallards, these teal rely on dabbling to collect plant material but also forage selectively for vegetation on and below the water surface.

Mallard food is mostly aquatic, including arrowhead, bur reed, duckweed, pondweed, rice cut-grass, smartweed, and spike rush. Mallards forage for water plants by sifting or dabbling rather than

Duckweed has been aptly named as a major source of food for ducks like this female Mallard and other waterfowl. *(Photo by Alexander Kolikov)*

plucking, which geese favor. (Mallards also eat insects, other arthropods, crayfish, and other crustaceans.)

While plant-eating aquatic birds depend on aquatic vegetation for food, some species of aquatic plants depend on these birds to disperse their seeds. Some of the seeds ingested by ducks pass through their digestive system capable of germination. Ducks often fly long distances during migrations, which plays an important role in helping plants disperse to different geographic zones.

NECTAR (FLOWERS)

Nectar is found in plant flowers, and it is one of the most recognized diets in the bird world: it is the primary food of hummingbirds. Nectar is also one of the simplest forms of food found in nature, but it varies in composition and sugar concentration among various plants (see the Native Flower-Nectar Sampler sidebar). Its primary function for plants is to attract pollinators.

Hummingbirds are widely recognized because of their close association with nectar. Although other types of birds, including chickadees, finches, orioles, warblers, and some woodpeckers, occasionally take advantage of this food source, they are not dependent on it.

Hummingbirds alter the amount of nectar they consume based on its concentration; the higher the concentration of sugars to water, the less they need to ingest. Nectars with high concentrations of its prime ingredients—natural forms of sugars—are also more viscous, requiring more time and effort to ingest, a shifting balance that hummingbirds must contend with. Studies of the food selections of hummingbirds show that the most commonly accessed sources are flowers with relatively dilute concentrations of sugars, about 26 percent by volume. Only 10 percent of their sources have concentrations of sugars of more than 35 percent by volume. These conclusions are from research conducted in the Caribbean islands and may differ from results in North America. In laboratory settings, the favored concentrations are sometimes higher but may not reflect what these birds prefer in the wild.

Another key finding from research into nectars is that hummingbirds can be very picky when given the chance. In a study of Rufous

NATIVE FLOWER-NECTAR SAMPLER

Abelia
Agave
Bee balm
Begonia
Bell flower
Bishop's hat
Blazing star
Bottlebrush
Buckwheat
Butterfly weed
Buttonbush
Camas
Canna
Cardinal flower
Catchfly
Chokecherry
Chuparosa
Clematis
Cleome
Clover
Comfrey
Coneflower
Coralbells
Delphinium
Dianthus
Dogwood
Firecracker plant
Flame flower
Flowering currant
Flowering quince
Four-o'clock
Foxglove
Gilia
Goats beard

Goldenrod
Gooseberry
Hawthorn
Hollyhock
Hosta
Impatiens
Jacobinia
Jewelweed
Joe-pye weed
Larkspur
Lilac
Lobelia
Lupine
Mallow
Malva
Manzanita
Milkweed
Mimosa
Monkey flower
Nicotiana
Obedient plant
Ocotillo
Oswego tea

Paintbrush
Penstemon
Penta
Rhododendron
Salmonberry
Salvia
Scarlet runner bean
Soapwort
Sunflower
Thistle
Touch-me-not
Trumpet bush
Trumpet vine
Twinberry
Verbena
Vervain
Wild azalea
Wild bergamot
Wild blueberry
Wild columbine
Wild iris
Yellow bells

A pair of Ruby-throated Hummingbirds feed on
bee balm flowers. *(Photo by Danita Delmont)*

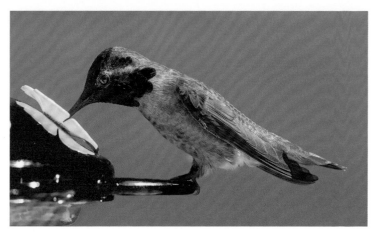

Hummingbirds, with their extreme need for energy to power their unique flight, are frequent visitors at backyard nectar feeders. *(Photo by Angel DiBilio)*

Hummingbirds, the birds preferred feeders with sucrose concentrations of 21 percent by volume more than those with a concentration of 19 percent by volume. Yet the same birds were not so selective between feeders with much higher concentrations and a much greater variation. When presented with concentrations of 48 percent or 72 percent, they showed little preference. This inconsistency likely involves viscosity, because it requires more energy for the tiny birds to extract heavier nectars, but it is also an advantage for the host plants. The "lighter" nectars force pollinators, in this case hummingbirds, to visit more flowers, a more effective pollination plan.

These tiny birds have fast metabolisms, burning through energy almost as rapidly as they extract it from their food, but they require time for their digestion to do its work. Most of the time during daylight hours, hummingbirds are resting, not feeding.

SAP

Sap is the liquid solution that circulates through plants to distribute water and nutrients. Trees and woody plants have two kinds of sap: an inner form called xylem is thin and carries water and nutrients from the roots to the leaves; an outer layer just under the bark, called phloem, is usually viscous and distributes nutrition from the leaves.

The nutrition that birds extract from sap mostly comes from the phloem, which varies among tree species and also fluctuates with the seasons. This sap is similar to nectar in its nutrient and sugar content, with the sugar—up to 30 percent of the sap—the primary target for birds.

Sapsuckers are named for this primary part of their diet, but other birds also seek out this nutritious liquid, including many woodpeckers and hummingbirds, as well as warblers and phoebes, among others. Sapsuckers constantly tap new access holes, an activity known to provide sap to at least thirty-five species, but none of these actively drill to access this food source.

Yellow-bellied Sapsuckers meet most of their nutritional needs with sap, though they also eat insects, other arthropods, and fruit. One estimate of their sap intake suggests they need at least 1.25 cups (290 milliliters) of sap per day to cover their energy needs, assuming

Hummingbirds are widespread in North America, feeding on a large array of flowering plants, including both native and introduced species. In this photo, a female Ruby-throated Hummingbird feeds at a red bird-of-paradise bush.

sap is their only food source. Drilling sap wells and extracting the content consumes up to half their waking hours during the winter, when sap is their predominate food source, but can take less time, depending on the type of tree and at other times of the year; preparing for and recovering from migration increases their need for energy.

Yellow-bellied Sapsuckers used their bills to drill holes in trees, with the objective of drinking the sap that collects in the holes. Depending on the tree, these birds produce both deep and shallow holes, which collect sap at different rates and with different viscosities. At least thirty-five other species of birds take advantage of sapsuckers' efforts and also drink this fluid. Insects that are attracted to the pooling and dripping sap are also targets for birds. *(Photo by Dennis W. Donohue)*

BIRD DIETS: ANIMALS

Eagles, hawks, owls, and other raptors are at the top of the avian food chain, embodying the status of carnivores within the bird world. Their range of animal prey includes mammals, other birds (eggs, nestlings, and adults), fish, amphibians, reptiles, aquatic invertebrates, and insects; insects are covered in an earlier chapter, so this chapter focuses on all the other animals that birds eat. For many raptors, prey may also include carrion.

But raptors aren't the only types of carnivorous birds; waterbirds also eat a variety of animals. The choice of prey is often linked to habitat. Raptors that frequent open fields primarily hunt rodents because these small mammals are the most common prey in that environment. Some hawks prefer nesting near open water, and in that habitat ducks and other waterbirds are favored. Ospreys choose aquatic habitats and eat fish.

Prey choices also vary according to the size of the hunter. In general, the larger the carnivorous bird, the larger its prey, but prey availability and time of year can override this factor. Also, for most North American raptors, females are larger than males, so females may hunt for larger prey than their male partners do.

Even large raptors, such as Swainson's Hawks, regularly include insects in their diet, though these selections are most likely to be larger types such as full-grown grasshoppers and dragonflies. Burrowing Owls, being small and nesting in burrows, mostly feed on insects that frequent the open areas they prefer for nesting, eating everything from termites to grasshoppers, but they also eat amphibians, reptiles, birds, and small mammals.

MAMMALS

Among the larger warm-blooded animals that larger raptors prey on, such as Bald Eagles, are muskrats, prairie dogs, rabbits, raccoons, and skunks. However, larger raptors, including Great Horned Owls, do not distinguish between these prey animals and any human pets

Clockwise from top: Cooper's Hawk with rabbit; Burrowing Owl with grasshopper; Barred Owl with vole; Peregrine Falcon with pigeon; American Kestrel consuming lizard. *(Photos, clockwise from top, by Elvor Kuchta, Martha Marks, Glass and Nature, Michal Ninger, Sergey Uryadnikov)*

that may be in the open, so small dogs and cats can be a regular part of their diet in urban and suburban areas.

Many raptors carry their prey to feeding perches after it is caught and killed (or at least stunned), reducing the chances of attack from other predators, such as coyotes, while on the ground. Therefore, raptors typically select prey that can be carried in the air. Talons are somewhat specialized for this task with a design that effectively grasps prey and helps hold it in flight; each type of raptor features minor variations in the shape and size of its talons, generally reflecting the size of preferred prey. Live prey pose a risk: they can bite, peck, and claw.

Peregrines feed on small mammals, especially squirrels and bats, and in the Arctic they feed on lemmings and ground squirrels; Peregrines can also be scavengers in parts of their range. Peregrine Falcons will sometimes consume their prey (or part of it) on the ground where it was caught and are known to sometimes consume smaller prey while flying. Eagles may also consume their prey on the ground, especially if they are hunting in open areas where there

are few perching sites. If prey can't be swallowed whole, it is dismembered into pieces for swallowing.

After prey are carried to feeding sites, the process of dismembering begins. Unless they capture prey that is relatively small, such as mice or voles, for example, most raptors

An increasing number of falcons and hawks gravitate to urban areas to take advantage of high densities of their preferred prey: rodents and small birds. This American Kestrel has established a nest in the wall of a century-old brick office building, an artificial cavity that effectively replaces a more traditional nesting site.

do not eat their prey whole, but tear it into pieces small enough to swallow. Raptors, unlike most other birds, are well equipped to reduce their prey to portions small enough to be swallowed in pieces if it is too large to be swallowed whole. This practice varies according to the size of the prey. The size of the pieces varies with the size of the raptor, but in general, the manageable pieces vary from 0.03 to 0.10 ounce (1 to 3 grams).

Raptors are not food wasters. Typically, large raptors devour more of their individual prey animals than small raptors do, and as the size of prey animals increases for any size raptor, less and less is consumed of their fur, bones, and entrails. Not much is left behind—typically only a scattering of feathers or fur and sometimes bones.

When prey is abundant, raptors may be picky eaters, consuming only choice parts. A large owl may use its bill to break open the head of a prey animal so that it can remove and eat the brains, but other raptors usually remove the head and discard it, except for smaller animals, which they ingest whole. Intestines are often ignored or discarded, but most raptors will selectively devour the major organs, primarily the liver and heart. The major focus is muscle mass. A published report from 1903 described a Great Horned Owl nest under which were scattered the bodies of 113 Norway rats, each having its skull broken open and the brains removed. Other citations also mention this result with other mammalian prey as well.

RODENTS

Worldwide, there are more than 1,500 species of rodent, with about 200 native to North America.

Smaller mammal prey include squirrels, mice, voles, rats, and other rodents. Long-eared Owls are woodland-based but they feed almost exclusively on open land, and as much as 98 percent of their overall food intake consists of small rodents, with voles at the top of the list. Voles can make up as much as half or more of their diet, though their prey across North America includes forty-five species of mammals.

Owls in most of North America are not common in urban areas, since they prefer quiet surroundings, but there are exceptions. Barn

An Eastern Screech-Owl has captured a mouse. *(Photo by Allen Schairer)*

Owls and Great Horned Owls are routine visitors in urban zones, on the hunt for familiar prey, especially mice, rabbits, rats, squirrels, and other small mammals.

Great Horned Owls are opportunistic predators, with diets that take advantage of changes in habitat, season, and prey availability. As large raptors, they typically select larger prey than that of other smaller owls. This is not a strict rule, however, and they just as often feed on small mammals such as voles and mice. In parts of their range, rabbits form the majority of their diet, and in others, birds are the most common. In the wild or in cities, they routinely kill and eat fish, raccoons, skunks, and snakes.

Some observers note that other owl species may also increasingly include urban areas for both hunting and nesting, especially Barred Owls. In a few cities, there have also been reports of urban nests for the Eastern Screech Owl, at least in Texas.

Barred Owls in the nonurban wild favor rodents for food, with mice and voles dominating their diet. A study of Barred Owls in urban areas of British Columbia, however, reported that in urban zones, they switched to the rodent prey that was more common in developed areas: roof rats (black rats) and Norway rats (brown rats). In

RODENT MENU

Rodents are a major source of food for most owl species in North America. As much as 70 percent or more of their foraging may consist of rodents, mostly small species. Just about any rodent can be a target, but the majority of owl prey are voles, mice, and gophers, with more than 200 species to choose from in North America. Most species in an owl's rodent diet are active at night, but owls may also hunt at dawn and dusk, expanding the selection of prey. Owls will typically swallow a small-sized catch whole, after the prey animal is dead. Other raptors also consume a lot of rodents, up to half or more of some raptors' diets, making these birds an effective control for rodent pests in both rural and urban areas.

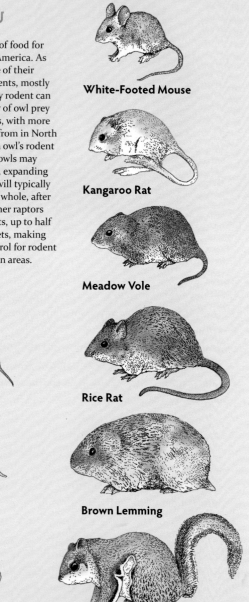

White-Footed Mouse

Kangaroo Rat

Meadow Vole

Rice Rat

Brown Lemming

Southern Flying Squirrel

Deer Mouse

Grasshopper Mouse

Pocket Mouse

British Columbia, there was a direct correlation between the number and percentage of rats in owl diets and the density of urban development: the more congested the development, the more rats and the greater the attraction for the owls. Rats made up more than 60 percent of these urban hunters' diet. A similar result is reported in the diet of Great Horned Owls nesting in Seattle, and parallel reports are made for cities in Europe.

BIRDS

Birds, especially passerines, are a part of many raptors' diets. Bird feeders are magnets for raptors, as they concentrate prey birds in confined spaces, but positioning the feeder close to trees or bushes improves the chances of escape for targeted birds.

Birds are a regular part of the Great Horned Owl's diet—some as large as turkeys; other raptors and even other owl species are also targeted. Long-eared Owls' prey across North America includes thirty-five species of birds. Barred Owls hunting in an urban area in North Carolina preyed more on birds, a possible consequence of the number of backyard bird feeders. Bald Eagles also target birds, especially ducks and other waterbirds.

The diet of the Sharp-shinned Hawk is suggested by one of its common names, bird hawk. Throughout its range, it is noted for preying on other birds, particularly passerines. This raptor is relatively comfortable in urban settings and often takes advantage of backyard bird feeders to ambush its prey. In one survey, Sharp-shinned Hawks were implicated in 35 percent of attacks on bird feeders nationally.

Peregrine Falcons have an established reputation as hunters, with the fastest diving speed of any bird and known success across a wide geographical area, increasingly including cities. Most falcon prey are other birds, typically caught in the air, and often relatively large compared to the Peregrine's size. Prey species frequently include American Robins, ducks, grackles, grebes, gulls, jays, orioles, pigeons, rails, terns, and woodpeckers—and bats.

This Red-tailed Hawk has captured a Northern Flicker on the ground and carried it to a perch. The raptor has not yet dispatched its prey and has begun stripping its feathers while the bird is still alive.

Birds are usually defeathered after capture and sometimes the wings are not consumed, as they contain little meat. Typically less of a bird's body is consumed than that of a mammal prey's.

AQUATIC PREY

Birds that feed in the water depend on a wide range of animal food sources, including fish, reptiles, amphibians, mollusks, and crustaceans and other arthropods, including aquatic insects (see the Aquatic Animal Menu sidebar).

Birds use a variety of tactics to acquire aquatic prey. At least thirty-eight feeding behaviors are associated with this habitat. Some of these prey are found close to the surface, where wading birds such as egrets forage, but diving birds such as loons can target fish swimming as deep as 200 feet (60 meters).

Within their range, Bald Eagles' preference is live fish, but they are known to capture and eat reptiles, amphibians, and crustaceans. Fish make up more than half of the Bald Eagle diet, with the remainder

AQUATIC ANIMAL MENU

A .Crayfish; B. Riffle beetle larva; C. Riffle beetle; D. Stonefly; E. Texas leech;
F. Dragonfly nymph; G. Caddisfly larva; H. River frog tadpole; I. Northern leopard
frog; J. Freshwater mussel; K. Rainbow trout

mostly being birds (28 percent) and mammals (14 percent). The ratio changes by season and local availability.

Ospreys in North America consume more than eighty species of fish, but in most inland freshwater habitats, the majority of their prey may be limited to only two or three species, the fish that are most common in their local habitats. Fish make up as much as 99 percent of their diet.

Ospreys generally catch fish too large to be swallowed whole. Captured fish can range in size from 11 ounces (312 grams) to more than 2 pounds (0.9 kilogram), weighing 10 percent to as much as 50 percent of an Osprey's own body mass. At the nest or feeding perch, they pluck pieces, starting at the head and working their way toward the tail. Every part of the fish is consumed, including the intestines, fish skin, and tail, but larger pieces and pieces with bones may not be fed to chicks. Fish that are not consumed right away may be left, usually in the nest itself, for later consumption.

Vision is the predominant sense used by birds to locate underwater prey. Cormorants and loons chase down fish and other prey by

Ospreys are very effective catching fish, with a success rate that is tied to their preference for familiar waters. *(Photo by Mark Metcalf)*

American White Pelicans, common in both fresh- and saltwater habitats, usually feed in groups. They do not dive like the Brown Pelican, but fish from the surface by using their bills to scoop prey from the water. Most of the time, they select fish that are less than 2 inches (5 centimeters) long, but are capable of swallowing those that are much larger. *(Photo by Ekaterina Krasnova)*

sight while swimming underwater; kingfishers and some other birds sight their prey and dive from above.

Birds that use their wings for propulsion underwater include auks, auklets, dippers, guillemots, puffins, and shearwaters, as well as murres, which can hunt for food as deep as 300 feet (91 meters). Many birds that swim underwater have shorter wings than nondiving species. Some birds that swim underwater use their wings to achieve speeds up to 4 miles (6.4 kilometers) an hour, similar to those that propel themselves with their feet. Common Murres can swim below the surface at almost 6 miles (9.7 kilometers) an hour. Even with wing propulsion, however, underwater swimmers may still use their feet to provide added push, although this is not common.

Diving petrels use their wings for propulsion underwater, though some diving birds may use a combination of feet and wings. Plunge divers, such as gannets, plummet into the water at speeds up to 60 miles (97 kilometers) per hour, helping them achieve depth quickly, more than 100 feet (30 meters) down in some cases. The Northern Gannet, like all underwater birds, hunts by sight, but it spots its prey from the air before it dives, unlike loons and cormorants, which hunt after submerging.

Most of the floating waterbirds we see rely on webbed feet for propulsion. Webbing is an adaptation that makes aquatic environments more productive for birds, allowing them to move around while foraging for animal and plant food sources. Webbing, and lobes as on the feet of grebes, also provides additional propulsion underwater.

Birds known for foot-propulsion, such as loons, have feet that are arranged relatively far back on their bodies, a position that gives their legs and feet more power in the water, although it makes them ungainly when walking on land. Grebes and loons paddle underwater by extending their feet to either side of their bodies; cormorants paddle with their feet under their bodies. The standard motion for birds swimming underwater is for both feet to stroke in unison, but all birds that swim on the surface use alternating strokes. Cormorants paddle with alternate feet on the surface, but while swimming underwater thrust with both feet simultaneously.

Loons, cormorants, and grebes, such as this Pied-billed Grebe with a kelpfish, hunt underwater by sight, outswimming fish and other aquatic prey with speed and agility. *(Photo by Sheila Fitzgerald)*

Most birds have hollow bones, a characteristic that lessens the burden of weight while flying, but loons' bones are dense and solid, making it easier for them to dive and remain underwater. Loons float low in the water when on the surface. Most of their dives are less than 200 feet (60 meters) deep, but they have been observed as deep as 600 feet (183 meters) in large bodies of water, including the Great Lakes.

In laboratory settings, captive loons have been observed swimming at speeds from 0.4 to 1.9 miles (0.6 to 3.1 kilometers) an hour, but they are likely capable of faster speeds in natural settings. The fastest speeds recorded for grebes is 2.7 miles (4.3 kilometers) an hour and for cormorants, 3.8 miles (6.1 kilometers) an hour. This pace may seem slow compared to the standard human walking speed of about 3 miles (4.8 kilometers) an hour, but it is fast enough to chase down most of the fish these underwater hunters prey on.

Canada Geese are considered herbivores, obtaining their food from plant sources both in and out of the water. One study, however, notes that fish may also be a part of the diet in some geese, as observed on several occasions. Individual geese caught multiple fish of various sizes, with small fish swallowed whole and larger ones shaken into pieces before being swallowed. Mallards have also been

Grebes and loons catch fish while swimming underwater, but usually surface before swallowing them. Left: Pied-billed Grebe *(Photo by Tom Reichner)*; right: Common Loon *(Photo by Brian Lasenby)*

observed catching and eating fish (although this is rare), feeding on fish carcasses discarded by anglers, and eating salmon eggs. Fish have also been caught and eaten by American Crows, Black and Eastern Phoebes, and Marsh Wrens, but this is also considered unusual.

A Great Blue Heron captures a catfish in a freshwater lake. *(Photo by Nancy Bauer)*

Little Blue Herons tend to travel farther and select smaller prey than larger herons and egrets; small fish such as anchovies, darters, killifish, and various minnows are among their targets. Great Egrets, with longer legs, are able to forage in deeper water than smaller wading birds, and although they can catch and swallow larger fish because of their size, often capture fish of smaller size that are more abundant because the fish are out of the range of hunters in shallower water. Great Egrets and Great Blue Herons demonstrate about the same outcome while hunting, roughly a 70 percent success rate.

Shorebirds—some sandpipers, plovers, and others—have diets that mostly consist of aquatic and terrestrial insects and other invertebrates, but also capture fish occasionally. In the shallow-water habitats where these birds forage, common small fish such as dace, minnows, and smelt are sometimes consumed.

AMPHIBIANS AND REPTILES

Amphibians, such as frogs and tadpoles, and reptiles, such as lizards and snakes and even alligators, are a regular part of the diet for many birds. Aquatic species such as shorebirds forage in shallow water, where this vertebrate prey is often abundant.

Some birds, such as cormorants, rely on a single practice: diving from the surface to locate prey underwater, where they chase it down and capture it. In the water, they float low, sometimes with only their heads and necks above the surface, and dive from a floating position.

A Double-crested Cormorant dives from the surface on an underwater hunting expedition, unlike raptors such as ospreys, who dive from the air, usually aiming directly at prey they have already spotted.

Using their wings and webbed feet for propulsion, they actively hunt for prey at depths of a few feet up to 60 feet (18 meters) below the surface. They typically stay submerged until they catch something to eat, including crayfish, fish, frogs, and similar aquatic animals, with underwater episodes that typically last under a minute. Feathers on cormorants and anhingas are less water-repellent than those of other swimming and diving birds because these species have no oil glands. To counter the effects of being in the water, they take frequent breaks and dry their feathers in the sun, often spreading their wings to maximize exposure.

Other birds, such as egrets and herons, exhibit a broader range of actions, stalking, chasing, or ambushing their prey from vantage points above the water's surface. Egrets sometimes employ their wings as a canopy to shade the water surface and reduce glare, improving their chances of spotting prey under the water, and the shadow may also attract prey. Wading birds also use their wings for stability while moving through the water, as well as to startle and flush prey.

Black-crowned Night Herons, Great Blue Herons, and Great Egrets sometimes use bait to improve their hunting success. This method, used most frequently by Green Herons, involves selecting an object as bait, dropping it on the water's surface, and then ambushing the fish or other animals that swim to it. The bait can be natural, such as

This Snowy Egret, like other egrets and herons, stalks its prey in shallow water along the banks of lakes and streams. Its stealthy approach and fast reflexes result in a high ratio of successful captures. Prey includes crayfish, fish, frogs, insects, small snakes, snails, and other animals that live in these habitats.

a dead or live insect or, as on several occasions noted by observers, scavenged pieces of bread left by humans. Such activity is more of a curiosity than a standard foraging method.

AQUATIC INVERTEBRATES

Aquatic invertebrates that birds eat include aquatic insects (beetles, brine flies, fly larvae, midges, water fleas, and many more), brine shrimp, crabs, crayfish, leeches, mussels, snails, and worms. Birds target these animals at various growth stages, from egg to adult, and benefit from their wide abundance in both freshwater and marine habitats. Many aquatic invertebrates also thrive year-round, providing food sources throughout the year.

Grebes spend most of their time in the water. A study of Eared Grebes at Mono Lake in California reported they spend up to 15 percent of their time underwater, seeking their primary food: brine shrimp—up to 90 percent of their diet. The grebe can reduce its buoyancy by trapping water within its feathers, which replaces air, allowing it to increase its dive depth; other waterbirds, including loons, have this ability as well.

Touch is an alternative to sight for birds foraging underwater or in mud; birds primarily use their bills to detect aquatic insects and other invertebrates, but may also use this practice for vegetation. The American Avocet is noted for "scything," moving its bill from side to side through mud as a foraging method. Egrets, herons, ibises, and storks forage this way at various times, probing with their bills but also occasionally feeling for targets with their toes. The feet of wading herons and other shallow water stalkers are also sometimes used to startle prey into movement, making them easier to spot. The diet of herons, ibises, and storks includes not only aquatic invertebrates but also birds, bird eggs, fish, and rodents and other small mammals.

Capturing prey on or under the water requires extremely fast reflexes, something water-feeding birds excel at. In response to tactile feedback while foraging, the Wood Stork can snap its bill closed in about 25 milliseconds. Birds have extended necks, with more vertebrae and flexibility than most animals, improving their ability to lunge at prey. Herons grab prey with a decisive thrust of the neck, which is flexible enough for them to strike forward, to the side, or downward equally well.

As these birds strike, most of the time they catch their prey with an open bill, but especially for species with longer, thinner bills, one or both bills may be used to spear the target. Once caught, prey must be subdued or killed before it can be swallowed, and this can be accomplished with a range of actions. Depending on the size of the prey, it may be repeatedly snapped with the bill, shaken, or bashed against a hard surface. To orient prey headfirst before swallowing, it is flipped and tossed with the bill to maneuver it into the right position. Big birds with small prey spend little time handling their catch; it is typically positioned and swallowed in a matter of seconds.

CARRION

Carrion is food for many more birds than vultures. Bald Eagles, for example, are noted for a diet that is a mix of live prey and carrion. From large birds such as eagles and hawks to small ones such as jays and magpies, many species find essential nutrition in the bodies of dead fish, mammals, and other birds.

The biggest problem for birds when it comes to carrion, at least with the bodies of larger animals, is access. Tough skin and thick fur pose barriers that some birds are unable to get through unless the dead animals are torn open by larger scavengers, such as badgers, bears, coyotes, large raptors, or wolves.

Ravens have a noted role in finding carrion. They partner with coyotes and wolves, as well as Bald Eagles, to locate new sources to scavenge. Ravens follow wolves on their hunting expeditions. Ravens are sometimes the spotters, using their aerial advantage point to spot roadkill, carcasses and gut piles left behind by hunters, and carrion hidden by mammalian carnivores in brush, ravines, or other natural cover.

Once a dead animal is discovered, the quicker the large carnivores arrive, the sooner carrion provides meals for smaller avian feeders. In a study of raptor scavenging in Arizona, researchers found that Common Ravens average less than three days before discovering a

In urban areas, birds are one of the most effective scavengers, although vultures are rarely seen. This American Crow has carried the body of a dead fox squirrel to a feeding perch, where it can defend its meal.

new carcass, and coyotes appear at about five days. The carcasses in this study included elk, mule deer, and pronghorn in a variety of habitats.

Eagles, ravens, vultures, and smaller birds have a pecking order at carrion feeding sites, with size determining rank. Most of the time, coyotes or other mammals dominate a feeding site, but Bald Eagles are known to challenge coyotes, and if eagles are present in enough numbers, they can force a single coyote to retreat. In the Arizona study, as many as eighteen eagles and thirty-two ravens showed up to feed at some carcasses.

Birds of all sizes feed on various parts of mammal carrion, including major and minor muscles, major organs, entrails, brains, soft tissue, and bone marrow if it's exposed. Eagles and ravens consumed a high of 95 pounds (43 kilograms) a day from a single carcass in the Arizona study, but the amounts from roadkill were smaller, less than 22 pounds (10 kilograms), where vehicle traffic interrupted feeding.

Peregrine Falcons, though highly skilled and effective aerial hunters, also use carrion as a food source. When hunting on the wing, immature falcons are sometimes less successful than adults, so for them, scavenging represents a more reliable food resource. Another factor in this relationship is the relative absence of competition when feeding on carrion. In their normal hunting activity, Peregrines are often attacked by other raptors looking for meals to steal.

In one study of Peregrines in coastal Washington, 29 percent of the food these birds ingested came from carcasses, mostly dead seabirds and waterbirds (90 percent of the total carrion prey). The researchers in this study believe that these falcons and others throughout their range may take advantage of carrion because it represents a more effective way to maximize access to food. The dead animals they fed on were typically larger than the live prey that is the Peregrine's principal food.

Vultures are known to consume even more carrion than eagles and ravens. Their digestive systems are strong enough and their digestive process lasts long enough to dissolve all sorts of animal tissue, including bone and fur, although they do sometimes regurgitate small pellets. There are three species of North American vultures—

Turkey Vulture, Black Vulture, and California Condor—but because of their rarity and limited range, California Condors are rarely seen.

The most common species is the Turkey Vulture, which is a significant part of the food chain throughout North America, finding and disposing of dead animals of all sizes. They devour everything from crickets to dead livestock and occasionally eat small prey alive. In a study from southern Pennsylvania, Turkey Vultures were found to feed mostly on dead domestic livestock (two-thirds of its diet), wild animals (mostly groundhogs and skunks), but also occasionally kitchen scraps, offal from livestock slaughter, and even insect larvae.

Turkey Vultures and Black Vultures may compete for animal carcasses where their ranges overlap, mostly in the southern United States. Both of these species have been traditionally blamed for killing young farm animals and spreading livestock disease, but research has proven these issues to be false.

Carrion also attracts a variety of insects that are active participants in the cycle of decomposition. Animal carcasses provide food

Turkey Vultures feed on the carcass of a dead deer. Vultures compete for carrion with other birds and mammals and face deadly consequences when they congregate around roadkill, with vehicle traffic a serious threat. *(Photo by Hayley Crews)*

Garbage dumps are prime feeding locations for many kinds of birds but are particularly attractive to scavengers such as crows, gulls, and ravens. *(Photo by Andrew Newark)*

for ants, beetles, flies, their maggots (fly larvae), and wasps, among other arthropods. Aggregations of these invertebrates provide a concentrated source of food for insect-eating birds, which may select carrion more for the insects than the meat.

A less desirable part of Bald Eagle foraging zones are human garbage dumps. Competing with crows, vultures, and other scavengers, Bald Eagles congregate at dumps to take advantage of a never-ending stream of leftovers, and they may suffer from the ingestion of plastics and other materials not intended for consumption. As open garbage dumps have been replaced by enclosed facilities, however, birds feeding in these zones have become relatively limited and uncommon.

BIRD DIET PROFILES

In this chapter, 130 of the most common birds in North America—species most often referred to or asked about in multiple field guides and online lists—are profiled by their type of diet. Some bird diets have been studied extensively, but many others lack detail, even if generalities are known. General food preferences are often the only reliable result from diet studies. Birds of the same species may target different foods from hour to hour or day to day and differ in what they ingest in different parts of their range; diets of individual birds of the same species may also vary because of individual preferences.

The 130 species included here are representative of the major types of birds in North America, including many that are familiar at backyard feeders. Most feeders are stocked with mixed seed, which covers the basic entries listed here. Food provided in feeders necessarily limits choices for birds to products available commercially and also lacks the wider variation found in nature, especially that of insects, although mealworms can fill this gap when provided.

Each entry in this chapter gives the bird's common name, scientific name, diet type, a list of general food preferences, and known feeder preferences. The items listed under Diet for each entry include both general and specific foods, with preferences noted when supported by information sources. The feeder preferences, if any, come from years of information collected by volunteers who contribute to FeederWatch, a valuable crowd-sourced database (see Resources).

Bird lovers often discover for themselves intriguing variations in the food choices of bird species visiting backyard bird feeders. Observers may notice preferences, such as for sunflower seeds that are hulled or whole or corn that is cracked or whole, and adjust future feed purchases to reflect what local birds prefer. Seeds that are popular one season may be ignored in another; different sizes of the same seed may trigger different reactions; undetectable (to humans) qualities may attract or deter.

Two excellent resources for detailed information about individual species in North America, including a photo of each bird, can be found online: Audubon's "Guide to North American Birds" and Cornell Lab of Ornithology's "Birds of North America" (see Resources).

ACADIAN FLYCATCHER

Empidonax virescens
Mostly insectivorous
Diet: Insects and other arthropods—ants, aphids, bees, beetles, caterpillars, cicadas, crane flies, crickets, damselflies, dragonflies, flies, grasshoppers, harvestmen (daddy longlegs), larvae of various insects, mosquitoes, moths, roaches, scorpion flies, sow bugs, spiders, termites, true bugs, wasps; berries and fruit—blackberry, dogwood, elderberry, sugarberry

AMERICAN AVOCET

Recurvirostra americana
Omnivorous
Diet: Insects and other arthropods—aquatic insects, brine shrimp, crustaceans, leeches, terrestrial insects, worms; mollusks, snails and other gastropods; small amphibians; small fish. Also seeds and foliage of aquatic plants.

AMERICAN BITTERN

Botaurus lentiginosus
Mostly piscivorous
Diet: Fish—catfish, eels, killifish, perch, pickerel, sticklebacks, suckers, sunfish; amphibians, salamanders, snakes; aquatic insects, crayfish and other crustaceans. Also small rodents.

AMERICAN COOT

Fulica americana
Omnivorous
Diet: Mostly plant material—foliage, roots, stems, tubers, seeds; aquatic and terrestrial plants; grasses and sedges; algae, buttonbush, cattail, coon tail, duckweed, eelgrass, ferns, hornwort, hydrilla, pondweed, smartweed, water milfoil, wild celery, wild rice, agricultural grains; aquatic insects and other arthropods—beetles, butterflies, crayfish and other crustaceans, flies, prawns, spiders, worms; fish; birds (eggs); mollusks, snails; tadpoles. Also carrion.

AMERICAN CROW

Corvus brachyrhynchos
Omnivorous
Diet: Insects and other arthropods—beetles, caterpillars, grasshoppers, spiders; amphibians, reptiles; birds—eggs, nestlings, adults; small mammals; seeds—agricultural grains; nuts; fruit; carrion. **Feeders:** Prefers cracked or whole corn, peanuts, suet, fruit, millet, oats, milo.

AMERICAN DIPPER

Cinclus mexicanus
Mostly insectivorous
Diet: Aquatic insects and other arthropods—beetles, larvae of various insects, mosquitoes, true bugs, worms; snails. Also fish roe, small fish less than 3 inches (7.6 centimeters).

AMERICAN GOLDFINCH

Spinus tristis
Mostly granivorous
Diet: Seeds—dandelion, elm, goldenrod, grasses, ragweed, sedges, sunflower, thistles, trees (alder, birch, cedar); insects—aphids, beetles, caterpillars. **Feeders:** Prefers niger, sunflower.

AMERICAN KESTRE L

Falco sparverius
Carnivorous
Diet: Large insects and other arthropods—beetles, butterflies, caterpillars, cicadas, crayfish and other crustaceans, dragonflies, grasshoppers, moths, scorpions, spiders; small rodents (mice, voles), shrews, bats; small birds; amphibians, reptiles; small fish.

AMERICAN REDSTART

Setophaga ruticilla
Mostly insectivorous
Diet: Insects and other arthropods—ants, aphids, bark lice, beetles, caterpillars, crane flies, flies, leafhoppers, midges, moths, small wasps, spiders; berries and other fruit.

AMERICAN ROBIN

Turdus migratorius
Omnivorous
Diet: Insects and other arthropods—beetles, butterflies, caterpillars, centipedes, earthworms, flies, millipedes, moths, sow bugs, spiders, termites; snails; seeds; berries and other fruit from more than fifty genera of fruiting plants. **Feeders:** Prefers sunflower, suet, peanut hearts, fruit, mealworms.

AMERICAN WHITE PELICAN

Pelecanus erythrorhynchos
Piscivorous
Diet: Fish—bass, carp, catfish, chub, jackfish, minnows, perch, pickerel, pike, salmon, shiners, sticklebacks, suckers, sunfish, trout—size ranges from 2 inches (5 centimeters) to 2 feet (0.6 meter), but usually selects smaller prey. Also crayfish, salamanders, tadpoles.

BALD EAGLE

Haliaeetus leucocephalus
Mostly piscivorous
Diet: Fish—bass, carp, catfish, herring, salmon, shad, suckers, trout; terrestrial birds, ducks and other waterbirds; crustaceans; mammals—muskrats, rabbits, raccoons, rats, squirrels; amphibians, reptiles; carrion.

BALTIMORE ORIOLE

Icterus galbula
Mostly insectivorous
Diet: Insects and other arthropods—ants, aphids, beetles, caterpillars, crickets, grasshoppers, midges, mosquitoes, spiders, termites, wasps; snails; nectar; berries and fruit. **Feeders** (uncommon): prefers suet, fruit.

BARN OWL

Tyto alba
Carnivorous
Diet: Mostly voles; birds; flying squirrels, lemmings, mice, moles, shrews, juvenile rats and rabbits.

BARN SWALLOW

Hirundo rustica
Mostly insectivorous
Diet: Mostly flying insects—bees, butterflies, crane flies, damselflies, dragonflies, flies, flying ants and termites, gnats, horseflies, flies, mayflies, mosquitoes, moths, wasps), beetles, crickets, grasshoppers, leafhoppers; snails. Also seeds; berries.

BARRED OWL

Strix varia
Carnivorous
Diet: Mostly small mammals—bats, mice, opossums, rabbits, rats, shrews, squirrels, voles; large insects and other arthropods; birds (up to the size of pheasants); amphibians, reptiles. Also crayfish, crabs; mollusks; fish.

BELTED KINGFISHER

Megaceryle alcyon
Mostly piscivorous
Diet: Mostly small fish. Also aquatic insects, crayfish, crustaceans; mollusks; frogs, lizards, reptiles, tadpoles; small mammals; young birds.

BLACK-CAPPED CHICKADEE

Poecile atricapillus
Omnivorous
Diet: Mostly insects and other arthropods—aphids, beetles, caterpillars, centipedes, flies, katydids, larvae of various insects, leafhoppers, moths, scale insects, spiders, treehoppers, true bugs, wasps; slugs, snails; seeds; berries and fruit; carrion. **Feeders:** Prefers sunflower, safflower, niger, suet, peanuts, mealworms.

BLACK-CHINNED HUMMINGBIRD

Archilochus alexandri
Mostly nectarivorous
Diet: Nectar—agave, columbine, firecracker bush, fireweed, hummingbird bush, honeysuckle, jacobina, lantana, larkspur, ocotillo, paintbrush, penstemons, sage, scarlet gilia, skyrocket, thistle, tree tobacco (at least ninety plant species); tree sap; small insects (ants, beetles, flies), spiders. **Feeders:** Sugar water.

BLACK-CROWNED NIGHT HERON

Nycticorax nycticorax
Mostly piscivorous
Diet: Fish; amphibians; aquatic insects, crayfish and other crustaceans, leeches and other worms, terrestrial insects; birds—eggs, nestlings; clams, mussels, squid; reptiles; rodents; carrion.

BLACK TERN

Chlidonias niger
Mostly piscivorous
Diet: Small fish; aquatic insects, crayfish and other crustaceans, leeches and other worms, spiders, terrestrial insects—caddisflies, crickets, damselflies, dragonflies, flying ants, grasshoppers, locusts, mayflies; amphibians, tadpoles; mollusks.

BLUE JAY

Cyanocitta cristata
Omnivorous
Diet: Plant material—seeds, agricultural grains; insects and other arthropods—beetles, butterflies, caterpillars, flies, grasshoppers, millipedes, spiders; berries and fruit; nuts—acorns, beechnuts, chestnuts, hazelnuts, hickory nuts; birds—eggs, nestlings; mollusks, snails; carrion. Also small rodents. **Feeders:** Prefers sunflower, safflower, suet, corn, peanuts, fruit, millet, milo, mealworms.

BREWER'S BLACKBIRD

Euphagus cyanocephalus
Omnivorous
Diet: Insects and other arthropods—aphids, beetles, butterflies, caterpillars, crickets, grasshoppers, small crustaceans, spiders, termites; seeds—agricultural grains, grasses and sedges; berries; snails. Also frogs; small rodents; birds—eggs, nestlings, adults.

BROWN-HEADED COWBIRD

Molothrus ater
Omnivorous
Diet: Seeds (grasses, agricultural grains); insects and other arthropods—beetles, caterpillars, grasshoppers, spiders.
Feeders: Prefers sunflower, cracked corn, peanut hearts, millet, oats, milo.

BROWN CREEPER

Certhia americana
Mostly insectivorous
Diet: Insects (eggs, pupae, larvae, caterpillars, and adults)—ants, aphids, bark weevils and other beetles, caddisflies, fruit flies, gnats, leafhoppers, moths, pseudoscorpions, sawflies, scale insects, spiders, true bugs; seeds. **Feeders:** Prefers sunflower, suet, peanut hearts.

BUFFLEHEAD

Bucephala albeola
Mostly insectivorous in freshwater habitats; crustivorous in saltwater habitats
Diet: Aquatic insects—beetles, crabs and other crustaceans, larvae of caddisflies, damselflies, dragonflies, mayflies, midges, water boatmen; small fish; snails and other mollusks (including zebra mussels); seeds and foliage of aquatic plants.

BULLOCK'S ORIOLE

Icterus bullockii
Omnivorous
Diet: Insects and other arthropods—beetles, butterflies, caterpillars, cicadas, crane flies, crickets, earwigs, flying ants, grasshoppers, leafhoppers, moths, scale insects, spiders, treehoppers, true bugs, walking sticks, wasps; berries and fruit—blackberry, cherry, mulberry, raspberry, serviceberry; nectar.

CANADA GOOSE

Branta canadensis
Mostly herbivorous
Diet: Aquatic and terrestrial plants (foliage, roots, shoots, stems, tubers, berry, seeds)—algae, forbs, grasses, legumes, pondweed, reeds, seaweeds, sedges, succulents; agricultural grains. Also aquatic insects, terrestrial insects, crustaceans; mollusks; small fish.

CANADA JAY

Perisoreus canadensis
Omnivorous
Diet: Insects and other arthropods—ants, bees, beetles, caterpillars, centipedes, crickets, flies, grasshoppers, spiders, true bugs, wasps; berries; birds—eggs, nestlings; fungi; small rodents; carrion. **Feeders:** Prefers sunflower, suet, peanuts, fruit, mealworms.

CANVASBACK

Aythya valisineria
Mostly herbivorous depending on location
Diet: Aquatic plants (foliage, roots, stems, buds, seeds, tubers)—grasses, sedges. Also aquatic insects—larvae and nymphs of caddisflies, damselflies, dragonflies, mayflies, midges; mollusks, snails; small fish.

CAROLINA CHICKADEE

Poecile carolinensis
Omnivorous
Diet: Insects and other arthropods—aphids, beetles, butterflies, caterpillars, larvae and eggs of various insects, moths, spiders, true bugs; seeds—ragweed, pine nuts, redbud; berries—blackberry, blueberry, honeysuckle, mulberry, poison ivy, Virginia creeper. **Feeders:** Prefers sunflower, safflower, niger, suet, peanuts, mealworms.

CAROLINA WREN

Thryothorus ludovicianus
Mostly insectivorous
Diet: Insects and other arthropods—ants, bees, beetles, caterpillars, crickets, grasshoppers, leafhoppers, millipedes, roaches, sow bugs, spiders, true bugs, wasps; snails; seeds—bayberry, poison ivy, smartweed, sumac, sweet gum; acorns; berries. **Feeders:** Prefers sunflower, suet, peanut hearts, mealworms.

CATTLE EGRET

Bubulcus ibis
Mostly insectivorous
Diet: Large insects and other arthropods—centipedes, crayfish and other crustaceans, crickets, earthworms, flies, grasshoppers, millipedes, moths, spiders. Also birds—eggs, nestlings, adults; frogs, snakes; leeches, ticks; small fish.

CEDAR WAXWING

Bombycilla cedrorum
Mostly frugivorous
Diet: Berries and fruit—cedar, dogwood, hawthorn, honeysuckle, juniper, madrone, mistletoe, mulberry, peppertree, raspberry, serviceberry, toyon; flowers; insects—ants, beetles, caterpillars, crickets, flies, grasshoppers, mayflies, scale insects, stoneflies, true bugs. Also tree sap. **Feeders:** Prefers fruit, mixed seeds.

CHIMNEY SWIFT

Chaetura pelagica
Insectivorous
Diet: Flying insects and other arthropods—bees, beetles, butterflies, caddisflies, crane flies, fleas, flying ants, houseflies, leafhoppers, mayflies, mosquitoes, moths, stoneflies, spiders, true bugs, wasps.

CHIPPING SPARROW

Spizella passerina
Omnivorous
Diet: Insects and other arthropods—beetles, caterpillars, flies, grasshoppers, leafhoppers, spiders, true bugs; seeds (agricultural grains, grasses, sedges)—bead grass, bindweed, chickweed, clover, crabgrass, dandelion, foxtail, knotweed, poverty weed, purslane, ragweed, wolf tail). **Feeders:** Prefers sunflower, niger, cracked corn, millet, milo.

COMMON GOLDENEYE

Bucephala clangula
Omnivorous
Diet: Aquatic insects, aquatic worms, crayfish and other crustaceans, crabs, leeches, shrimp; frogs; mollusks; small fish, pondweed and other aquatic vegetation (foliage, seeds, tubers).

COMMON GRACKLE

Quiscalus quiscula
Omnivorous
Diet: Insects and other arthropods—bees, beetles, caterpillars, crayfish, crickets, earthworms, grasshoppers, spiders; birds—eggs, nestlings; frogs, lizards; small rodents; small fish; snails; acorns; seeds; berries and fruit. Also agricultural grains. **Feeders:** Prefers sunflower, safflower, suet, cracked corn, peanuts, fruit, millet, oats, milo.

COMMON LOON

Gavia immer
Mostly piscivorous
Diet: Small fish up to 10 inches (25 centimeters)—bluegill, chub, minnows, perch, rock cod, shad, suckers. Also amphibians; aquatic insects, crayfish and other crustaceans, leeches; mollusks; snails.

COMMON MERGANSER

Mergus merganser
Mostly piscivorous
Diet: Fish (up to 50 fish species)—chub, minnows, salmon, sculpin, shad, suckers, sunfish, trout; aquatic insects—beetles, caddisflies, caterpillars, crane flies, dragonflies, mayflies, true flies, water striders. Also mussels; shrimp, spiders.

COMMON MURRE

Uria aalge
Mostly piscivorous
Diet: Fish (about 36 species)—anchovies, cod, capelin, haddock, herring, pollock, rockfish, smelt. Also crustaceans, aquatic worms; squid.

COMMON NIGHTHAWK

Chordeiles minor
Insectivorous
Diet: Insects (more than 50 species)—beetles, caddisflies, crickets, flying ants, grasshoppers, mayflies, mosquitoes, moths, termites, true bugs, wasps.

COMMON RAVEN

Corvus corax
Omnivorous
Diet: Birds—eggs, nestlings, adults; insects and other arthropods—beetles, caterpillars, grasshoppers, moths, scorpions, spiders; fish; frogs, lizards, reptiles; rodents and other small mammals; seeds; berries and fruit; carrion. Also agricultural grain. **Feeders** (uncommon): prefers sunflower, suet, cracked corn, peanuts.

COMMON TERN

Sterna hirundo
Mostly piscivorous
Diet: Fish (about 55 species) up to 6 inches (15 centimeters)—alewives, anchovies, butterfish, capelin, hake, herring, mummichog, pollock, rockling, sand lance, shad, shiners, silversides, smelt, sticklebacks; aquatic worms, crustaceans, insects, leeches; squid.

COOPER'S HAWK

Accipiter cooperii
Carnivorous
Diet: Mostly medium-sized and smaller birds— blackbirds, crows, doves, flickers, grouse, jays, juncos, pheasants, pigeons, quail, robins, sparrows, starlings; small mammals—bats, chipmunks and other rodents, rabbits and hares. Also amphibians, reptiles; fish; insects. **Feeders:** Targets doves, juncos, sparrows, starlings.

DARK-EYED JUNCO

Junco hyemalis
Omnivorous
Diet: Insects and other arthropods—ants, beetles, butterflies, caterpillars, flies, grasshoppers, moths, spiders, true bugs, wasps; seeds—grasses, sedges. Also berries; agricultural grains. **Feeders:** Prefers sunflower, safflower, niger, cracked corn, peanut hearts, millet, oats, milo.

DOUBLE-CRESTED CORMORANT

Phalacrocorax auritus
Mostly piscivorous
Diet: Fish usually 6 inches (15 centimeters) or less—alewives, bass, capelin, carp, catfish, cod, drum, eels, flounder, goby, hake, herring, minnows, perch, salmon, shad, shiners, smelt, stickleback, suckers, sunfish, walleye. Also aquatic insects, crayfish and other crustaceans, shrimp; amphibians, frogs, snakes; mollusks.

DOWNY WOODPECKER

Dryobates pubescens
Mostly insectivorous
Diet: Insects and other arthropods—ants, aphids, beetles and beetle larvae, caterpillars, gall wasps, moths, scale insects, spiders, true bugs; snails. Also acorns; seeds; berries; sap, inner bark. **Feeders:** Prefers sunflower, safflower, suet, peanuts, mealworms.

EASTERN BLUEBIRD

Sialia sialis
Omnivorous
Diet: Insects and other arthropods—beetles, butterflies, caterpillars, centipedes, crickets, earthworms, grasshoppers, mosquitoes, moths, sow bugs, spiders; snails; berries and fruit. **Feeders:** Prefers suet, peanut hearts, fruit, mealworms.

EASTERN KINGBIRD

Tyrannus tyrannus
Mostly insectivorous
Diet: Insects and other arthropods—bees, beetles, caterpillars, crickets, flies, flying ants, grasshoppers, leafhoppers, spiders, wasps. Also berries and fruit.

EASTERN PHOEBE

Sayornis phoebe
Mostly insectivorous
Diet: Insects and other arthropods—ants, bees, beetles, butterflies, caterpillars, crickets, flies, grasshoppers, millipedes, mosquitoes, moths, spiders, ticks, true bugs, wasps. Also berries.

EASTERN SCREECH-OWL

Megascops asio
Carnivorous
Diet: Large insects and other arthropods—beetles, crayfish, crickets, earthworms, grasshoppers, moths, spiders; small mammals (about 138 vertebrates)—bats, mice, moles, shrews, voles; small birds; frogs, lizards. Also small fish.

EASTERN TOWHEE

Pipilo erythrophthalmus
Omnivorous
Diet: Insects and other arthropods—ants, bees, beetles, caterpillars, centipedes, crickets, grasshoppers, millipedes, moths, sow bugs, spiders, true bugs, wasps; snails; small amphibians, small reptiles; acorns; seeds; berries and fruit. Also plant material (buds, flowers, foliage). **Feeders:** Prefers sunflower, cracked corn, peanut hearts, millet, milo.

EASTERN WHIP-POOR-WILL

Antrostomus vociferous
Insectivorous
Diet: Insects—ants, bees, beetles, caterpillars, earthworms, flies, grasshoppers, mosquitoes, moths, wasps.

EASTERN WOOD-PEWEE

Contopus virens
Mostly insectivorous
Diet: Insects and other arthropods—bees, beetles, butterflies, flies, flying ants, grasshoppers, millipedes, moths, spiders, true bugs, wasps.

EUROPEAN STARLING

Sturnus vulgaris
Omnivorous
Diet: Mostly insects—beetles, butterflies, caterpillars, earthworms, flies, grasshoppers, moths, spiders; snails; seeds; berries. Also nectar. **Feeders:** Prefers sunflower, suet, corn, peanuts, fruit, millet, oats, milo.

FERRUGINOUS HAWK

Buteo regalis
Carnivorous
Diet: Small to medium-sized mammals—rabbits and hares, rodents; birds; insects; snakes.

GRAY CATBIRD

Dumetella carolinensis
Omnivorous
Diet: Insects and other arthropods—ants, beetles, caterpillars, crickets, grasshoppers, millipedes, spiders, true bugs; berries and fruit. Also small fish.

GREAT BLUE HERON

Ardea herodias
Mostly piscivorous
Diet: Mostly fish—bass, flounder, gunnel, perch, sculpin, smelt, stickleback. Also aquatic and terrestrial insects, crustaceans; birds; frogs, salamanders, snakes, turtles; rodents.

GREAT HORNED OWL

Bubo virginianus
Carnivorous
Diet: Mostly mammals—opossums, rabbits and hares, raccoons, skunks, small rodents; amphibians, reptiles; birds. Also crayfish, large insects (beetles, crickets), earthworms.

GREATER ROADRUNNER

Geococcyx californianus
Mostly carnivorous
Diet: Insects and other arthropods—beetles, caterpillars, centipedes, crickets, flies, grasshoppers, locusts, millipedes, scorpions, spiders, true bugs; birds (eggs, nestlings, adults)— small rodents— ground squirrels, mice, rats, voles; frogs, lizards, reptiles; berries; seeds.

GREEN HERON

Butorides virescens
Mostly piscivorous
Diet: Mostly fish—carp, catfish, eels, goby, minnows, pickerel, shad, sunfish. Also aquatic insects, crayfish and other crustaceans, earthworms, leeches; frogs; small rodents; snails, tadpoles.

GREEN-WINGED TEAL

Anas crecca
Mostly herbivorous
Diet: Aquatic and terrestrial plants—pondweed; seeds—grasses and sedges. Also aquatic insects, crustaceans; mollusks.

HAIRY WOODPECKER

Dryobates villosus
Mostly insectivorous
Diet: Insects and other arthropods—ants, beetles, caterpillars, larvae of various insects, millipedes, spiders; berries; seeds; nuts. Also sap. **Feeders:** Prefers sunflower, safflower, suet, peanuts, mealworms.

HERRING GULL

Larus argentatus
Omnivorous
Diet: Fish—alewives, bass, capelin, catfish, drum, eels, herring, mackerel, perch, sand lance, shiners, smelt, suckers, sunfish; insects and other arthropods—ants, aquatic and terrestrial worms, beetles, butterflies, caterpillars, crane flies, crustaceans, flies, grasshoppers, moths; birds (eggs, nestlings, adults)—cormorant, eider, gull, puffin, tern; frogs; mollusks, snails, squid; berries; rodents; carrion.

HORNED LARK

Eremophila alpestris
Omnivorous
Diet: Insects—beetles, caterpillars, grasshoppers; seeds—agricultural grains, grasses, sedges. Also snails; spiders; berries.

HOUSE FINCH

Haemorhous mexicanus
Mostly herbivorous
Diet: Plants (buds, flowers, berries and fruit, seeds)—amaranth, chickweed, knotweed, mullein, pigweed, poison oak, sunflower, thistle, wild mustard. Also agricultural fruit; insects—aphids, caterpillars. **Feeders:** Prefers sunflower, safflower, niger.

HOUSE SPARROW

Passer domesticus
Mostly herbivorous
Diet: Seeds—agricultural grains, bristle weed, chickweed, crabgrass, grasses, knotweed, ragweed, sedges, sunflower. Also insects and other small arthropods—ants, bees, beetles, caterpillars, grasshoppers, moths, wasps. **Feeders:** Prefers sunflower, cracked corn, peanut hearts, millet, milo.

HOUSE WREN

Troglodytes aedon
Mostly insectivorous
Diet: Insects and other arthropods—ants, bees, beetles, caterpillars, crickets, flies, grasshoppers, leafhoppers, mayflies, millipedes, mosquitoes, moths, spiders, true bugs, wasps; snails.

INDIGO BUNTING

Passerina cyanea
Omnivorous
Diet: Insects and other arthropods—aphids, beetles, caterpillars, cicadas, grasshoppers, mayflowers, moths, other flying insects, spiders, worms; seeds—goldenrod, grasses, thistles, plants (buds, pollen, flowers, foliage); berries.

KILLDEER

Charadrius vociferous
Mostly insectivorous
Diet: Insects and other arthropods—ants, beetles, caterpillars, centipedes, crayfish and other crustaceans, dragonfly larvae, earthworms, fly larvae, grasshoppers, spiders, webworms; snails. Also seeds—amaranth, arrowhead, grasses, pigweed, sandspur, sedges, rushes.

LEAST SANDPIPER

Calidris minutilla
Mostly insectivorous
Diet: Insects and other arthropods—ants, crustaceans, flies, fly larvae, grasshoppers. Also aquatic worms, horseshoe crab eggs; snails; seeds of aquatic plants.

MALLARD

Anas platyrhynchos
Omnivorous
Diet: Mostly plant material (roots, stems, tubers, seeds of aquatic and terrestrial plants, agricultural grains); insects—larvae of dragonflies and other flies; acorns; crustaceans, earthworms, shrimp; frogs, tadpoles; mollusks, snails; small fish.

MARSH WREN

Cistothorus palustris
Insectivorous
Diet: Insects and other arthropods—ants, bees, beetles, caterpillars, crickets, damselflies, flies, grasshoppers, larvae of aquatic and terrestrial insects, leafhoppers, mosquitoes, moths, spiders, true bugs, wasps.

MOUNTAIN BLUEBIRD

Sialia currucoides
Omnivorous
Diet: Insects and other arthropods—ants, bees, beetles, caterpillars, cicadas, crickets, flies, grasshoppers, mosquitoes, spiders; berries and fruit—buffalo berry, currant, grape, hackberry, juniper, mistletoe, serviceberry, sumac; seeds.

MOURNING DOVE

Zenaida macroura
Granivorous
Diet: Seeds—agricultural grains, amaranth, bristle grass, chickweed, crabgrass, dove weed, goosefoot, grasses, knotweed, pokeweed, poppies, purslane, ragweed, sedges, smartweed, spurges, sunflowers. **Feeders:** Prefers sunflower, safflower, niger, corn, peanut hearts, millet oats, milo.

NORTHERN BOBWHITE

Colinus virginianus
Omnivorous
Diet: Mostly seeds (up to 650 plant species)—agricultural grains, grasses, legumes; insects and other arthropods—bees, beetles, caterpillars, crickets, flies, grasshoppers, leafhoppers, spiders, wasps; acorns; plants (buds, foliage, roots); berries and fruit; snails.

NORTHERN CARDINAL

Cardinalis cardinalis
Omnivorous
Diet: Mostly seeds—bristle grass, dove weed, grasses, knotweed, panic grass, sedges, smartweed; plants (buds, flowers, foliage); berries and fruits—blackberry, grape, hackberry, mulberry; insects and other arthropods—ants, beetles, caterpillars, centipedes, crickets, dragonflies, flies, grasshoppers, lacewings, leafhoppers, mayflies, spiders, stinkbugs, true bugs. Also slugs, snails.
Feeders: Prefers sunflower, safflower, cracked corn, peanut hearts, millet, milo.

NORTHERN FLICKER

Colaptes auratus
Mostly insectivorous
Diet: Insects—mostly ants, beetles, caterpillars, crickets, grasshoppers, termites. Also berries and fruit—black gum, dogwood, hackberry, poison ivy, Virginia creeper, wild cherry; seeds; nuts. **Feeders:** Prefers sunflower, safflower, suet, cracked corn, peanuts, millet.

NORTHERN HARRIER

Circus hudsonius (formerly cyaneus)
Carnivorous
Diet: Small mammals—mice, rats, shrews, small rabbits, voles; birds—doves, flickers, small ducks and other waterbirds, songbirds; large insects; frogs, lizards, snakes. Also carrion.

NORTHERN MOCKINGBIRD

Mimus polyglottos
Omnivorous
Diet: Mostly insects and other arthropods—ants, bees, beetles, caterpillars, grasshoppers, spiders, wasps; berries—beautyberry, blackberry, black gum, buckthorn, cedar, elderberry, grape, hackberry, holly, sumac, Virginia creeper. Also earthworms; small lizards, snails. **Feeders:** Prefers sunflower, suet, peanut hearts, fruit.

NORTHERN PINTAIL

Anas acuta
Omnivorous
Diet: Aquatic and terrestrial plants and seeds—agricultural grains, algae, arrowhead, bulrush, grasses, musk grass, pondweed, sedges, smartweed, water lily, water milfoil, wigeon grass, wild millet; insects—beetles, crustaceans, earthworms, fly larvae, other larvae; snails. Also mollusks; small fish.

NORTHERN SAW-WHET OWL

Aegolius acadicus
Carnivorous
Diet: Mostly small rodents—lemmings, mice, shrews, voles; insects—beetles, grasshoppers; small birds.

NORTHERN SHRIKE

Lanius borealis
Carnivorous
Diet: Mostly large insects and other arthropods—ants, bees, beetles, bumblebees, caterpillars, flies, grasshoppers, spiders, wasps; small birds—crossbills, doves, finches, robins, sparrows, starlings, warblers, waxwings, wrens; rodents—mice, lemmings, shrews, voles; lizards; carrion.

NORTHERN SHOVELER

Spatula clypeata
Omnivorous
Diet: Insects and other arthropods—aquatic insects, crustaceans, water fleas; seeds; plants—hornwort, plankton, pondweed; mollusks, snails.

OSPREY

Pandion haliaetus
Piscivorous
Diet: Fish (more than 80 species) 4–12 inches (10–30 centimeters)—bass, carp, catfish, chub, flounder, herring, menhaden, mullet, perch, pollock, salmon, shad, smelt, suckers, trout, whitefish.

OVENBIRD

Seiurus aurocapilla
Mostly insectivorous
Diet: Insects and other arthropods—ants, beetles, caterpillars, earthworms, flies, mosquitoes, spiders, true bugs; snails; seeds.

PEREGRINE FALCON

Falco peregrinus
Carnivorous
Diet: Mostly birds (77 to 99 percent of its diet, more than 429 species)—ducks and other waterbirds, geese, gulls, loons, songbirds. Also amphibians; insects—crickets, grasshoppers; small mammals; carrion.

PIED-BILLED GREBE

Podilymbus podiceps
Mostly piscivorous and insectivorous
Diet: Crayfish and other crustaceans, aquatic insects—beetles, dragonfly nymphs, leeches, true bugs; frogs, tadpoles; mollusks; small fish. Also aquatic plants.

PINE SISKIN

Spinus pinus
Mostly granivorous
Diet: Seeds (forbs, grasses, sedges, trees)—alder, birch, chickweed, dandelion, elm, hemlock, maple, ragweed, sunflower, tamarack; plants (buds, flowers, shoots); nectar; pine nuts. Also insects—aphids, caterpillars, scale insects, spiders. **Feeders:** Prefers sunflower, niger.

PURPLE MARTIN

Progne subis
Insectivorous
Diet: Insects—aphids, bees, beetles, butterflies, caddisflies, crane flies, crickets, damselflies, dragonflies, flying ants, grasshoppers, houseflies, leafhoppers, mayflies, mosquitoes, moths, robber flies, spiders, termites, treehoppers, true bugs, wasps.

RED CROSSBILL

Loxia curvirostra
Mostly granivorous
Diet: Mostly pine nuts—Douglas fir, hemlock, pine, spruce; seeds—alder, birch, box elder. Also insects and other arthropods—aphids, beetles, caterpillars, gall insects, larvae of various insects, spiders; berries.

RED-BREASTED NUTHATCH

Sitta canadensis
Omnivorous
Diet: Insects and other arthropods—ants, beetles, caterpillars, flies, leaf bugs, spiders; seeds (grasses, sedges); pine nuts. Also berries and fruit. **Feeders:** Prefers sunflower, suet, peanuts, mealworms.

RED-HEADED WOODPECKER

Melanerpes erythrocephalus
Omnivorous
Diet: Insects and other arthropods—ants, beetles, caterpillars, cicadas, earthworms, flies, grasshoppers, grubs, spiders; seeds; nuts; berries and fruit (agricultural fruit).

RED-TAILED HAWK

Buteo jamaicensis
Carnivorous
Diet: Birds (small and medium-sized, up to pheasant size); small to medium-sized mammals— bats, rabbits and hares, rodents; large insects; frogs, snakes. Also carrion.

RED-WINGED BLACKBIRD

Agelaius phoeniceus
Omnivorous
Diet: Insects and other arthropods—ants, beetles, caterpillars, crustaceans, grasshoppers, grubs, spiders; snails; seeds (agricultural grains, grasses, sedges). Also berries and fruit. **Feeders:** Prefers sunflower, corn, peanut hearts, millet, oats, milo.

RING-BILLED GULL

Larus delawarensis
Omnivorous
Diet: Insects and other arthropods—beetles, butterflies, caterpillars, crustaceans, earthworms, flies, spiders; small rodents—mice, shrews, voles; fish—alewives, perch, smelt, sticklebacks; seeds.

RING-NECKED DUCK

Aythya collaris
Omnivorous
Diet: Aquatic plants (stems, foliage, roots, tubers, seeds)—algae, arrowhead, coon tail, goosefoot, grasses, hydrilla, pondweed, sedges, smartweed, water lily, water shield, wild celery, wild millet, wild rice; aquatic insects—aphids, aquatic worms, caddisflies, crane flies, crustaceans, dragonflies, leeches, midges, nymphs of various insects, spiders; mollusks, snails.

RING-NECKED PHEASANT

Phasianus colchicus
Omnivorous
Diet: Seeds—agricultural grains, bristle grass, bur cucumber, burdock, clover, dandelion, dayflower, foxtail, knotweed, ragweed, skunk cabbage, smartweed, sunflower; plants (foliage, roots); insects—ants, beetles, caterpillars, crickets, earthworms, fly larvae, grasshoppers, spiders; snails; berries and fruit—blackberry, dogwood, elderberry, grape, hawthorn, nightshade, sumac; nuts—acorns, hazelnuts. **Feeders:** Prefers sunflower, corn.

ROCK PIGEON

Columba livia
Mostly granivorous
Diet: Seeds (agricultural grains, grasses, sedges)—crabgrass, goosegrass, knotweed, pigweed; insects, earthworms; berries and fruit—poison ivy, pokeberry; acorns. **Feeders:** Prefers sunflower, safflower, corn, peanuts, millet.

ROSE-BREASTED GROSBEAK

Pheucticus ludovicianus
Omnivorous
Diet: Insects—ants, bees, beetles, caterpillars, gall insects, grasshoppers, sawflies, scale insects, spiders, true bugs, wasps; seeds—agricultural grains, milkweed, pigweed, smartweed, sunflower; snails; berries and fruit—blackberry, elderberry, juneberry, mulberry, raspberry, serviceberry; plants (foliage, buds, flowers)—beech, elm, hickory.

RUBY-THROATED HUMMINGBIRD

Archilochus colubris
Mostly nectarivorous
Diet: Nectar (mostly tubular flowers)—bee balm, bergamot, black locust, buckeye, cardinal flower, catchfly, columbine, coralberry, cross

vine, evening primrose, fireweed, gentian, honeysuckle, paintbrush, jewelweed, larkspur, morning glory, penstemon, pinks, thistle, touch-me-not, trumpet creeper, trumpet flower, tulip tree, vervain, wolfberry; insects—aphids, bees, eggs of various insects, fruit flies, gnats, mosquitoes, small caterpillars, spiders. Also sap. **Feeders:** Sugar water.

RUFFED GROUSE

Bonasa umbellus
Herbivorous
Diet: Plants (buds, catkins, foliage, twigs)—mostly aspen, beech, birch, clover, dock, dogwood, grape, greenbrier, hawthorn, hazelnut, mountain laurel, oak, sumac, willow; acorns; berries and fruit. Also insects.

SANDHILL CRANE

Antigone canadensis
Omnivorous
Diet: Mostly plants (foliage, roots, stems, tubers)—bur reed, grasses, rockweed, sedges, silverweed, water lily; seeds (agricultural grains); insects—beetles, caterpillars, crayfish, earthworms, grasshoppers; rodents—mice, lemmings; birds—eggs, nestlings; frogs, lizards, snakes; acorns; berries.

SAVANNAH SPARROW

Passerculus sandwichensis
Omnivorous
Diet: Insects and other arthropods—beetles, butterflies, caterpillars, crustaceans, damselflies, dragonflies, midges, millipedes, mites, moths, other flies, spiders; seeds (forbs, grasses, sedges); berries; mollusks, snails.

SCARLET TANAGER

Piranga olivacea
Mostly insectivorous
Diet: Insects—ants, aphids, bees, beetles, butterflies, caterpillars, cicadas, dobsonflies, earthworms, flies, grasshoppers, hornets, leafhoppers,
locusts, moths, sawflies, scale insects, spiders,
spittlebugs, termites, wasps; snails; berries
and fruit—bayberry, blackberry, black gum,
chokeberry, elderberry, grape, huckleberry, juneberry, mulberry, raspberry,
serviceberry, strawberry, sumac.

SEMIPALMATED PLOVER

Charadrius semipalmatus
Insectivorous
Diet: Insects—aquatic worms, beetles, caterpillars, crustaceans, earthworms, fly larvae,
horseshoe crab eggs, spiders; small mollusks,
snails. Also seeds.

SHARP-SHINNED HAWK

Accipiter striatus
Mostly avivorous
Diet: Small birds (passerines, up to quail size);
large insects; bats, rodents—ground squirrels,
mice, voles; frogs, lizards, snakes.

SNOW BUNTING

Plectrophenax nivalis
Omnivorous
Diet: Mostly seeds—agricultural grains,
amaranth, aster, crowberry, bilberry, bristle
grass, dock, goldenrod, knotweed, other grasses,
other sedges, poppy, ragweed, saxifrage; insects—beetles, caterpillars,
crane flies, other flies, spiders, true bugs. Also small crustaceans; leaves.

SONG SPARROW

Melospiza melodia
Omnivorous

Diet: Seeds—agricultural grains, amaranth, bristle grass, clover, dock, pigweed, knotweed, other grasses, panic grass, ragweed, sheep sorrel, smartweed, sunflower; insects and other arthropods—ants, assassin bugs, beetles, caterpillars, crane flies, crickets, earthworms, grasshoppers, grubs, larvae of various insects, leafhoppers, leaf rollers, mayflies, midges, small crustaceans, spiders, true bugs; snails; berries and fruit—blackberry, blueberry, cherry, mulberry, raspberry, strawberry. **Feeders:** Prefers sunflower, safflower, niger, cracked corn, peanut hearts, millet, milo.

SORA

Porzana carolina
Omnivorous

Diet: Insects and other arthropods—beetles, crickets, dragonflies, flies, grasshoppers, true bugs; seeds (agricultural grains, grasses, sedges)—bristle grass, duckweed, foxtail, knotweed, smartweed, wild millet, wild rice; plants (foliage of aquatic plants); snails.

SPOTTED TOWHEE

Pipilo maculatus
Omnivorous

Diet: Insects and other arthropods—ants, beetles, caterpillars, crickets, grasshoppers, millipedes, moths, sow bugs, spiders, true bugs, wasps; seeds—amaranth, chickweed, dock, nightshade, smartweed, thistle; berries and fruit—cherry, coffeeberry, gooseberry, honeysuckle, poison oak, sumac; acorns. **Feeders:** Prefers sunflower, cracked corn, peanut hearts, millet, milo.

STELLER'S JAY

Cyanocitta stelleri
Omnivorous
Diet: Seeds; acorns; berries and fruit; insects and other arthropods—bees, beetles, caterpillars, grasshoppers, moths, spiders, wasps; birds—eggs, nestlings.

SWAINSON'S THRUSH

Catharus ustulatus
Omnivorous
Diet: Mostly insects and other arthropods—ants, beetles, caterpillars, crane flies, crickets, flies, grasshoppers, moths, spiders, true bugs, wasps; berries and fruit—blackberry, brier, elderberry, huckleberry, raspberry, sumac, twinberry.

TREE SWALLOW

Tachycineta bicolor
Mostly insectivorous
Diet: Insects and other arthropods—ants, bees, beetles, butterflies, caddisflies, damselflies, dragonflies, grasshoppers, flies, flying ants, mayflies, mosquitoes, moths, sand fleas and other small crustaceans, spiders, stoneflies, true bugs, wasps, water boatmen; berries and fruit—bayberry, dogwood, Virginia creeper, wax myrtle; seeds (grasses and sedges).

TUFTED TITMOUSE

Baeolophus bicolor
Omnivorous
Diet: Insects and other arthropods—ants, bees, beetles, caterpillars, eggs and larvae of various insects, fly scale insects, spiders, treehoppers, true bugs, wasps; seeds; acorns; snails. **Feeders:** Prefers sunflower, safflower, niger, suet, peanuts, mealworms.

TURKEY VULTURE

Cathartes aura
Carnivorous
Diet: Carrion—mostly mammals; birds; amphibians, reptiles; invertebrates; fish. Also live insects.

WARBLING VIREO

Vireo gilvus
Mostly insectivorous
Diet: Insects and other arthropods—aphids, beetles, caterpillars, grasshoppers, scale insects, spiders, true bugs, wasps; berries and fruit—bunchberry, dogwood, elderberry, poison oak, pokeweed, sumac; snails.

WESTERN MEADOWLARK

Sturnella neglecta
Omnivorous
Diet: Mostly insects—ants, bees, beetles, butterflies, caterpillars, crickets, grasshoppers, larvae of various insects, spiders, true bugs, wasps; snails; seeds—agricultural grains, bristle grass, fiddle neck, filaree, other grasses and sedges, poppies, sunflowers, tar weed. **Feeders:** (uncommon): prefers sunflower, cracked corn.

WHITE-BREASTED NUTHATCH

Sitta carolinensis
Mostly insectivorous
Diet: Insects—aphids, ants, beetles, caterpillars, gall insects, larvae of various insects, moths, scale insects, spiders, treehoppers; seeds—agricultural grains, hawthorn, other grasses and sedges, sunflower: nuts—acorns, pine nuts. **Feeders:** Prefers sunflower, safflower, suet, peanuts, mealworms.

WHITE-THROATED SPARROW

Zonotrichia albicollis
Omnivorous
Diet: Insects and other arthropods—ants, beetles, caterpillars, damselflies, flies, millipedes, spiders, true bugs, wasps; seeds (grasses, sedges, trees)—elm, hazel, maple, ragweed, smartweed; berries—blueberry, bunchberry, cranberry, dogwood, grape, raspberry, sumac; snails. **Feeders:** Prefers sunflower, cracked corn, millet, milo.

WILD TURKEY

Meleagris gallopavo
Omnivorous
Diet: Mostly plants (foliage, buds, roots, bulbs); seeds—agricultural grains, ash, bristle grass, crabgrass, dog weed, dove weed, hackberry, hawthorn, ironweed, other grasses and sedges, panic grass, witch hazel; insects—ants, bees, beetles, caterpillars, centipedes, crayfish and other crustaceans, crickets, flies, grasshoppers, spiders, true bugs, walking sticks, wasps; nuts—acorns, beech, black cherry, pine nuts; berries and fruit—cabbage palm, grape, juniper, manzanita; frogs, lizards, snakes; snails.

WILSON'S PHALAROPE

Phalaropus tricolor
Mostly insectivorous
Diet: Insects and other arthropods—mostly aquatic insects, beetles, brine flies and other flies, crustaceans, shrimp, true bugs. Also seeds (aquatic plants).

WILSON'S SNIPE

Gallinago delicata
Mostly insectivorous
Diet: Insects—crustaceans, earthworms, larvae of insects, leeches, spiders; mollusks; frogs; seeds; plants.

WOOD DUCK

Aix sponsa
Omnivorous
Diet: Mostly seeds—agricultural grains, ash, bur reed, coon tail, cow lily, dayflower, duckweed, elm, maple, panic grass, pondweed, smartweed, tupelo, water milfoil, water shield, water lily, water primrose, wild millet, wild rice; insects—ants, beetles, butterflies, caterpillars, crustaceans, flies, moths, spiders, true bugs; acorns; snails; berries and fruit.

WOOD THRUSH

Hylocichla mustelina
Omnivorous
Diet: Insects and other arthropods—ants, beetles, butterflies, caterpillars, crickets, earthworms, flies, grasshoppers, millipedes, moths, sow bugs, spiders, wood lice and other crustaceans; berries and fruit—black gum, blueberry, cherry, dogwood, elderberry, grapes, jack-in-the-pulpit, holly, pokeweed, serviceberry, spicebush, Virginia creeper; mollusks, snails. Also small salamanders.

YELLOW-BELLIED SAPSUCKER

Sphyrapicus varius
Omnivorous
Diet: Sap; insects and other arthropods—ants, beetles, caterpillars, centipedes, crickets, flies, grasshoppers, larvae of various insects, mayflies, moths, spiders, stoneflies, treehoppers, true bugs, wasps; berries and fruit. Also inner bark. **Feeders:** Prefers suet, mealworms.

YELLOW-BILLED CUCKOO

Coccyzus americanus
Mostly insectivorous
Diet: Insects and other arthropods—ants, beetles, caterpillars, cicadas, crickets, flies and fly larvae, grasshoppers, insect larvae, katydids, spiders; berries and fruit—blackberry, elderberry, grapes, mulberry; birds —eggs, nestlings; frogs. Also lizards.

YELLOW-BREASTED CHAT

Icteria virens
Omnivorous
Diet: Insects and other arthropods—ants, bees, beetles, caterpillars, cicadas, crickets, grasshoppers, mayflies, moths, praying mantis, spiders, true bugs, wasps; berries and fruit—blackberry, blueberry, elderberry, grape, raspberry, strawberry.

YELLOW WARBLER

Setophaga petechia
Mostly insectivorous
Diet: Insects and other arthropods—beetles, butterflies, caterpillars, damselflies, flies, mayflies, midges, moths, mosquitoes, spiders; berries.

CHALLENGES AND SOLUTIONS

In dense urban zones, neighborhoods that lack mainstream grocery stores are called food deserts. Most of the time, these neighborhoods are downscale and have lower-than-average income levels, high crime rates, and other significant characteristics that are undesirable to most residents. Market forces typically create food deserts—high crime rates and low rates of personal spending make it harder for grocery businesses to generate and maintain profits.

Biologists Desirée Narango, Douglas Tallamy, and Peter Marra have added a new meaning to this term. They suggest that urban areas create "food deserts" for wildlife, particularly insects and birds. It's not that urban areas always have less variety in vegetation than natural landscapes—often, there are plentiful and diverse plantings, in residences and parks—but that these green spaces do not reflect the original diversity of native vegetation. Insects and birds suffer without access to the food sources they have adapted to, even if there appears to be a plentiful supply.

Other challenges facing birds include invasive species, toxins in the environment, and extinctions threatening not only birds' food sources but bird species as well.

Since more people in North America live in and around cities than in the countryside, it makes sense to pay attention to the attributes of both urban and rural areas as they relate to birds, insects, and other wildlife. Birds in cities, farmlands, and wilderness face different threats, but they share major problems that can be addressed with solutions ranging from habitat conservation to reducing pollutants.

AN INTRODUCED INVASION

On March 6, 1890, sixty European Starlings that had been captured in Europe were released in North America. The group behind this release, the American Acclimatization Society, had a well-defined goal: to bring every bird named in the works of William Shakespeare to Central Park in New York City. Along with the starlings,

The Lesser Goldfinch is one of the few native bird species that has survived the urbanization of North America, finding adequate food sources and few threats to its existence in cities and suburbs. This specimen is perched on a fence in a San Francisco neighborhood. Less-fortunate species for the heavily developed Bay Area include the Bank Swallow, California Clapper Rail, Caspian Tern, and Western Snowy Plover, all threatened by loss of habitat and pollution.

which required two attempts before a self-supporting colony was established, they also brought over the Bullfinch, Skylark, and Song Thrush, which did not thrive. The full complement of birds mentioned in Shakespeare's works tops 600 species, but it was the starling that has left a lasting impression in its new home.

Starlings have been so successful in the New World—they number about 200 million in North America—that the population on this continent is estimated to make up more than one-third of the total number of the species worldwide. Their range in North America is pretty much complete: coast to coast and from the Arctic to the Gulf of Mexico.

These birds carry a negative reputation with them: they are more aggressive competitors for food than native species; they outcompete native species for nesting sites; they group together in colonies that can decimate cereal crops; and the quantity of droppings from

European Starlings (as well as Rock Pigeons and House Sparrows) are natural scavengers. They create health problems in crowded metropolitan zones where they replace some of their natural diet with the garbage and food scraps humans leave behind. *(Photo by Robert Szymanski)*

their communal roosting areas fosters the spread of diseases, especially histoplasmosis.

The introduction of the House Sparrow (initially called the English Sparrow) to North America preceded the European Starling by decades, but it has had much the same impact. In sheer numbers, they outcompete native species and make a pest of themselves in cities, parks, and at backyard feeders, by devouring bird food, as well as feasting in large numbers on commercial crops. These birds, however, have also been impacted by the same threats that are harming native species, and surveys report their numbers are declining, both in North America and in England, part of their native range.

From the perspective of conservation, invasive species of both plants and animals are bad news. Whether they are introduced accidentally or purposely, the visible results are often a threat to native species, local habitats and ecosystems, and sometimes human inhabitants. Nevertheless, invasions happen, and with birds, it is worth considering a broader perspective that includes their benefits.

Starlings are a nuisance in both cities and the countryside because of their numbers. The effect of their competition on native birds, however, may not be as dire as often assumed. A study published in 2003 concluded that only one American bird group, sapsuckers—Red-breasted Sapsucker, Red-naped Sapsucker, Williamson's Sapsucker, and Yellow-bellied Sapsucker—had experienced a population decline because of starlings. Several other bird species, including bluebirds, were negatively affected in some ways but not decisively.

The Rock Pigeon is not native to North America and did not arrive here by accident, yet it is an established species with a preferred niche in urban areas, where discarded human food is a consistent part of its diet.

At home in the city, European Starlings also thrive in rural habitats, where they compete with native birds for insects, seeds, and other food. *(Photo by Petr Simon)*

On the positive side, starlings are omnivores, eating seeds, fruits, berries, and invertebrates, especially insects. The groups of starlings that forage in open fields can have a significant negative impact on crop pests—like many other birds, they tend to select insects over grain because of the high protein content of insects. Observers note that a significant amount of time spent foraging involves digging and probing with their bills in the soil as they hunt for invertebrates such as beetles, crickets, grasshoppers, larvae of butterflies and moths, snails, and worms.

This range of targets encompasses most of what are considered agricultural and garden pests. Studies of starling diets demonstrate that animal matter makes up about half of the food they ingest, on average, with a reported maximum of 97 percent (from a spring feeding period). A single starling eats from 0.3 to 0.8 ounce (7–23 grams) of animal-based food per day, and it typically does so while feeding in a flock of dozens to hundreds of birds—large starling flocks can number in the thousands, although this is rare.

TOXINS

Humans' desire to continually improve our agricultural food supply and protect against natural threats, such as rodents and insects, has introduced toxic substances of many different kinds. There are insecticides to improve crop yields; poisons to kill hungry and disease-carrying rodents; lead ammunition and fishing products to increase hunting and fishing success; mercury to improve industrial processes; and plastics to provide the modern conveniences of countless products. With the success of these chemical weapons, however, comes increasing damage to the environment and the plants and animals that live within it.

INSECTICIDES

Various chemicals have been employed for centuries as tools to control unwanted insect pests, with improvements continually sought. The most modern group of weapons in this fight are compounds known as neonicotinoid insecticides (neonics for short), which are used to coat seeds for plants that otherwise would be hosts to aphids, leafhoppers, leaf miners, thrips, scales, and whiteflies—a widely varied group of biting and sucking pests that can cause severe crop losses before harvest. (Although these compounds do not exist in nature, they were developed from one that is: nicotine.)

Neonics—the best-known is clothianidin—don't provide complete protection but instead a window of safety during the initial growth period after seeds germinate, because they are systemics: distributed internally in a plant throughout its structure, from roots

During the 1939 planting season, this Montana farmer loads farm equipment with poison to deal with an infestation of grasshoppers. Chemicals in this era were very effective at killing the insect pests they targeted, but they also harmed other insects, as well as birds and mammals in the vicinity. *(Photo from Library of Congress)*

to flowers. These compounds are also toxic to animals other than insects, including birds.

Agricultural use: Seed-eating birds are at risk from treated seeds used for agricultural crops; among the largest crops produced in North America are corn, soybeans, wheat, canola (rapeseed), rice, and sorghum. Application guidelines for neonics are formulated to reduce exposure to birds by limiting the availability of seeds: the normal application, planting seeds below the surface, puts most seeds out of sight and reach of most bird species. Additionally, modern planting equipment greatly reduces the number of individual seeds that are spilled or fail to be buried.

Neonics not only are used as seed coatings but also are sprayed directly on crops later in the growing cycle. Whether the compounds are applied as a seed coating or as a spray, up to 95 percent leaches away, ending up in air, soil, and water. Various studies report that traces of neonics have been found in most of the surface water throughout the planet.

Insect-eating birds are also affected by neonics. One of the broader threats from these compounds is damage to populations of aquatic insects. One study reports that caddisflies, mayflies, and midges are most affected, which must impact the birds that rely on these insects for food. Another negative effect of neonics on birds is that fewer pest insects on plants means a reduction in a vital food resource for other animals, including predatory insects that feed on these pests—another loss of a food resource for insectivorous birds.

Neonics are the latest generation of pesticides used in agriculture, replacing organophosphates and carbamates, which are more potent and cause more direct and indirect harm to birds and other wildlife. Despite the improvements, though, neonics are banned from some agricultural use, such as crops grown on public lands managed by the US Fish and Wildlife Service, and there is continuing pressure to limit or end their use in commercial applications.

Toxic gardens: Farmers are not the only people using neonics. Backyard gardeners are part of the extended market for insecticides as well. Some flowering plants are routinely treated in greenhouses before distribution to nurseries and big-box retailers. Public concern, primarily because of the link to colony collapse disorder in bees, has led to new labeling on plants sold at retail outlets, and some local and national plant outlets have instituted a self-imposed ban on neonic use.

Nevertheless, these products are widely available in a variety of spray containers, marketed for use on roses, other flowers, shrubbery, trees, vegetables, and houseplants. Such products include appropriate disclaimers and guidelines for use, but nothing requires consumers to follow those directions.

Birds that ingest neonics, through direct exposure or by ingesting insects that have been exposed, can suffer from a variety of symptoms, including reduced body mass, an impaired ability to navigate while flying, and reduced reproductive cycles. The effects can be lethal if enough is ingested. Research studies so far have shown that bird poisoning by neonics is not a frequent occurrence, at least in North America and Europe, where regulations are strictest. However, there are proven links between exposure to neonics and health risks to honeybees: neonics are one of the suspected factors in colony collapse disorder.

Cotton's success story: Chemical weapons have been part of human responses to agricultural threats for thousands of years, with many different compounds adapted for use, though all were variations of natural mineral or botanical products until the modern era. Cotton, which once ruled as the king of Southern agriculture, was devastated by boll weevils in the 1890s when this invasive species moved into the United States from Mexico as well as other parts of the world, including South America.

By the early 1900s, biologists knew that at least twenty-eight species of birds were active predators of the boll weevil, including blackbirds, cowbirds, flycatchers, grackles, meadowlarks, orioles, quail, sparrows, and wrens. Some of these natural predators specialized by season: blackbirds and meadowlarks fed on the weevils in winter; orioles concentrated their feeding in summer. Birds also were effective predators for the cotton leafhopper, cotton leaf perforator, and cotton leaf worm, among other traditional cotton pests.

In the late 1930s, agricultural chemicals such as calcium arsenate were widely available to control weeds and insect pests. This farmer is hand-dusting plants on his truck farm in southern New Jersey. *(Photo from Library of Congress)*

Beneficial insects were at work from the beginning as well, preying on boll weevils, pink bollworms (another major invertebrate pest of cotton), and less damaging pests, as reported in scientific investigations as early as 1879, before the weevils were first reported outside of Mexico. In several cases in the 1920s, farmers dusted their cotton fields with calcium arsenate—a potent compound in favor at the time—and successfully destroyed weevils, but they subsequently lost even more of their crops to aphids, which had previously been eaten by insect predators killed by calcium arsenate. The pink bollworm emerged as a key destructive invader in the South by the 1920s.

Birds obviously did not end losses for cotton growers, or the problem would not have become epidemic. Nor did any effect from other natural predators, including small mammals and dozens of insect species, stop the epidemic. Because of the recurring pestilence of this weevil, cotton crops became a prime target for pesticides. However, in the early decades of the boll weevil infestation, no chemicals, including DDT (dichlorodiphenyltrichloroethane), had a significant effect in the long term. Boll weevils developed resistance to this post–World War II compound in about ten years.

Up through the 1970s, cotton was estimated to be the target of one-third to one-half of all agricultural insecticides in the United States. During the long-running era of chemical warfare on the two cotton pests, however, the collateral damage included birds, mammals, and beneficial insects, not to mention harmful effects on humans and the environment.

The combination of these two destructive insects (and others as well, though none as damaging as the weevil and bollworm) triggered one of the first major explorations into insect pests and their relationship with agricultural crops, including extensive entomological research and advances in crop science. Thus, cotton was one of the first crops for which widespread nonchemical defenses were implemented in addition to chemicals, prompted by the significant amount of monetary damage growers faced. These methods include crop rotation, changes in seeding cycles, development of cultivars for pest resistance, government-mandated bans on movement of cotton seed or harvested cotton beyond defined zones (to reduce the spread of insects), and, most important, carefully timed use of pesticides for maximum effectiveness.

This multipronged approach, in combination with the continuing use of pesticides, led to a dramatic reduction in crop losses from both of these major pests, as well as statements from various experts that the complete eradication of one or more pests was possible. As of 2019, several regions in the South have declared that the boll weevil and/or the pink bollworm have been eradicated, which technically means they are no longer considered a threat. Cotton cultivation has a large impact, which means it can provide a pivotal role as a bellwether example for developing and applying new and better systems of pest control, utilizing the great economic leverage that such a megacommodity provides.

Bird success stories: Beginning in 1885, the US Department of Agriculture ran a research program for fifty-five years (ending in 1940) to study the role of birds in agricultural pest control. Shortly after this program was ended, the era began of DDT and large-scale chemical warfare against insect crop pests. Researchers studying this field in modern times note that some of these studies were flawed because of cultural biases ("good" insects and "bad" insects for example), deficient testing methods, and other drawbacks, yet the general results mirror what is valid today: birds have an ongoing value to commercial agriculture.

At least 220 species of North American birds are known to be predators of insects that are considered agricultural pests. These birds include blackbirds, buntings, crows, egrets, flickers, grackles, gulls, herons, jays, magpies, meadowlarks, nutcrackers, starlings, swallows, terns, warblers, and woodpeckers. Raptors are also often cited as beneficial to agricultural crops because they prey on small mammals such as mice and rats that feed on crops. In some studies, specific insectivorous bird species were found feeding on insect pests of ten or more crops. These included various blackbirds and sparrows, Barn Swallows, Common Nighthawks, Dickcissels, Eastern Bluebirds, Eastern Kingbirds, Eastern Meadowlarks, Horned Larks, Killdeer, Mourning Doves, and Western Kingbirds.

In decades of studies, specific bird species have been noted for their beneficial targeting of significant crop pests, among them armyworms, corn borers, corn earworms, corn wireworms, cut-worms, grasshoppers, and stinkbugs. In order of importance, agri-cultural crops with the highest associations with beneficial birds were sorghum, soybeans, grain corn, winter wheat, oats, and barley

As invasive Japanese beetles spread west from the East Coast, the much-maligned House Sparrow has become a predator of this pest, in this case eating two at a time.

This Eurasian Tree Sparrow consumes an insect pest in an apple orchard in Europe. *(Photo by Natalia Bachkova)*

(even though each of these crops also had some negative associations with bird species, which means the birds also fed on the crops).

In the 1990s, California apple orchards were a test subject to determine what effect birds had on one of the major insect pests for this fruit, the codling moth. Birds mostly targeted the larvae of this moth, especially during the winter off-season, reducing the size of the larval population by a factor of 11 to 99 percent.

California vineyards were the site of an experiment to increase the population of insect-eating birds, especially Western Bluebirds, by adding artificial nest boxes to active growing zones. The study reported that these insectivorous birds were significantly effective at reducing insects near to their nest boxes but had a positive effect elsewhere in the vineyards as well.

RODENTICIDES

Safe nesting areas, access to food, and limited competition may attract owls to cities and suburbs, but there are also risks not found in their traditional habitats. Multiple reports note a rising death toll in owls and other raptors from ingesting poisons used to control urban rodent pests. These rodenticides, especially those known as second-generation anticoagulant rodenticides (SGARs), end up being absorbed in the bodies of the birds that feed on rodents that have been dosed with SGAR baits. As much as 70 to 90 percent of the urban owls—Barred Owls and Great Horned Owls—tested in some areas have accumulations of SGARs, and 100 percent of the carcasses of dead owls in some urban zones test positive for SGARs. Bait stations intended for rats are also sometimes used as food resources by tree squirrels, other small mammals, pets, and even some songbirds, with a similar outcome.

SGARs are currently favored over first-generation anticoagulants because of their increased effectiveness. The first generation of products (warfarin, pindone, and others) required multiple feedings to produce mortality in the rodents they were intended for, but the second-generation poison produces the desired effects with fewer feedings, often only one. Following ingestion, death can be delayed from several days to several weeks.

The SGAR baits used in modern rodent traps are slow-acting; rodents continue foraging before they die, giving raptors, as well as other scavengers, opportunity to ingest the same poison.

Rodent traps baited with SGARs are a familiar element in the modern cityscape, although most people are unaware of their presence. They are placed outside fast-food outlets, restaurants, supermarkets, and any retail or wholesale facility where food is handled or stored. Traps are designed to sequester SAGR-infused bait inside enclosures with openings small enough to prevent entry to animals other than rats and mice.

Once these rodents leave a trap, however, the poison travels with them. The consequence is the same for unintended targets, including cats, dogs, and wildlife. Owls and other predators, such as foxes and coyotes, that ingest SGARs along with their prey become "collateral damage" in the war against vermin. A quest for alternatives is underway.

The latest generation of rodent traps are widely distributed at buildings where food is served or sold. The SGAR baits they contain are effective and safer than poisons used in previous rodenticides, but at the cost of significant danger to raptors whose prey has been contaminated with the bait.

LEAD POISONING

Lead as a toxic element is a well-publicized danger in buildings, with national restrictions banning its use and mandating remediation, primarily in paint and plumbing. This established protocol is aimed at protecting people, particularly children, but lead is just as damaging to other animals, including pets and wildlife. In areas away from cities, the primary focus on lead as a toxin has been aimed at the lead ammunition and weights used in hunting and fishing.

The lead in hunting ammunition continues to be a deadly threat to birds and other wildlife. Alternatives are gradually replacing this traditional material.

Multiple studies have well documented the problems of lead ingestion by birds and its toxic aftermath. The primary source to date has been shotgun pellets, which birds ingest as they forage in wetlands, where waterfowl are traditionally targeted by hunters.

A study of lead ingestion by loons reported that 23 percent of recovered carcasses contained lead objects: 48 percent of the

Lead poisoning is a major cause of declining health and death in waterfowl. This carcass of a Common Loon was not tested for cause of death. *(Photo by Kirk Hewlett)*

ingested objects were lead sinkers, 19 percent were lead jigs, and the remainder a mixed lot of split shot, bullets, shotgun pellets, and unidentified pieces containing lead. The most important conclusion from this report was that every loon carcass showed evidence of lead poisoning: the digestive systems of fish-eating birds typically have a lower pH level than birds with other diets and therefore they absorb ingested lead quicker.

Loons acquire lead from two sources: direct ingestion from foraging for grit on lake bottoms and indirect ingestion from capturing fish that have loose fishing gear attached. Ducks also forage for grit on lake bottoms; a Mallard that ingests a single size 4 lead shot has a 20 percent chance of dying from lead poisoning.

Lead poisoning is usually a death sentence. A single bullet shard the size of a grain of rice is enough lead to kill a bird as large as a vulture or an eagle. Although these shards may be expelled along with feathers, fur, and bone fragments, some of the lead will have already leached into the digestive system, where it leads to health problems in the host bird.

Bald Eagles, at the top of their food chain, are the most recognized victims of exposure to lead. Across North America, lead is a known factor in eagle deaths and poisonings that do not result in death.

Eagles acquire lead from two sources: most is from direct ingestion of lead bullet fragments from hunter-killed deer carcasses—including stripped carcasses and viscera of properly field-dressed carcasses—and some is from indirect ingestion of other scavenger animals such as coyotes that have fed on these remains.

Recent reports indicate that the number of deaths is increasing even as the number of hunters declines. The Bald Eagle population has been expanding in recent decades, placing more of them in harm's way, one of the reasons for the increase in effects on them from lead. Meanwhile, lead poisoning from ammunition is the leading cause of death for California Condors, an endangered species, also from exposure to the carcass of slain game animals.

Alternatives are available for both lead ammunition and lead fishing gear. Alternatives to lead include copper, steel, tungsten, bismuth, and various alloys of copper and tungsten. Fishing sinkers, jigs, and other items made with replacement materials, including bismuth, steel, tin, and tungsten-nickel alloy, are on the market. Nonlead rifle ammunition is sometimes referred to as "green bullets," and its leading proponent is the US military, which began phasing out lead ammunition (for some calibers) in 2010. A ban on the use of lead shot for hunting waterfowl on federal land has been in effect since 1991, and several states are in line to follow suit. A general trend is underway for additional local, state, and federal legislation to address this issue, and widening public support will likely make this a national priority in coming years.

MERCURY POISONING

The toxicity of mercury is well known, and regulations and safety guidelines for its use in products and manufacturing are widely implemented. Mercury emissions from mining, cement production, power plants, crematories, factories, and other sources is regulated and has been reduced over recent decades. Yet mercury poisoning continues to be a problem in the environment, because even minute amounts work their way up the food chain, ultimately affecting many animals, including birds.

Mercury can leak into the environment from some lightbulbs and batteries if they are not disposed of properly.

The mercury problem for birds, other wildlife, humans, and the environment persists because of uneven safety practices around the world as well as within North America. The problem is also compounded by the nature of mercury itself, which transforms to its most toxic form—methylmercury—on exposure to microorganisms in the environment. Methylmercury becomes concentrated in fish, shellfish, and their predators, including seabirds, posing the greatest harm from this element.

In birds, mercury affects reproduction success, survivability of eggs, digestion, and other internal physiologies. The migration behavior of birds is affected, as well as brain activity associated with birdsong. Numerous studies document mercury's harm to many bird species, especially those active in and around water, including avocets, cormorants, egrets, grebes, herons, loons, Mallards, pelicans, plovers skuas, stilts, and terns, and, as well as falcons, flycatchers, pheasants, robins, sparrows, swallows, and wrens.

Annually, worldwide accumulations of mercury (including from natural sources, manmade emissions, and reemissions from handling and chains of usage) are estimated to be from about 5,500 to 8,800 tons (5,000 to 8,000 metric tons). Despite strong support worldwide to limit mercury emissions, no dramatic improvements are expected.

PLASTIC POLLUTION

Plastics are the new public enemy number one in the environmental community, and with good reason. Beginning in the 1950s, the production and use of single-serving plastic containers expanded dramatically, generating an unprecedented tidal wave of plastics that flooded the world. Even as landfills captured record amounts of used plastics, large quantities drifted into the environment, much of it concentrated in oceans. An estimated 60 to 80 percent of all marine debris is plastic.

The remnants of a plastic fishing net likely caused the death of this Northern Gannet, but the greater threat from plastic throughout the world is not as visible. Microplastics—degraded bits of plastic debris—are small enough to be ingested, and they are increasing in quantity in most ecosystems. *(Photo by Andrew Balcombe)*

The total amount of plastic debris in oceans, estimated at 275 million tons (250 million metric tons), includes microscopically small particles (microplastics), beads, pellets, shards, bags, fishing line, and a wide variety of discarded plastic products, from shoes to containers. Regulations, processes, and technology already exists to confine plastic debris to appropriate holding areas or to recycle it, but these actions are not being followed: an estimated 6 to 14 million tons (5 to 13 million metric tons) of plastic is added to oceans annually. The problem posed by microplastics is unsolved.

This accumulation of plastic in the world's oceans is increasingly having an impact on the diets of both seabirds and shorebirds. Birds ingest plastics directly, in tiny particles and larger pieces, as well as indirectly, by ingesting fish and shellfish that have themselves ingested tiny particles. The entire oceanic food chain is already afflicted: invertebrates, mussels, oysters, prawns, fish, birds, sea turtles, and marine mammals. In 2019, American lobsters were first reported to be part of this growing list.

Plastic has permeated the entire food chain for birds. A recent study of Turkey Vultures in Chile reported that more than 80 percent of the pellets ejected by these scavengers contained plastics. Researchers believe the plastic comes from waste commonly found along roadsides, garbage dumps, and other areas where vultures forage. Black Vultures in Mexico have also been reported consuming such nonfood items. Up to 40 percent of these birds' pellets included plastic bags and rubber bands, as well as glass, cloth, and similar material.

In North America, California Condors are also known to be ingesting this artificial material from scavenging. Turkey Vultures and Black Vultures are frequent visitors to garbage sites, so it is likely that the problem also occurs in the US and Canada, though the results of ingesting plastic by these scavengers is unknown.

Although plastic pollution is under increasing scrutiny, it is still poorly measured. The latest estimate suggests that the amount worldwide has increased ten times since 1980.

EXTINCTIONS

The current estimated total of plant and animal species on the planet is 8 million, including 5.5 million species of insects. Yet the relative abundance of native species—plant and animal—found in most of the largest terrestrial habitats has dropped by 20 percent or more.

In 2019, a major scientific study reported that since 1900, species of seed-bearing plants have been going extinct at an average rate of three a year. Extinction is part of the natural cycle of nature, but this rate is considered abut 500 times higher than what would be expected from natural causes. In North America during the same time period, the rate varies from zero to ten plant species per year going extinct, depending on location. The scientists involved in this project believe the overall rate is an understatement of the actual problem.

The Intergovernmental Science-Policy Platform on Biodiversity and Ecosystem Services released a report in May 2019 supported by research from around the world and a review of about 15,000 sources. It concluded that around 1 million animal and plant species are currently threatened with extinction, the largest number ever estimated. The chair of this organization, Sir Robert Watson, observed, "The health of ecosystems on which we and all other species depend is deteriorating more rapidly than ever. We are eroding the very foundations of our economies, livelihoods, food security, health and quality of life worldwide." The time left for many species is estimated to be mere decades.

PINECONE CATASTROPHE

Pine nuts are a widespread source of food for insects, mammals, and birds—for some birds species, they are a crucial resource. In parts of western North America, some pine forests are suffering from the direct and indirect consequences of climate change. Pine forests in the West and Southwest suffer from a rise in average temperatures and prolonged droughts—effects of a changing climate—along with the spreading damage from infestations from several types of pine beetles.

Warmer average temperatures have extended the range of white pine blister rust, a nonnative fungus, and mountain pine beetles.

The beetles' natural range formerly was confined by normal seasonal cycles of winter cold; extreme low temperatures killed off the beetle larvae that otherwise ended up killing trees. As extreme low temperatures gradually get less severe, the beetles have a larger range in which to expand.

The overall impact of the mountain pine beetle has yet to be seen, but the effects stretch from the southern Rocky Mountains to British Columbia. In Colorado alone, 3.4 million acres (1.4 million hectares) of forest—mostly ponderosa and lodgepole pine trees—have been killed by the beetles. Birds that use the cone seeds for food have been affected the most. In parts of their range, the abundance and productivity of these pines has decreased by more than 70 percent since 2003, with a corresponding drop in the number of Pinyon Jays. But the consequences have also bolstered the survival of other birds, such as those that nest in cavities (dead trees often provide more shelter than live ones) and bark drillers, which have an almost limitless supply of insects to target for foraging.

White-bark pines are affected by this epidemic of pine beetles, as well as the spread of white pine blister rust even as some individual trees have developed resistance to the fungus. This high-altitude pine, one of the most threatened of the cone-producing conifers, is a noncommercial species—trees are typically not large enough for lumber. Yet it is considered a keystone species because of the number of animals, from insects to bears to seed-eating birds such as Clark's Nutcracker, that depend on them for food.

In Crater Lake National Park, Oregon, a Clark's Nutcracker feeds on pine nuts in a white-bark pine tree. *(Photo by Robert Mutch)*

In parts of their range, white-bark pine trees have declined by as much as 90 percent, a level that biologists believe is not enough to sustain some birds that depend on their seeds. Not only are Clark's Nutcrackers dependent on their seeds, but the seeds are also dependent on these birds for dispersal and the long-term survivability of their species. These birds can carry viable seeds up to 14 miles (22.5 kilometers) from their origin.

An action plan is underway to offset this pinecone catastrophe. Seeds from rust-resistant white-bark pine trees are being collected and cultivated, with young trees raised in nurseries and replanted in affected zones. There is yet no practical solution developed in response to the mountain pine beetles, but researchers are working on a variety of remedies, though these may be of use only in confined areas.

ENDANGERED BIRDS

Since 1971, the National Audubon Society has researched and reported on North American bird species that are threatened by a reduction in their natural range or otherwise experiencing a decline in population. Of more than 300 North American species on the latest list, some are projected to lose more than half of their current range by 2050 and the rest a similar loss by 2080.

Climate change: The Audubon Climate Report now includes species that are seriously threatened by climate change. The report assumes that the current rate of climate change will continue at its present pace, but it does not factor in losses from development, the potential for some birds to successfully shift their current geographical preferences to other zones, or additional cascading effects—good and bad—that may be triggered by climate change.

Habitat loss: Even as more people strive to support birds in urban environments, fewer birds are sustained by our developed environment. Development is not a uniform process; it encompasses a range of changes, including increasing human population density, escalating traffic, an upsurge in background noise, rising levels of chemical toxins used in gardens and parks, and swelling numbers of domesticated predators—mostly house cats. These factors are

A few of the North American birds that are in danger on state or federal endangered species lists or reported as "common species in steep decline" (clockwise from upper left): Greater Prairie-Chicken, Willow Flycatcher, Piping Plover, Loggerhead Shrike, Golden-cheeked Warbler *(Photos, clockwise from upper left, by Danita Delmont, Martha Marks, Dawn J. Benko, Bouke Atema, Michael Armentrout)*

Urban and suburban sprawl continuously removes native habitats from the landscape, reducing the acreage needed to support native plants and the birds that depend on them. *(Photo by Tim Roberts Photography)*

found in all kinds of neighborhoods, including office parks and downtown zones.

In one of the longest-running studies on record, a bird census in Cambridge, Massachusetts, outlines what happens as development replaces native habitats. Beginning with a population of about 26,000 in the 1860s, Cambridge now has more than 114,000 residents, with added infrastructure for housing, schools, and retail support. In the Cambridge study, a rapid and sustained loss of tree cover marked much of the period of development, and between the 1860s and 2012, the number of species of breeding birds declined from twenty-six to twelve. This negative change was influenced by the introduction of invasive species, the increasing use of pesticides, and the loss of wild habitat. The only species that remained constant through this 150-year stretch were American Robins, Blue Jays, and Gray Catbirds. Another key finding from this survey was that insectivorous birds declined the most, though there was a slight increase in the last several decades of the study. (This is not the only such study, with similar findings elsewhere in North America and with parallel results in Europe.)

But in the last several decades in Cambridge, the trend of habitat loss has been reversed. Green space, open space, parks, riparian zones, and private gardens are now a routine part of planning for office and residential neighborhoods. In this geographical region, originally characterized by hardwood forests, these measures are unlikely to ever re-create what was there before in what is now an urban landscape. But development can mitigate the loss of native habitats, not just in parks and green space; a variety of greenery, from tall and dense vegetation to trees, can encourage nesting birds. None of this may adequately replace native terrain, but appropriate landscape features can accommodate birds and the food sources they need.

The US Geological Survey has a large-scale, ongoing study, the North American Breeding Birds Survey, which began in 1966 with the objective of developing reliable estimates of population changes. Many research projects based on this core data provide pertinent insights into the effects that climate change and other factors have had on birds. This includes species that have shifted zones of maximum abundance northward as a result of a warming climate and negative effects from the loss of native grassland due to rural development and the degradation of land used for agriculture.

Trees provide an obvious benefit by harboring insects that support insectivorous birds, but they also provide buffers and barriers to the urban noise that can discourage bird activity. One of the most negative effects of urbanization on environmental values is the loss of trees as cities grow. A study in Brazil concluded that trees have a positive effect for birds in relation to noise, one of the most recognized negatives of urban life, by providing a buffer from the sounds of traffic, people, and other aspects of city life. Trees also have an innate value for birds as sources of shelter and food. Street trees were studied to determine the effects of their number and size on influencing local bird populations. The urban areas with the most and largest trees had the greatest diversity of bird species as well as the largest number of birds, with the number of native tree species an important factor. Increasing the number of street trees can also reduce crowding and dependence on greenery in parks by the birds that find them beneficial.

HOW TO SUPPORT BIRDS

Support for birds has always begun at a grassroots level, from individuals. One of the most notable efforts arose in the last quarter of the nineteenth century, when bird feathers, even entire bodies of dead birds, were a major fashion trend for women's clothing in Europe and North America, primarily as adornments for hats. These desirable accessories launched a wide-scale quest for plumage, severely impacting populations of some birds.

At the peak of this trend, up to forty species of North and South American birds were targeted for their feathers, including hummingbirds, egrets, kingfishers, herons, parrots, ospreys, woodpeckers, larks, and gulls. On March 21, 1888, at a single wholesale auction in London, 12,000 hummingbird skins were sold, shipped in from ports in North and South America. Between 1904 and 1911, 152,000 hummingbirds were imported for the feather auctions in London. A single feather dealer is reported to have purchased more than 400,000 hummingbirds from a single source in the West Indies.

Following World War I, airplanes were widely used to apply chemicals to agricultural crops. This biplane is spraying insecticide on a farm field in New Jersey in 1936. *(Photo from Library of Congress)*

As the fashion industry increasingly bolstered such use of feathers, some nature lovers became alarmed. Individuals, including both consumers and ornithologists, spoke out against this trend. Groups including the Royal Society for the Protection of Birds, founded in 1889 in Great Britain, and the Audubon Society, founded in 1896 as a state organization in Massachusetts, were initially formed just to fight against this exploitation.

By the early years of the twentieth century, individuals and groups began to achieve success by promoting public awareness and fostering industry restrictions, but it took decades before feathers were no longer considered fashionable. These days, birds are under even greater threat, and citizen action is once again needed.

PROTECT GARDENS AND LAWNS RESPONSIBLY

In the garden, foliage, flowers, and vegetables are prime targets for insect pests, the traditional foe of gardeners. Insecticides, including many in the past that were toxic to humans, became a traditional weapon against these pests. Before the widespread availability of chemical fertilizers in the early twentieth century, however, farming and gardening were organic by necessity, but both inorganic and organic compounds began to dominate the war against insects in both gardens and agricultural fields.

In the early 1900s, arsenic and arsenic-based compounds were the first commercially based products to target insect pests: Paris Green, Scheele's Green, and London Purple were three such products, which also included copper, calcium, or lead. In the first phase of this chemical war on insects, the main concern about potential harm focused on mammals, especially humans, with a reported outcome that was generally favorable, at least in comparison to the deadly effects of other chemicals then available.

DDT (dichlorodiphenyltrichloroethane) was discovered in 1939, and within a few years it was extensively used; its discoverer, Swiss chemist Paul Müller, received the Nobel Prize in Medicine for this work. Other compounds from this era included dieldren, chlordane, and parathion. Because of DDT's immediate effectiveness and

Pesticide sprayers used to be made out of metal and dispensed chemicals that are now banned. Modern sprayers have replaced the metal with plastic and the chemicals with less-lethal compounds (to humans), but birds and beneficial insects still suffer. *(Photo by Cigdem)*

relatively low cost, it was a tough battle to push back against its use, even in the face of compelling evidence.

In Long Island Sound, New York, one study measured the presence of DDT at 3 parts per million (ppm) in the local estuaries, escalating to 0.5 ppm in minnows, 2 ppm in larger fish, and 25 ppm in Ospreys, which feed almost exclusively on fish. This increase of 10 million times in concentration led to major reproductive complications for Ospreys and a sharp decline in their population, along with similar declines for other avian predators such as Bald Eagles and Brown Pelicans. The result was even more dire for Peregrine Falcons, which were wiped out throughout the eastern part of the country.

This story, by now well known, has not had a happy ending despite the ban on DDT (in effect as of December 31, 1972) and the population recoveries by these birds. DDT and its by-products still lurk in sediment in many places where it was widely used, and it is still being manufactured in a few places outside the Western Hemisphere even though a near-total global ban is in effect.

MODERN INSECTICIDES

What does this mean for backyard gardens? Insecticides have been developed far beyond the compounds available in our grandparents' era, and the chemistry of agriculture has benefited considerably from the lessons learned about DDT. However, the latest generation of insecticides are considerably more effective at much smaller doses than the previous compounds. Much less is needed to kill, because they are much more harmful, at least to their intended targets.

Among these new insecticides are neonicotinoids (neonics), which are absorbed into plants and are less threatening to mammals, including humans. Active in a plant's pollen, they can be toxic to bees and other pollinators, as well as to beneficial insects that prey on plant pests. Some of these newer compounds are now referred to as persistent organic pollutants (POPs), which have been banned by treaty in 176 countries as of 2011. The United States is not one of these countries.

As much as 10 percent of the total land area of the United States is subject to annual treatment with pesticides. The majority is agricultural, which accounts for almost 80 percent of the total use of these chemicals. With modern farming equipment, chemicals used on fields can be accurately and continually controlled, limiting excess applications and potential contamination. As business operators, farmers benefit by not wasting money on unnecessary pesticide use.

This does not always hold true for backyard gardeners. Gardeners are not only much less savvy about insecticide use than farmers, they also tend to use too much—as much as ten times more pesticides (per unit of land) on lawns than farmers use on crops. This kind of overuse is not always the fault of gardeners, however, as products packaged for residential use are allowed to contain up to thirty times the concentration of active ingredients as products intended for agricultural applications.

Even if insecticides are carefully applied, backyard gardens are not appropriate environments for chemical insect control. Studies confirm that insecticides and herbicides reduce the diversity of lifeforms, especially in aquatic environments, where these compounds end up even when used with care.

For many agricultural crops, monoculture is a driving trend that has increased the size of fields and reduced the diversity of plant and insect species, directly impacting birds. Monoculture also greatly benefits from widespread use of agricultural chemicals that are also a threat to this diversity. *(Photo by 3doorsofsun)*

Indeed, almost all birds eat insects, at least during part of their annual feeding activities, especially when raising young. One of the main roles of the bird-friendly garden is to provide an insect-friendly environment. Unfortunately for mainstream flower and vegetable gardens, which idealize the concept of flawless foliage, this means abandoning the main modern tool used for this end: chemical insecticides.

HERBICIDES AND GENETIC MODIFICATION

In the past few decades, pesticide use in agriculture has remained steady or declined because of the increasing use of genetically modified (GM) crops, which require fewer applications and smaller quantities. Roundup-ready and *Bacillus thuringiensis* (Bt)–infused crops are the major applications for GM. However, even with these modern approaches, the basic threat remains because of the natural ability of insects to evolve in response to threats. The long-term effects of GM plants are also still under review, with some evidence that there may be other unintended consequences.

The main ingredient in Roundup and similar products is glyphosate, which is not considered dangerous to insects, birds, and other animals. Formally, it is declared to be "low in toxicity," but other ingredients added to commercial products that contain glyphosate are a potential threat. The direct risk to birds and insects from these and other weed killers is the destruction of habitat.

One potent example comes from a sharp decline in the number and density of milkweed plants in and around corn and soybean fields in the Midwest, where glyphosate has been frequently used for years. More than 70 percent of these plants, an estimated 850

Conservation programs involving farms find that adjusting planting schedules may benefit both farmers and wildlife, by timing planting and harvests before and after large numbers of migrating birds fly through. These Northern Pintails and Mallards have gleaned leftover corn from the previous season in a field in North Dakota. *(Photo by Patrick Ziegler)*

million, are no longer alive in the area affected. The loss of milkweed plants is the key suspect in a continuing decline in the population of monarch butterflies, which depend on milkweed as the host for their eggs. By changing the planting and harvesting schedules—earlier or later—farmers can avoid direct exposure of some crop chemicals to migrating birds that are known to target this kind of food. Seeds planted later generate crops that mature later, and vice versa, although local weather patterns and variations in growing cycles can limit implementation.

For many gardeners, specific circumstances can favor insecticides, for appropriate reasons: mosquitoes carry West Nile virus and other diseases affecting people and pets; wasps and bees sting; Japanese beetles consume roses and other plants. But in the process of waging war against these insects, is a countermeasure more harmful than needed? Birds are collateral damage in almost every attack against threats to lawns and gardens. The costs are heavy—and rising.

HEALTHY ALTERNATIVES

The emergence of organic gardening after World War II promotes gardening that does not rely on compounds that come from non-natural sources. The term "organic gardening" is credited to Jerome Rodale, who introduced it in the twentieth century. A well-regarded alternative for organic growers is pyrethrum, a natural compound produced from the dried flowers of the chrysanthemum plant, with the natural ability to kill insects. Its use dates back more than 2,000 years; most of the modern commercial products are synthetic versions called pyrethroids. There are other products from natural sources, including dormant oils (neem extracts and others) and insecticidal soaps.

Unfortunately, although most such products pose little or no threat to birds or humans, they are indiscriminate in which insects they kill, and some, including pyrethrums, are particularly toxic for bees. Water sprays and hand picking are the only reliably safe methods of dealing with insect pests, although backyard chickens are noted for preying on such insects.

GROW BIRD-POSITIVE PLANTS

Plants that provide the most effective support for insects and birds are those that are native to a locality, which in some cases may vary from one mile to the next. Altitude, water table, wind patterns, slope pitch and direction, and soil type, among other factors, all contribute to the natural environment in which local plants have developed over very long periods of time, at least since the last ice age. The insects and birds that have developed along with them benefit most from flora that fits the location.

However, most gardens are a mix of native and nonnative plants and might also have some invasive species, such as bindweed. Native insects visit bindweed flowers, a benefit to the insects, and a few seed-eating birds are known to eat the seeds—the Chipping Sparrow, for one—although this adds to the invasiveness of this weed because the ingested seeds can remain viable if they pass through a bird's digestive system.

The Russian olive tree, an introduced species in North America, is considered a problem plant. However, the berries on this tree attract insects, birds, and mammals. Although this species is not desirable as a new planting, established trees support birdlife. *(Photo by Anna Gratys)*

In another example, Russian olive trees were brought to North America in the early 1900s as ornamentals and widely planted in the western states for windbreaks and soil stabilization. They are now considered highly invasive in many areas. Yet the fruit, similar in appearance to standard olives, is sought out by at least fifty species of birds and other animals.

Gardening that includes nonnative plants is not a threat to birds as long as no harmful compounds are used to support those plants' growth. The bird-friendly garden, however, goes beyond "do no harm" to become a support system for what human development often leaves behind: the natural legacy of place. This is a relatively new concept; until recent decades, the advice in gardening guides, books, and almanacs focused on protecting flowers and produce from predators, including birds.

Vegetable and flower gardens are a traditional part of most cultures in North America, from sustenance farmers to middle-class families, although the concept of organic gardening did not become a focus until after World War II. Vintage seed catalogs did not provide products that were intended to attract and sustain birds or other wildlife. *(Photo from Library of Congress)*

Even if invasive plants can have some value for birds and insects, there are reasons to prefer the natives. Bindweed, for example, spreads voraciously across gardens, lawns, and fields and has yet to attract insect predators in North America that might help restrain its spread.

LAWNS

Lawns are part of the problem of nonnative plantings, even though they provide some ornamental value as well as food for wildlife. Bluegrass, the dominant lawn grass in North America, is a native of Europe and North Asia but has been adapted to flourish in every growing zone in North America.

The most serious issue with bluegrass and other standard lawn grasses is what's required to keep them looking green and lush. This requires lots of water, which is in perennially short supply in parts of the continent, and the lushness also relies on doses of chemicals to control insects, other arthropods, rusts, mildew, and fungal diseases. Not only are insects and other targeted pests felled, so are other arthropods that are beneficial—and all of these invertebrate life-forms provide food for birds.

American Robins are currently thriving in part because their omnivorous diet includes earthworms, which are readily found in

Insect pests, such as these caterpillars of the white cabbage butterfly, can be controlled with many products. Chemicals that repel or harm these caterpillars, however, also cause harm to other insects, some of which provide benefit by preying on these pests. Birds may also be harmed, but the biggest loss is to the long-term health of a garden by removing a source of food for insect-eating birds. *(Photo by MagicBones)*

healthy lawns. Studies have determined that robins are most active in lawns within the thirty minutes after mowing, when earthworms are most accessible, and the spread of the robin population has mirrored the spread of suburban developments.

However, some home owners consider earthworms a pest because as they surface, they create unsightly piles of castings. This attitude may be compounded in neighborhoods controlled by covenants that require home owners to maintain lawns with a uniform neatness.

Even though there are no commercial products designed specifically to target only earthworms, various chemical agents, including those that contain carbaryl or imidacloprid, are a widespread threat to insects and other arthropods, beneficial species and pests alike, as well as the birds that feed on them—such as the American Robin, which is particularly affected.

Bluegrass is not the only choice for suburban lawns; cultivars of native grasses work as well but require less care and, most important, less water. Among these are buffalo grass, red fescue, and St. Augustine grass; a non-grass option is clustered field sedge.

A suburban lawn is not a healthy habitat for birds like this American Robin unless it is safe for earthworms. *(Photo by Breck P. Kent)*

BIRD-FRIENDLY YARDS

For decades, some gardeners have made an extra effort to plant flowers, shrubs, and trees that attract and benefit birds and beneficial insects. In recent years, this grassroots activity has blossomed into a movement, supported by increasing awareness that such planting is not just personally rewarding, it has become a vital step in thwarting the diminishing capacity of the planet to support its wildlife.

Bird feeders and birdhouses were an initial stage of this development, which has now greatly expanded to include permanent plantings and water sources for birds. The value of plants that support birdlife goes well beyond the supplementary food source represented by feeders. For one thing, with the exception of suet and mealworms, feeders provide little support for insect-based bird diets—the diet of most North American bird species.

Most of the time, nectar-loving birds and bees are not very picky about the source of this essential food, although hummingbirds sometimes discriminate between the concentration of sugars available. Plants that provide nectar in North America include native and introduced species, particularly in flower gardens, and both are instrumental in supporting these flying pollinators.

To be truly bird-friendly, gardens need to be more than a source of nectar, though. Seeds, flower buds, foliage, nuts, or fruit are also part of the diet for wildlife. Many of these animals depend on specific plants that are not only native to North America, but native to local habitats and ecosystems.

Most insect-eating birds, such as this Downy Woodpecker, will select suet over other food offered at bird feeders. Suet feeders traditionally were a chore to maintain because home owners had to make the suet themselves. In the current well-supported market for bird feeders, prepackaged suet cakes are widely available, and some will hold up well in warm weather. *(Photo by Mike Truchon)*

Most suppliers of seeds, garden plants, shrubs, and trees categorize their offerings by recommended standard plant zones, type of soil, and sun exposure.

However, just because a plant is recommended for a standard growing zone, it isn't necessarily appropriate for local birds and insects. For example, within limits, as gardeners in Maine can grow plants that survive as well as in Southern California, but this does not mean that the same plants are equally supportive of birds and insects in such distinctly different geographic locations. Bird-friendly gardens benefit if these zone recommendations are augmented by local relevancy.

The goal of bird-friendly yards is year-round support for both insects and birds. In zones where the majority of birds migrate away for the winter, the goal remains the same. Annuals and perennials of various plant species can provide a continuum of buds, blossoms, seeds, and fruit—food for birds—throughout a growing season and beyond. Appropriate local native plants will already be primed to also support the insects and other arthropods that have complementary year-round relationships with local birds.

Fortunately, it's easy for gardeners and homeowners to find suitable "locally correct" plants. Large and small municipalities across Canada and the United States are home to one of the most useful resources created by people: libraries. These provide books, magazines, local information on a wealth of subjects—including birds and gardening—and, in most places, access to the internet. Web browsers link questions to answers and are increasingly populated with guidelines, databases, and advice at the local and state level. The best resource at libraries is librarians. When in doubt, ask. Below are some other resource ideas.

- Local bookstores
- Retail garden and nursery stores
- Agricultural extension office and agents
- Local gardening groups
- Master gardeners
- Local colleges and universities
- Municipal park departments
- Local or regional botanical gardens and arboretums
- Local links for national organizations
- Catalogs and websites of native seed companies

BE FEEDER FRIENDLY

Do bird feeders help or harm birds? Because birds will always appear and consume the food offered to them in feeders, many people believe that the birds must not be getting enough food from natural sources. An argument is also made that luring birds away from natural sources harms their connection to the wild and they will come to depend on artificial sources for sustenance.

The reality is that feeding birds supplements normal diets rather than replaces them. A study published in 2015 reported that, in general, the health of individual birds is improved with access to feeders. Specifically, their antioxidant levels increase, feather growth is faster, and physiological stress is reduced. On the negative side, the spread of infectious diseases can increase when feeders are not kept clean.

As natural habitats shrink, from the effects of a warming climate and development, feeders may provide beneficial assistance to species as risk. Several studies suggest this is already the case, both in North American and England. Positive results include earlier dates at which eggs were laid (which improves the chances for survival of nestlings), larger clutch sizes, shorter times between successful clutches, improved protection of eggs from predators, and earlier fledging (which also improves the survival rate). At the same time, studies have looked at the effects when feeders are removed, and they reveal that birds are able to adjust without negative effects, indicating that dependency on feeders is not an issue.

UNWANTED BIRDS

Bird feeding does have unintended consequences. Feeders attract not only birds that are welcome but also those that are not. Corvids, including crows, jays, and magpies, are thought to spend up to

It's not difficult to find seeds for plenty of native grasses and plants in most regions.

75 percent of their time foraging on human-derived food sources, although mostly not from dedicated feeders. This type of diet is linked to increases in their populations, and bird feeding may also have a similar effect on Rock Pigeon and House Sparrow populations, which most bird feeders do not welcome. Rock Pigeons and House Sparrows are nonnative species that many bird lovers would like to exclude. This bias is personal and often not subject to discussion, but these species are here to stay, and they have redeeming features.

Concentrations of birds in and around feeders also attract predators, including raptors, which prey on feeder birds. Some bird lovers find it difficult to observe visits by raptors, which are there to plunder smaller birds as part of their natural feeding habits. However, raptors can reduce the predatory pressure on threatened bird species that are not frequent visitors to feeders. That is, birds that are not attracted to feeders, because of diet or habitat preferences, are less likely to be captured by raptors if the raptors are busy stalking feeder birds. If birds are to be supported, it is difficult, if not inappropriate, to sort birds into good guys and bad guys.

OTHER UNWANTED VISITORS

Bird feeders are not always the object of affection. Neighbors and even home owners themselves understand the downsides of such structures. For most feeder minders, one of the major complaints is the arrival of mice, rats, and other opportunistic uninvited guests, which can include coyotes, raccoons, skunks, and even bears. These visitors are attracted by bird food and can create unhealthy or dangerous situations.

No single solution is applicable for these animals. Bird food that has spilled from feeders must be removed routinely to reduce the chances that it will develop into a permanent resource for these interlopers. Mice and rats are the most common visitors, and it requires diligence to remove opportunities for them to gain access to human living spaces. On the plus side, over time their presence attracts raptors as well, especially at night, when owls are on the prowl.

The single greatest perceived pest with bird feeders is squirrels. Bird lovers, as with most adults, either love or hate these rodents but have a particular concern about squirrel raids on bird feeders. Not only do squirrels consume more food than birds, but they can also be destructive, gnawing their way into feeders and outdoor feed containers and monopolizing feeding platforms. Squirrels have evolved to be cunning seekers of food with a wide range of appetite, opportunists that greatly benefit from the addition of feeders to their urban environment.

There are no complete solutions. Several companies manufacture squirrel-proof feeders, which can provide some protection, though at a cost. Commercial antisquirrel baffles are also available to discourage poaching. Some bird lovers have also tried dosing bird feed with hot peppers, though this will not deter hungry squirrels. Squirrels eating pepper-laced bird food do not stop eating, but suffer through the pain of the active ingredient, capsicum, which birds cannot detect.

Though not a perfect solution, the most practical method of dealing with squirrels is to provide a separate, well-stocked alternative dining platform. As long as squirrel feeders are filled with suitable food (sunflower seeds are the most coveted), the bird feeders are less likely to be a target. Placement is also important, with bird-feeding zones kept far enough away from squirrels to reduce the chance of raiding; 10 feet or more (3.5 meters) is a recommended separation. Squirrels may have a mixed reception in yards and gardens but, as the most common wild mammals urban dwellers are likely to see in the city, they deserve consideration.

FEEDER FOOD

Sunflower seeds: It's no surprise that sunflower seeds are the number-one favorite food in bird feeders. These seeds yield the highest value nutrition of all commercial plant-based sources, are widely available at reasonable prices, and appeal to the widest variety of species—squirrels included. Not all sunflower seeds are equal, however.

Whole sunflower seeds are categorized as either black oil or gray-striped. The former is a general category representing hybrids developed for high oil content (a few suppliers label these as "dark oil");

the latter are also known as confectionary seeds, characterized by larger seed sizes.

Sunflower seeds are packaged in three primary types for bird feeders. The main market is for whole black oil seeds, which have high oil content and relatively thin hulls, making them accessible even to smaller birds. Striped sunflower seeds, commonly used in snack products for humans,

Black oil sunflower seeds

are larger than black oil seeds but have thicker, harder hulls, making them less accessible for small birds such as sparrows and finches. (Some bird-food suppliers offer a mix of the two varieties, with gray-striped seeds mostly appealing to larger birds.) Hulled seeds are also available, whole or as chips, a popular alternative to many birds because the kernels take less time and effort to consume.

The best seeds for feeders are the black oil type, which have the most oil content, compared to striped snack-type seeds. Black oil seeds are easier to break open, even by larger birds. For those birds that do not have the bill size and strength to break through sunflower hulls, shelled seeds are an option; these are sometimes packaged as sunflower hearts. Another option is broken seeds, which are sometimes labeled as sunflower chips. Either of these provide just as much nutrition as the whole variety, but additional care with them is necessary because they are more vulnerable to oxidation and moisture. They also offer an advantage that appeals to some feeder owners: no mess made from discarded hulls. The sunflower seed industry sorts seed chips into three categories—fine, medium, and coarse—that represent the relative size of the chips, but these categories are not typically reflected on consumer packaging.

An estimated 2,000 different sunflower varieties have been developed since the commercialization of the plant began, although some of these are no longer in circulation. Most of the modern black oil hybrids are developed from the perodovik cultivar. There is little difference among types of black oil seeds, and large suppliers usually combine batches from different farms and different sunflower varietals.

The commercial market for black oil sunflower includes seed supplies treated with insecticides and fungicides, which can greatly improve yields but have remnant toxic effects for birds. Because of the vulnerability of birds within the food chain, extra care is essential when selecting sunflower seeds for feeders. Ideally, people who use bird feeders will use organic seeds, a critical feature for all feeder food. Birds can quickly accumulate harmful chemical compounds such as insecticides, preservatives, and herbicides. Even if these compounds are mostly concentrated in the sunflower seed shells, which are typically discarded by most birds, the residue is still toxic and can still cause harm. Certified organic feed from recognized dealers can cost more, but in a growing climate of environmental threats, the only other option for organic seeds is to grow your own sunflowers, which can limit what is available for the birds.

Other than being organic, the most important factor for sunflower seeds is freshness. Seeds, as with most plant products, lose nutritional value with time and are best used within a year of harvest. Use storage containers that keep seeds dry, and put the containers in a dark place. Any stored seed that is exposed to moisture will quickly develop mildew or other damage and should be safely disposed of, since it can become toxic. Commercial sunflower seed is raw, not roasted, and does not include salt; roasted, salted sunflower seeds are for people, not birds.

Peanuts: This nonnative food for birds provides affordable and nutritious fare in feeders. Peanuts, whole or shelled, are one of the most common foods used in feeders and attract a wide variety of birds, as well as squirrels. Whole peanuts may be difficult or impossible for smaller birds to break into. Shelled and/or peanut pieces are an appropriate alternative.

The nutritional value in peanuts is linked to freshness, although once placed in a feeder, these legumes rarely last long enough to grow stale. Even if peanuts are carefully stored in cool, dry conditions, it

Peanuts

is best to use them within a few months of purchase. Avoid discount suppliers, which often rely on out-of-date supplies. A bigger problem with peanuts is heat and moisture, which can quickly produce mold, presenting potential health risks from aflatoxin, a natural compound produced by fungus.

Either raw or roasted peanuts are acceptable, but raw peanuts can contain natural compounds that inhibit production of a key enzyme necessary for digestion, which can cause problems for birds. Roasting raw peanuts at 300 degrees Fahrenheit (about 150°C) for twenty to thirty minutes neutralizes these compounds but does not destroy aflatoxin. Because this and other toxic compounds can contaminate peanuts at their point of origin, peanut sourcing should be limited to well-established brands with trusted supply sources. Salted peanuts are not acceptable as bird food.

Niger: Sometimes packaged as "thistle seed," niger (also spelled nijer and Nyger, a registered trademark of the Wild Bird Feeding Industry, a trade organization) comes from a plant not native to North America. Most niger is imported from Africa, India, Nepal, and Myanmar (Burma); it originated in Nigeria, where it is more commonly known as the African yellow daisy.

In the past few decades, niger has become a major commercial product, with more than 50,000 tons (45,350 metric tons) sold annually in the United States. The seed can be imported into North

America only after it has been treated to prevent germination, a heat-based process that does not affect the nutritive value of the seed. Though this treatment is promoted as a way to stop unwanted weeds from arriving along with the niger, it is not required and has been ineffectively applied in some batches, according to individual reports. Farmers and amateur gardeners in Canada and the United States have acquired some of these untreated niger seeds and experimented with growing it on local soils. There are suppliers that offer North American-grown niger for feeders and websites that promote the seeds for gardens. Although there are no known dangers from growing this plant in North America, there are risks, including potential dangers for native plants if niger escapes cultivation and competes with native plants in the wild.

Niger seeds are used to stock thistle feeders. Although not native to North America, these seeds provide welcome nutrition to birds that rely on small seeds. Finches and other species that flock to thistle feeders consume the seeds one at a time, first using their tongue and bill to remove the husks.

Niger is a nutritious choice for seedeaters and a beneficial supplement to natural food sources. This seed works well in thistle feeders because of the shape and size of the seeds, thistle feeders are actually designed to dispense niger. Native thistle eaters, such as the American Goldfinch, are easily attracted to thistle feeders serving niger. Other species that are attracted include Black-capped Chickadees, Carolina Chickadees, Common Redpolls, Dark-eyed Juncos, Inca Doves, Mourning Doves, Pine Siskins, Song Sparrows, and Tufted Titmice.

Corn: In comparison to feeder bird seeds, corn is one of the best sources of nutrition and one of the few that is native to North America. Feeders are routinely supplied with one or both varieties of corn, whole or cracked kernels, especially in mixed feeds. Cracked kernels will likely attract more birds than whole kernels, as they are more accessible to smaller species. A wide range of birds are attracted to this food, including birds that some consider nuisances—House Sparrows, Rock Pigeons, and Starlings—in addition to squirrels and the usual risk of other rodents, such as mice and rats.

Corn for feeders is field corn, one of the most common commodity crops in North America, which is produced for animal feed, cooking oil, fuel (ethanol), and a wide variety of chemical compounds. Field corn differs from sweet corn, the variety grown in vegetable gardens, which represents only about 1 percent of total annual corn production. The biggest difference is in sugar content.

Sweet corn has been developed to maximize sweetness, and people eat it when the ears are immature, still alive, and growing. In dried form, sweet corn loses most of its sweetness (sugars convert to starch as moisture decreases) and has about the same nutritional value as field corn. Properly dried sweet corn will work just as well in feeders as field corn.

Field corn, also called dent corn because of the characteristic indentation in the end of each kernel, is intended to be used dry and contains less sugar and more starch than sweet corn. One bushel of fresh field corn yields about 14 pounds (6.4 kilograms) of dried kernels, with an average ear holding from 600 to 800 kernels.

Seed corn that is produced for gardens and agricultural use may be treated for protection against insects, rodents, birds, and other predators. This treatment is typically indicated by color, usually a red dye. Bird feeders should never be stocked with any seed that has

Cracked corn

such treatment, which is certain to be toxic. Corn for feeders, like other popular bird foods, is best purchased as a commodity specifically packaged for this purpose, and as with other feeder products, organic is recommended.

Corn, like peanuts, is susceptible to contamination with aflatoxin. The contamination can be at the source or it can develop from exposure to heat and moisture during storage. As with other feed sources, with time the nutritional value decreases and potential for contamination increases. Avoid buying corn in quantities that last longer than a few months, and while it is being used, store the corn in airtight containers in a cool, dry location protected from unwelcome intruders, especially insects and rodents.

Safflower seeds: The safflower plant is native to Asia, but it has been grown in the Americas since at least the 1700s. Hybrid varieties began to appear in the mid-1950s, increasing the percent of oil and expanding the market. Another introduced plant, safflower is gaining popularity among consumers as an alternative to wheat. Safflower seeds are grown in Canada and the United States, but most of the current market is for cooking oil, which is naturally low in saturated fatty acids compared to other oils.

Safflower seed is also a standard part of most bird-feed mixes, providing nutritive value at low cost. Some birds in North America may avoid these seeds, likely because of unfamiliarity, but taste and

Safflower seeds

nutritional content, particularly high levels of protein and fat, can attract their attention over time. Anecdotal observations suggest that safflower seeds do not attract squirrels, although that may also change over time.

As with other seeds, supplies of safflower seeds for bird feeders should come from trusted packagers, and organic certification is important. Storage also follows standard guidelines: airtight containers in a cool, dry location. Seeds lose nutritive value over time, and storage time should be limited to months, not years.

Some birding organizations suggest that this grain deserves use with care if birds such as blackbirds, House Sparrows, and European Starlings are frequent visitors to feeders. These species, and a few others, seem to be more attracted to this seed than others, and such organizations say it is inappropriate to contribute to these species' well-being, as their diets are already heavily influenced by human practices, especially agriculture.

Millet: A familiar grain in Europe since at least the Middle Ages, millet originated in various forms in Asia and Africa. The major types are barnyard, brown-top, foxtail, pearl, and proso. Some are grown as forage for animals, while others produce seeds that are used for both animal and human food. Today, variations of foxtail and proso millets are the most common commercial types grown in North America. Proso millet is the type used for bird food, but elsewhere in the world, it is primarily a cereal seed for human consumption, providing more protein and iron than wheat or rice.

Proso millet is available in two types, white and red, with white reportedly more popular than red with some bird species. Birds that are attracted to this seed include cardinals, finches, grosbeaks, juncos, and siskins. Some birding resources caution against confusing these small round seeds with milo (see below), which has similar color, size, and shape, because milo is considered an inferior food source that is avoided by birds.

Proso millet is not widely available by itself but is a component of mixed-feed packages. It may provide the most value to birds when scattered on the ground or spread in low-mounted trays,

Millet

because its greatest appeal is to ground-feeding birds. Storage guidelines are the same as for other small seeds.

Some birding organizations suggest that this grain deserves use with care if birds such as blackbirds, European Starlings, and House Sparrows are frequent visitors to feeders, for the same reasons mentioned above for safflower seeds.

Milo: The seeds of the grain sorghum plant, milo is native to Africa and widely grown in North America, in more acreage than barley or oats. In Africa, milo has traditionally provided food for humans, but on this continent, it is primarily a staple for livestock and a source of biofuel (ethanol). Higher in protein and fat than corn, it has recently attracted attention as a niche alternative for artisan baking. It has a long history in the bird-feed industry, but not without controversy.

Among many bird lovers and feeders, milo has a bad reputation. Many birding sources state that birds do not eat this seed and it is used only as an inexpensive filler in cheap mixed feeds. At least some of this is correct: milo is the cheapest of all bird foods and is widely, if not universally, found in the least-expensive mixes on the market. It is also missing, deliberately, from high-end feed products.

However, birds do eat it, as reported from Cornell Lab of Ornithology seed preference tests, with Curve-billed Thrashers, Gambel's Quails, and Steller's Jays among species that selected milo over sunflower seed. Few birds can be said to prefer other seeds to sunflower seeds, but some species will consume milo, both as a foraging resource

Milo

and in bird feeders. In general, it seems to be more popular among western birds than those in the eastern US. Among the birds that eat milo are Band-tailed Pigeons, California Quail, California Towhees, Chipping Sparrows, Common Ground Doves, Dark-eyed Juncos, Mourning Doves, Northern Cardinals, Red-winged Blackbirds, Song Sparrows, Spotted Towhees, and White-crowned Sparrows.

The bottom line? If in doubt, leave it out.

Other seeds: Canary seed, canola (rapeseed), flaxseed, oats, rice, and wheat are among the "fillers" often found in inexpensive feed mixes. There are always birds that will eat these seeds, given the opportunity and lack of alternatives, but these feeds rank low in preference in several comparative studies.

Fruit: Commercially available fruit for bird feeders is the dried variety, usually offered in mixed lots of berries and pieces of other fruit. Standard mixes include raisins, dried apples, cherries, cranberries, and sometimes other fruit.

Fresh fruit in feeders is a larger project, requiring more diligence on the part of bird lovers, but can encompass as wide a selection as the market or orchard permits: apples, blueberries, grapes, melons, oranges, peaches, and so on. Anything larger than a grape should be cut into a few pieces, though not necessarily bite-size.

Baltimore Oriole on citrus feeder

Birds that are attracted to dried and fresh fruit include American Robins, Baltimore Orioles, Black-billed Magpies, Blue Jays, Bohemian Waxwings, Canada Jays, Cedar Waxwings, Eastern Bluebirds, Hermit Thrushes, Northern Mockingbirds, Pine Grosbeaks, Red-bellied Woodpeckers, and Yellow-rumped Warblers.

Food mixes: Packaged feeder fill is most often sold as mixes of various seeds. Sunflower seeds and peanuts are the most prevalent, with other content varying widely. Some suppliers carefully select ingredients that attract certain kinds of birds, and some mixes deliberately avoid content that attract the "wrong" kind of birds (such as European Starlings, House Sparrows, or Rock Pigeons).

The biggest factor in selecting mixes is quality. Higher quality in feeder mixes aims at the highest nutritive value, avoiding low-quality nutritive ingredients altogether and controlling supply chains to ensure purity. Birds do not fare well from residual chemicals that are often used in agricultural production, especially insecticides. Bird-food mixes often are offered as value-driven products, which is a legitimate plus for consumers, but not if it harms the birds to which it will be fed.

Suet: In its traditional form, suet is the fat removed from its cushioning around the kidneys in beef (sometimes mutton was also a source) and used for cooking or for making tallow candles. In the modern era, when beef fat (by itself, anyway) is no longer part of

Bird food mix

the American diet, it lives on (if in name only) as suet for bird feeders. This type of suet begins with a base of animal fat that can come from a variety of mammals other than cows.

Among bird-feeder options, suet is about the only commercial alternative, along with mealworms, to vegetarian bird food. Packaged suet products are typically blocks of congealed fat that is often mixed with seeds, dried fruit, and other feeder basics. Although susceptible to dripping in hot weather, the suet in commercial

Suet

products is formulated to make it heat-resistant (but still better in cold weather than warm). Some companies offer nondrip varieties that have added ingredients to keep the contents from melting in the heat. Homemade recipes abound on websites, and some do not contain the namesake fat, replacing it with peanut butter or other solid edibles.

Suet feeders are designed to accommodate the suet blocks, which are usually manufactured in a standard size: roughly 5 inches by 5 inches by 1 inch (12.7 centimeters by 12.7 centimeters by 2.5 centimeters). These are typically wire cages that, when filled with the suet blocks, are suspended about 6 feet (1.8 meters) above the ground, a height that is comfortable for the birds it attracts. Squirrels are likely to raid any suet feeder they can get to, so special care in placement and squirrel-proofing is prudent.

Many birds that are attracted to seed feeders are omnivorous and are also attracted to suet. Among the species noted for favoring suet are the American Crow, Brown Creeper, Bushtit, Canada Jay, chickadees, Curve-billed Thrasher, Eastern Bluebird, Northern Mockingbird, Red-bellied Woodpecker, wrens, and Yellow-rumped Warbler.

Mealworms: Along with suet, mealworms are the only commercially available bird food that is not plant based. Mealworms, the larval form of a darkling beetle species, are usually available at pet and bird supply stores in freeze-dried form. Some bird lovers note that this desiccated form is unappetizing to the birds that show up at their feeders, these birds either ignoring the worms altogether or discarding them once they taste them. Other observers, however, report that the dried form is readily accepted and eagerly ingested.

The reality is that different bird species may have different preferences, and individuals of the same species may react differently. In any case, dedicated feeder hosts can provide live mealworms if they can find a supplier. If bird-related retailers do not stock live mealworms, others that do are reptile stores and some fishing-bait stores.

Another option is "mealworm ranching": growing these insects at home. As with other insects, there are four life stages (egg, larva, pupa, adult), which can be simply managed in small containers. Adult and larval forms can thrive on a diet of dried oats with little care. Raising mealworms is also a great project for kids, providing a hands-on lesson about insects, life cycles, and food chains.

Birds that are particularly attracted to mealworms in backyard feeders include the American Robin, Black-capped Chickadee, Black-crested Titmouse, Bushtit, Cactus Wren, Carolina Wren, Downy Woodpecker, Eastern Bluebird, Hermit Thrush, Pygmy Nuthatch, Varied Thrush, and Yellow-bellied Sapsucker.

Nectar: Nectar mixes are readily available at a variety of retail outlets, and recipes provide directions for producing homemade versions. Nectar feeders are often considered hummingbird-specific, but the sugar water they dispense can also attract other species. Baltimore Orioles, Red-bellied Woodpeckers, and some warblers also find the sweet contents

Live mealworms are a preferred feeder food for many bird species but are not widely available at retail outlets, and when they are, they can be expensive. Dried mealworms, which provide more nutrition per unit of weight, are carried at most birding stores, but some birds may not find them tempting. A solution for do-it-yourselfers is to grow your own live mealworms. The worm itself is the larval stage of a species of darkling beetle, and large numbers are produced in a short time.

compelling, even if they lack the specialized bills and tongue that hummingbirds use for access.

Nectar requires some diligence in feeder use to protect birds. Feeders have to be kept clean and the liquid contents fresh to avoid spoilage. Insects and other unwanted visitors also require attention if their numbers get

Hummingbird feeders are designed to hold nectar.

out of control, as the syrup that nectar feeders dispense is a potent attractor for a wide range of life-forms, mostly bees and wasps (but also ants and earwigs).

KEEP LEARNING

Bird lovers in North American benefit from a wealth of resources, support systems, and ways to expand personal knowledge about the avian world. Many opportunities involve a range of options that provide participation that can accommodate a range of work situations and lifestyles.

Local and national organizations support birds, other wildlife, and conservation. Membership helps fund their activities and provides members with forums, expert opinions, activities, and, often, publications with content of particular value.

Along with national organizations that involve appropriate subject areas for birders, local groups provide support that turns abstract philosophies into action. Friends, neighbors, and local experts are allies in the movement to appreciate, support, and expand efforts to strengthen protection for the avian world. Although action on a national scale is a necessary part of the pro-wildlife movement, action becomes more immediate and personal at the local level. People form the core of meaningful change, beginning with awareness and communication.

Starting points for expanding knowledge about birds and participating in birding-related activities include local and national birding organizations, natural-history museums, public gardens, zoos and wildlife centers, and parks—local, state, and national. In many cities, retail outlets provide significant resources for bird-watchers and home owners who have bird feeders.

National chains such as Wild Birds Unlimited and independent bird stores are a natural center of knowledge about birds, with staff members who have personalized and local information—and not just limited to bird feeders and bird feed. Most of these shops publish newsletters, provide web content, offer hands-on activities—bird walks, introductions to birding, etc.—and are often local centers of activities that involve conservation.

For specific organizations and allies, see Resources.

EVENTS

The birding industry is well established throughout the continent, with regional and national events that cater to the subject. There

Sandhill Cranes aggregate in large flocks at the beginning and end of their migration, with birding events timed to support viewing opportunities in Colorado, Nebraska, and other locations. Other migratory species are also the focus of unique festivals that attract a full spectrum of birding enthusiasts, from amateur to professional. *(Photo by Sherry Saye)*

Bird lovers become citizen scientists by participating in Project FeederWatch, an increasingly important research program based on observations of bird feeders. *(Photo by Marty Pitcairn)*

are more than 130 multiday birding festivals annually in Canada and the United States, plus more outside of the continent. *BirdWatcher's Digest*, a bimonthly consumer magazine, provides a list of these events on its website. This listing includes local, regional, and national dates, with many events dedicated to specific birds: cranes, eagles, hummingbirds, et cetera.

Bird festivals appeal to bird lovers of all ages and can provide a personalized introduction for newcomers as well as opportunities to gain advanced knowledge. Many festivals are organized near viewing areas where there is access to bird viewing supported by knowledgeable guides. Some of these festivals are timed to coincide with migratory flights of specific species, such as Sandhill Cranes and raptors.

For specific events and organizations, see Resources.

CITIZEN SCIENCE

"Citizen science" is an established way that enthusiasts without credentials, means, or backing of the formal sciences can become involved. Citizens of all ages who already pursue personal interests

On the left, volunteers from the Bird Observatory of the Rockies measure and band a Yellow Warbler near Denver. On the right, a Harris's Hawk is measured and banded in a suburban backyard in Tucson, Arizona, by staff members of the Department of Ecology and Evolutionary Biology at the University of Arizona. *(Photo on right by Gregory McNamee)*

connected to natural history, including horticulture and wildlife, can volunteer to participate in field studies and more.

Project FeederWatch: In the birding community, one of the best programs for personal connection to science is Project FeederWatch. From November through April, birders count the number and species of birds that visit feeders. People of all ages from classrooms, nature centers, and birding groups participate by sending periodic reports to the project site, which is run as a joint venture by the Cornell Lab of Ornithology and Bird Studies Canada. The project has been underway since the mid-1970s and has thousands of participants. The resulting data provides detailed statistics that define and track the activities and general health of birds in wintering habitats, helping determine species that are at risk or threatened.

Bird observatories: Another option for hands-on activity are the bird observatories found throughout the continent, often at sites along migration routes or within conservation zones. Science-based programs are at the core of these facilities, but they rely on volunteer support, and education is often a top priority. In the United States and Canada, there are about sixty bird observatories, most with their own websites that provide background information and descriptions of available activities.

Bird banding: Observatories, local birding groups, and other science-based organizations sometimes support citizen involvement in bird banding activities as part of their missions. These are run by experienced personnel but often allow visitors and sometimes include hands-on experiences as part of banding programs.

For specific information and organizations, see Resources.

ACKNOWLEDGMENTS

The subject of this book had its initial motivation from a night-time expedition searching for owls in the Connecticut countryside in 1969, led by Paul Spitzer (now Dr. Paul Spitzer, ornithologist), a classmate at Wesleyan University. Decades later, as this project was initiated, researched, illustrated, and written, direct and indirect support was generously provided by Gregory McNamee, Ed O'Brien, Jon Zahourek of Anatomy in Clay Centers, Scott Menough of Wild Birds Unlimited, Garth Spellman of the Denver Museum of Nature and Science, Terry Chesser of the American Ornithological Society, Christopher Richard, Greg Goodrich, Cheryl Opperman, and Marilyn Auer.

Special thanks to Deborah Hofmann (David Black Literary Agency) and Kate Rogers and the diligent staff at Mountaineers Books. Thanks also to Dennis Paulson, for reviewing an early draft and offering many helpful suggestions.

The following institutions provide invaluable resources online: American Bird Conservancy, American Birding Association, Audubon Society, Auraria Library, Bird Observatory of the Rocky Mountains, Cornell Lab of Ornithology, Denver Public Library, the Library of Congress Image Collection, Norlin Library at the University of Colorado, Penrose Library at the University of Denver, and the Tattered Cover.

RESOURCES

PROFESSIONAL PUBLICATIONS

Avian Conservation and Ecology, Society of Canadian Ornithologists
The Auk, American Ornithological Society
The Condor, American Ornithological Society
Journal of Field Ornithology, Association of Field Ornithologists
Journal of Raptor Research, Raptor Research Foundation
Living Bird, Cornell Lab of Ornithology
Open Ornithology Journal, Bentham Open
Waterbirds, Waterbird Society
Wilson Journal of Ornithology, Wilson Ornithological Society

CONSUMER PUBLICATIONS

Audubon Magazine, Audubon Society, audubon.org
Bird Conservation, American Bird Conservancy, abcbirds.org
Birder's World, birdwatchingdaily.com
Birding Magazine, American Birding Association, aba.org
   /magazine
Bird Life, Bird Life International, birdlife.org/birdlife-magazine
Birds & Blooms Magazine, birdsandblooms.com
Bird Watching Magazine, birdwatchingdaily.com
Bird Watcher's Digest, birdwatchersdigest.com
North American Birds, American Birding Association, aba.org
   /north-american-birds
Watching Backyard Birds, watchingbackyardbirds.com

ORGANIZATIONS AND AGENCIES

American Bird Conservancy, abcbirds.org
American Birding Association, aba.org
American Ornithological Society, americanornithology.org
American Prairie Reserve, americanprairie.org
Audubon Society, audubon.org

bird festivals, birdwatchersdigest.com/bwdsite/explore
/festivals.php

Bird Freak, birdfreak.com

bird observatories, birdnet.org/info-for-ornithologists
/observatories/

Birds of North America, Cornell Lab of Ornithology, birdsna.org

common names of insects, Entomological Society of America,
entsoc.org/common-names

Ducks Unlimited, ducks.org

eBird, ebird.org

Guide to North American Birds, Audubon Society, audubon.org
/bird-guide

Institute for Bird Populations, birdpop.org

International Wildlife Rehabilitation Council, theiwrc.org

Lady Bird Johnson Wildflower Center, wildflower.org

National Audubon Society, audubon.org

National Parks Conservation Association, npca.org

National Sunflower Association, sunflowersnsa.com

National Wildlife Federation, nwf.org

National Wildlife Refuge Association, refugeassociation.org

Native Seed Network, nativeseednetwork.org

Native Seeds Search, nativeseeds.org

Nature Conservancy, nature.org

Ornithological Council, birdnet.org

Partners in Flight, partnersinflight.org

plants database, Natural Resources Conservation Service, US
Department of Agriculture, plants.sc.egov.usda.gov

Project FeederWatch, Cornell Lab of Ornithology, feederwatch.org

Purple Martin Conservation Association, purplemartin.org

Sand County Foundation, sandcountyfoundation.org

Sierra Club, sierraclub.org

US Fish and Wildlife Service, fws.gov/birds/bird-enthusiasts
/bird-watching.php

Waterbird Society, waterbirds.org

Wild Bird Feeding Industry, wbfi.org

Xerces Society, xerces.org

PRODUCT SOURCES

Applewood Seed Co., applewoodseed.com

Bird Feeders Etc., birdfeedersetc.com

Droll Yankees, drollyankees.com

Duncraft, duncraft.com

Ernst Seeds, ernstseed.com

Kaytee Products, kaytee.com

Native American Seed, seedsource.com

Perky Pet, perkypet.com

Petco, petco.com

Petsmart, petsmart.com

Prairie Moon Nursery, prairiemoon.com

Roundstone Native Seed LLC, roundstoneseed.com

Shooting Star Native Seeds, shootingstarnativeseed.com

Spence Restoration Nursery, spencenursery.com

Urban Birder, theurbanbirder.com

Wildflower Farm, wildflowerfarm.com

Wild Birds Unlimited, wbu.com

Wild Foods 4 Wildlife, wildfoods4wildlife.com

BIBLIOGRAPHY

GENERAL

Alderfer, Jonathan, ed. *National Geographic Complete Birds of North America*. Washington, DC: National Geographic Society, 2006.

Backhouse, Frances. *Woodpeckers of North America*. Ontario, Canada: Firefly Books, 2005.

Baicich, Paul J., Margaret A. Barker, and Carrol L. Henderson. *Feeding Wild Birds in America: Culture, Commerce, and Conservation*. College Station: Texas A&M University Press, 2015.

Barker, Margaret A., and Jack Griggs. *The Feeder Watcher's Guide to Bird Feeding: Cornell Bird Library Guide*. New York: HarperCollins, 2000.

Baumel, Julian J., et al., eds. *Handbook of Avian Anatomy*. Cambridge, MA: Publications of the Nuttall Ornithological Club, 1993.

Bent, Arthur Cleveland. *Life Histories of North American Cuckoos, Goatsuckers, Hummingbirds, and Their Allies*. Mineola, NY: Dover Publications, 1989. First published by Smithsonian Institution, 1940.

Brooke, Michael, and Tim Birkhead, eds. *The Cambridge Encyclopedia of Ornithology*. Cambridge, UK: Cambridge University Press, 1991.

Buchmann, Stephen L., and Gary Paul Nabhan. *The Forgotten Pollinators*. Washington, DC: Island Press, 1996.

Bull, John, and John Farrand. *National Audubon Society Field Guide to North American Birds, Eastern Region*. New York: Alfred A. Knopf, 1996.

Burton, Robert. *Bird Flight*. New York: Facts on File, 1990.

Cullina, William. *Native Trees, Shrubs, and Vines*. Boston: Houghton Mifflin, 2002.

Dunn, Erica H., and Diane L. Tessaglia-Hymes. *Birds at Your Feeder*. New York: W. W. Norton, 1999.

Elbroch, Mark. *Animal Skulls: A Guide to North American Species.* Mechanicsburg, PA: Stackpole Books, 2006.

Elbroch, Mark, and Eleanor Marks. *Bird Tracks and Sign: A Guide to North American Species.* Mechanicsburg, PA: Stackpole Books, 2001.

Elkins, Norman. *Weather and Bird Behavior.* Calton, UK: T. & A. D. Poyser Ltd., 1983.

Enderson, Jim. *Peregrine Falcon: Stories of the Blue Meanie.* Austin: University of Texas Press, 2005.

Floyd, Ted. *How to Know the Birds.* Washington, DC: National Geographic Partners, 2019.

———. *Smithsonian Field Guide to the Birds of North America.* New York: HarperCollins, 2008.

George, J. C., and A. J. Berger. *Avian Myology.* Cambridge, MA: Academic Press, 1966.

Gill, Frank B. *Ornithology.* 2nd ed. New York: W. H. Freeman, 1995.

Goodman, Donald C., and Harvey I. Fisher. *Functional Anatomy of the Feeding Apparatus in Waterfowl.* Carbondale: Southern Illinois University Press, 1962.

Gould, Stephen Jay, ed. *The Book of Life: An Illustrated History of the Evolution of Life on Earth.* New York: W. W. Norton, 2001.

Hickman, Cleveland P. *Integrated Principles of Zoology.* New York: McGraw-Hill, 2008.

Hill, Geoffrey E. *Bird Coloration.* Washington, DC: National Geographic Society, 2010.

Hutchinson, Rev. H. N. *Extinct Monsters: A Popular Account of Some of the Larger Forms of Ancient Animal Life.* London: Chapman & Hall, 1896.

Kaiser, Gary W. *The Inner Bird: Anatomy and Evolution.* Vancouver: University of British Columbia Press, 2007.

Kaplan, Gisela, and Lesley J. Rogers. *Birds: Their Habits and Skills.* St. Leonards, Australia: Allen & Unwin, 2001.

Kaufman, Kenn. *Kaufman Field Guide to Birds of North America.* Boston: Houghton Mifflin, 2000.

King, A. S., and J. McLelland, eds. *Form and Function in Birds.* Cambridge, MA: Academic Press, 1985.

Kolbert, Elizabeth. *The Sixth Extinction*. New York: Bloomsbury Publishing, 2014.

Kress, Stephen W. *The Audubon Society Guide to Attracting Birds*. 2nd ed. Ithaca, NY: Cornell University Press, 2006.

———. *National Audubon Society: The Bird Garden*. New York: Dorling Kindersley, 1995.

Krochmal, Arnold, and Connie Krochmal. *Uncultivated Nuts of the United States*. Washington, DC: US Forest Service, US Department of Agriculture, 1982.

Leahy, Christopher W. *Birdwatcher's Companion: North American Birdlife*. Princeton, NJ: Princeton University Press, 2004.

Lovette, Irby J., and John W. Fitzpatrick. *The Cornell Lab of Ornithology Handbook of Bird Biology*. 3rd ed. Hoboken, NJ: John Wiley & Wiley, 2016.

Lucas, Alfred M., and Peter R. Stettenheim. *Avian Anatomy: Integument*. Washington, DC: Avian Anatomy Project Agricultural Research Service, US Department of Agriculture, 1972.

Mahnken, Jan. *The Backyard Bird-Lovers Guide*. North Adams, MA: Storey Publishing, 1996.

Marshall, A. J., ed. *Biology and Comparative Physiology of Birds*. Cambridge, MA: Academic Press, 1960.

Martin, Alexander C., Herbert S. Zim, and Arnold L. Nelson. *American Wildlife and Plants: A Guide to Wildlife Food Habits*. Mineola, NY: Dover Publications, 1961. First published by McGraw-Hill, 1951.

Maxon, Martha Anne. *The Real Roadrunner*. Norman: University of Oklahoma Press, 2005.

National Geographic Society. *Field Guide to the Birds of North America*. 2nd ed. Washington, DC: National Geographic Society, 1987.

Peterson, Roger Tory. *A Field Guide to Western Birds*. 3rd ed. Boston: Houghton Mifflin, 1990.

Powell, Hugh, Brian Scott Sockin, and Laura Erickson, eds. *All About Backyard Birds*. Apex, NC: Cornell Lab Publishing Group, 2017.

Powell, James Lawrence. *Night Comes to the Cretaceous*. New York: W. H. Freeman, 1998.

Proctor, Michael, Peter Yeo, and Andrew Lack. *The Natural History of Pollination*. Portland, OR: Timber Press, 1996.

Proctor, Noble S., and Patrick J. Lynch. *Manual of Ornithology: Avian Structure and Function*. New Haven, CT: Yale University Press, 1993.

Rüppell, Georg. *Bird Flight*. New York: Van Nostrand Reinhold, 1975.

Schmauss, Anne, Mary Schmauss, and Geni Krolick. *For the Birds: A Month-by-Month Guide to Attracting Birds to Your Backyard*. New York: Stewart, Tabori, & Chang, 2008.

Sekercioglu, Cagan H., Daniel G. Wenny, and Christopher J. Whelan, eds. *Why Birds Matter*. Chicago: University of Chicago Press, 2016.

Shufeldt, R. W. *The Myology of the Raven*. New York: Macmillan, 1890.

Sibley, David Allen. *The Sibley Guide to Birds*. New York: Alfred A. Knopf, 2000.

Sorenson, Sharon. *Birds in the Yard Month by Month*. Mechanicsburg, PA: Stackpole, 2013.

Stokes, Donald, and Lillian Stokes. *Stokes Field Guide to the Birds of North America*. New York: Little, Brown, 2010.

Stubbendieck, James, Stephan L. Hatch, Neal M. Bryan, and Cheryl D. Dunn. *North American Wildland Plants*. 3rd ed. Lincoln: University of Nebraska Press, 2017.

Stutchbury, Bridget. *The Private Lives of Birds*. New York: Walker, 2010.

Todd, Kim. *Sparrow*. London: Reaktion Books, 2012.

Vander Wall, Stephen B. *Food Hoarding in Animals*. Chicago: University of Chicago Press, 1990.

Waldbauer, Gilbert. *How Not to Be Eaten: The Insects Fight Back*. Berkeley: University of California Press, 2012.

———. *What Good Are Bugs?* Cambridge, MA: Harvard University Press, 2003.

Ward, Peter D. *Rivers in Time: The Search for Clues to Earth's Mass Extinctions*. New York: Columbia University Press, 2000.

Whittow, G. Causey, ed. *Sturkie's Avian Physiology*. 5th ed. Cambridge, MA: Academic Press, 2000.

Witzany, Guenther, ed. *Biocommunication of Animals*. New York: Springer, 2014.

Zimmer, Carl. *The Tangled Bank: An Introduction to Evolution*. Greenwood Village, CO: Roberts and Co., 2010.

HOW BIRDS EVOLVED

Abourachid, Anick, and Elizabeth Höfling. "The Legs: A Key to Bird Evolutionary Success." *Journal of Ornithology* 153 (May 17, 2012): 193–198.

Black, Riley. "What Doomed the Pterosaurs?" *Smithsonian Magazine*, March 13, 2018, online.

Brusatte, Stephen L., Jingmai K. O'Connor, and Erich D. Jarvis. "The Origin and Diversification of Birds." *Current Biology* 25, no. 19 (October 5, 2015): 888–98.

Carrano, Matthew T., and Patrick M. O'Connor. "Bird's-Eye View." *Natural History* 114, no. 4 (May 2005): 42–47.

Dyke, Gareth. "Winged Victory." *Scientific American* 303, no. 1 (July 2010): 70–75.

Field, Daniel J. "Big-time Insights from a Tiny Bird Fossil." *Proceedings of the National Academy of Sciences* 114, no. 30 (July 25, 2017): 7750–52.

Heinrich, Bernd. "Flow Behavior: The Evolution of Sex Appeals." *Natural History* 127, no. 1 (October 2018): 9–11.

Jarvis, Erich D., et. al. "Whole-genome Analyses Resolve Early Branches in the Tree of Life of Modern Birds." *Science* 346, no. 6215 (December 12, 2014): 1320–31.

Jetz, W., et al. "The Global Diversity of Birds in Space and Time." *Nature* 491 (November 15, 2012): 444–48.

Ksepka, Daniel T., and Michael Habib. "Giants of the Sky." *Scientific American* 314, no. 4 (April 2016): 64–71.

Misof, Bernhard, et. al. "Phylogenomics Resolves the Timing and Pattern of Insect Evolution." *Science* 3466, no. 6210 (November 7, 2014): 763–67.

Oliveros, Carl H., et al. "Earth History and the Passerine Superradiation." *Proceedings of the National Academy of Sciences* 116, no. 16 (April 16, 2019): 7916–25.

Raikow, Robert J., and Anthony H. Bledsoe. "Phylogeny and Evolution of the Passerine Birds." *BioScience* 50, no. 6 (June 2000): 487–99.

Richardson, Lauren A. "Birds, Blooms, and Evolving Diversity." *PLoS Biology* 16, no. 10 (October 4, 2018), online.

Singer, Emily. "How Dinosaurs Shrank and Became Birds." *Quanta Magazine*, June 2, 2015. www.quantamagazine.org/how-birds-evolved-from-dinosaurs-20150602.

Thomas, Gavin H. "An Avian Explosion." *Nature* 526, no. 7574 (October 2015): 516–17.

THE ANATOMY AND PHYSIOLOGY OF HOW BIRDS EAT

Amo, L., et.al. "Predator Odour Recognition and Avoidance in a Songbird." *Functional Ecology* 22 (2008): 289–93.

Averett, Nancy. "The Sniff Test." *Audubon Magazine,* January-February 2014, online.

Backus, Spencer B., et.al. "Mechanical Analysis of Avian Feet." *Royal Society Open Science* 2, no. 2 (February 2015), online.

Bandyopadhyay, Promode R., Henry A. Leinhos, and Aren M. Hellum. "Handedness Helps Homing in Swimming and Flying Animals." *Nature*, 2013, online.

Baumhardt, Patrice E., et.al. "Do American Goldfinches See Their World Like Passive Prey Foragers?" *Brain, Behavior and Evolution* 83, no. 3 (June 2014): 181–98.

Beason, Robert C. "Through a Bird's Eye: Exploring Avian Sensory Perception." Animal and Plant Health Inspection Service, US Department of Agriculture, 2003. aphis.usda.gov.

———. "What Can Birds Hear?" *Proceedings of the 21st Vertebrate Pest Conference,* no. 78 (2004): 92–96.

Benkman, Craig W. "A Crossbill's Twist of Fate." *Natural History* 101, no. 12 (December 1992): 38–44.

Berger, Cynthia. "True Colors." *National Wildlife* 50, no. 5 (August-September 2012), online.

Bhattacharyya, B. N. "Avian Jaw Function: Adaptation of the Seven-Muscle System and a Review." *Proceedings of the Zoological Society* 66, no. 2 (2013): 75–85.

Birkhead, Tim. "Do Birds Smell?" *Bird Table,* spring 2012, 12–13, online.

Bock, Walter J. "Avian Cranial Kinesis Revisited." *Acta Ornithologica* 34, no. 2 (1999): 115–22.

Bock, Walter J., and Waldron DeWitt Miller. "The Scansorial Foot of the Woodpeckers, with Comments on the Evolution of Perching and Climbing Feet in Birds." *American Museum Novitiates*, March 1959, online.

Boström, Jannika E., et al. "Ultra-Rapid Vision in Birds." *PLoS One* 11, no. 3 (March 18, 2016), online.

Bowen, Richard. "Digestive Anatomy and Physiology of Birds." Colorado State University, online.

Bright, Jen A., et.al. "The Shapes of Bird Beaks Are Highly Controlled by Nondietary Factors." *Proceedings of the National Academy of Sciences*, May 10, 2016, online.

Brooke, M. de L., et al. "The Scaling of Eye Size with Body Mass in Birds." *Proceedings of the Royal Society* 266, no. 1417 (November 1998): 405–12.

Chen, C. C. W., and K. C. Welch. "Hummingbirds Can Fuel Expensive Hovering Flight Completely with Either Exogenous Glucose or Fructose." *Functional Ecology* 28, no. 3 (2014): 589–600.

Clark, Larry. "Odor Detection Thresholds in Tree Swallows and Cedar Waxwings." *The Auk* 108, no. 1 (January 1991): 177–80.

Clay, Zanna, et al. "Food-associated Vocalizations in Mammals and Birds." *Animal Behaviour* 83 (2012): 323–30.

Cohen, Steven M., et al. "Audibility Thresholds of the Blue Jay." *The Auk* 95 (July 1978): 563–68.

Cook, Robert G. "The Comparative Psychology of Avian Visual Cognition." *Current Directions in Psychological Science* 9, no. 3 (June 2000): 83–89.

Corfield, Jeremy R., et al. "Diversity in Olfactory Bulb Size in Birds Reflects Allometry, Ecology, and Phylogeny." *Frontiers in Neuroanatomy* 9, no. 102 (July 2015), online.

Cracraft, Joel. "The Functional Morphology of the Hind Limb of the Domestic Pigeon." *Bulletin of the American Museum of Natural History* 144, no. 3 (1971), online.

Csermely, Davide, et al. "Prey Killing by Eurasian Kestrels: The Role of the Foot and the Significance of Bill and Talons." *Journal of Avian Biology* 29, no. 1 (1998): 10–16.

Davis, Brian. "The Scoop on Duck Bills." Ducks Unlimited, ducks. org.

Davis, Jamie K. "Evolution of a Bitter Taste Receptor Gene Cluster in a New World Sparrow." *Genome Biological Evolution* 2 (2010): 358–70.

Dawson, William R. "Evaporative Losses of Water by Birds." *Comparative Biochemical Physiology* 71, no. 4 (1982): 495–509.

Donatelli, Reginaldo J. "Jaw Musculature of the Picini." *International Journal of Zoology*, 2012, online.

Dooling, Robert J., et al. "Auditory Sensitivity and Vocalizations of the Field Sparrow." *Bulletin of the Psychonomic Society* 14, no. 2 (1979): 106–8.

Eisthen, Heather L. "Why Are Olfactory Systems of Different Animals So Similar?" *Brain Behavior and Evolution* 59, nos. 5–6 (2002): 273–93.

Elsahy, Deena Ahmed. "The Passive Perching Mechanism in Passeriformes Birds." Undergraduate Honors Thesis Collection, Butler University, Indianapolis, IN, 2014.

Engels, William L. "Tongue Musculature of Passerine Birds." *The Auk* 55, no. 4 (October 1938): 642–50.

Estrella, Sora M., and José Masero. "The Use of Distal Rhynchokinesis by Birds Feeding in Water." *Journal of Experimental Biology* 210 (2007): 3757–62.

Exnerová, Alice, et al. "Importance of Colour in the Reaction of Passerine Predators to Aposematic Prey." *Biological Journal of the Linnean Society* 88, no. 1 (2006): 143–53.

Firestein, Stuart. "How the Olfactory System Makes Sense of Scents." *Nature* 413, no. 6852 (September 13, 2001): 211–18.

Fisher, Harvey I. "Some Aspects of the Kinetics in the Jaws of Birds." *Wilson Bulletin* 67, no. 3 (September 1955): 175–88.

Fisher, Harvey I., and Eleanor E. Dater. "Esophageal Diverticula in the Redpoll." *The Auk* 78, no. 4 (October 1961): 528–31.

Fowler, Denver W., et al. "Predatory Functional Morphology in Raptors." *PLoS One* 4, no. 11 (November 2009): e7999, online.

Freire, R., et al. "Minor Beak Trimming in Chickens Leads to Loss of Mechanoreception and Magnetoreception." *Journal of Animal Science* 89, no. 4 (April 2011): 1201–6.

Gardner, Leon L. "The Adaptive Modifications and the Taxonomic Value of the Tongue in Birds." *Proceedings of the US National Museum* 67, no. 19 (1925): 1–49.

Gentle, Michael, and John Breward. "The Bill Tip Organ of the Chicken." *Journal of Anatomy* 145 (1986): 79–85.

Gill, Frank B. *Ornithology.* 2nd ed. New York: W. H. Freeman, 1995.

Gionfriddo, James P., and Louis B. Best. "Grit-Use Patterns in North American Birds: The Influence of Diet, Body Size, and Gender." *Wilson Bulletin* 108, no. 4 (1996): 685–96.

Greenwold, Matthew J., et al. "Dynamic Evolution of the Alpha and Beta Keratins Has Accompanied Integument Diversification and the Adaptation of Birds into Novel Lifestyles." *BMC Evolutionary Biology* 14, no. 249 (2014), online.

Gwinner, Helga, et al. " 'Green Incubation': Avian Offspring Benefit from Aromatic Nest Herbs Through Improved Parental Incubation Behaviour." *Proceedings of the Royal Society B: Biological Sciences* 285 no. 1880 (2018), online.

Hagelin, Julie C., and Ian L. Jones. "Bird Odors and Other Chemical Substances: A Defense Mechanism or Overlooked Mode of Intraspecific Communication?" *The Auk* 124, no. 3 (July 2007): 741–61.

Harriman, A.E. and R.H. Berger. "Olfactory Acuity in the Common Raven." *Physiological Behavior* 36 (1986): 257–62.

Hausmann, Laura, et al. "Improvements of Sound Localization Abilities by the Facial Ruff of the Barn Owl." *PLoS One* 4, no. 11 (November 2009): e7721, online.

Heffner, H. E., and R. S. Heffner. "Auditory Perception." *Farm Animals and the Environment*, 1992, 159–84, online.

Hemert, Caroline Van, et al. "Microanatomy of Passerine Hard-Cornified Tissues: Beak and Claw Structure of the Black-capped Chickadee." *Journal of Morphology* 273, no. 2 (2012): 226–40.

Iwasaki, Shin-ichi. "Evolution of the Structure and Function of the Vertebrate Tongue." *Journal of Anatomy* 201, no. 1 (2002): 1–13.

Johnston, Nancy E. "The Avian Tongue." Golden Gate Audubon Society, June 2014, online.

Jung, J. Y., et al. "Structural Analysis of the Tongue and Hyoid Apparatus in a Woodpecker." *Acta Biomaterialia* 37 (March 2016): 1–13.

Karasov, William H. "In the Belly of the Bird." *Natural History* 11 (November 1993): 32–38.

Kassarov, Luka. "Are Birds Able to Taste and Reject Butterflies Based on 'Beak Mark Tasting'? A Different Point of View." *Behaviour*, 1999, 965–81, online.

Kieron´czyk, Bartosz, et al. "Avian Crop Function: A Review." *Annals of Animal Science* 16, no. 3 (April 2016): 653–78.

King, A. S., and J. McLelland, eds. *Form and Function in Birds*. Cambridge, MA: Academic Press, 1985.

Klump, G. M., et al. "The Hearing of an Avian Predator and Its Avian Prey." *Behavioral Ecology and Sociobiology* 18, no. 5 (1986): 317–23.

Konishi, Masakazu. "How the Owl Tracks Its Prey." *American Scientist* 100, no. 6 (November-December 2012): 494–503.

Krogis, Anna. "On the Topography of Herbst's and Grandry's Corpuscles in the Adult and Embryonic Duck-bill." *Acta Zoologica* 12, nos. 2–3 (1931): 241–63.

Langlois, Isabelle. "The Anatomy, Physiology, and Diseases of the Avian Proventriculus and Ventriculus." *Veterinary Clinics Exotic Animal Practice* 6, no. 1 (2003): 85–111.

Lavin, Shana R., et al. "Morphometrics of the Avian Small Intestine Compared with That of Nonflying Mammals." *Physiological and Biochemical Zoology* 81, no. 5 (2008): 526–50.

Lederer, Robert J. "The Role of Avian Rictal Bristles." *Wilson Bulletin* 84, no. 2 (June 1972): 193–97.

Liu, Hong-Xiang, et al. "An Update on the Sense of Taste in Chickens." *Journal of Nutrition and Food Science* 8, no. 2 (May 2018): 686.

Lovette, Irby J., and John W. Fitzpatrick. *The Cornell Lab of Ornithology Handbook of Bird Biology.* 3rd ed. Hoboken, NJ: John Wiley & Wiley, 2016.

Lucas, Frederic A. "The Tongues of Birds." *Report of the National Museum*, 1895, 1003–23, online.

MacMillen, Richard E. "Water Economy of Granivorous Birds." *The Condor* 92, no. 2 (1990): 379–92.

Macwhirter, Patricia. "Rhamphotheca." In *Handbook of Avian Medicine*, 2nd ed., 25–55, Tully et. al., eds (Philadelphia: Saunders, 2009).

Marshall, A. J., ed. *Biology and Comparative Physiology of Birds.* Cambridge, MA: Academic Press, 1960.

Martin, Graham R. "Through Birds' Eyes: Insights into Avian Sensory Ecology." *Journal of Ornithology* 153 (2012): S23–S48.

———. "What Is Binocular Vision For? A Birds' Eye View." *Journal of Vision* 9, no. 11 (2009): 1–19.

Martin, Graham R., and D. Osorio. "Vision in Birds." In *The Senses: A Comprehensive Reference*, 25–52, Basbaum et. al. (New York: Elsevier, 2010).

Mason, J. Russell and Larry Clark. "Avoidance of Cabbage Fields by Snow Geese." *Wilson Bulletin* 108 (1996): 369–71.

Matsuzaki, Osamu. "Numbers of Olfactory Receptor Cells and Fine Structure of Olfactory Nerves in Various Birds." *Zoological Science* 12, no. 1 (1995): 117–23.

Moore, Bret A., Diana Pita, et al. "Vision in Avian Emberizid Foragers." *Journal of Experimental Biology* 218 (2015): 1347–58.

Moore, Bret A., Luke P. Tyrrell, et al. "Does Retinal Configuration Make the Head and Eyes of Foveate Birds Move?" *Nature/Science Reports* 7 (2017), online.

Ödeen, Anders, et al. "Evolution of Ultraviolet Vision in the Largest Avian Radiation: The Passerines." *BMC Evolutionary Biology* 11, no. 313 (2011), online.

O'Rourke, Colleen T., et al. "Hawk Eyes I: Diurnal Raptors Differ in Visual Fields and Degree of Eye Movement." *PLoS One* 5, no. 9 (September 2010): e12802, online.

Ortega, Laura J. "Avian Visual Perception: Interocular and Intraocular Transfer and Head-bobbing Behaviour in Birds." Diss., Bochum, Germany: International Graduate School of Neuroscience, 2005.

Pecsics, Tibor, et al. "The Cranial Morphometrics of the Wildfowl." *Ornis Hungarica* 25, no. 1 (2017): 44–57.

Pendergraft, L.T. and J.M. Marzluff. "Fussing over Food: Factors Affecting the Vocalizations American Crows Utter around Food." *Animal Behaviour* 150 (2019): 39–57.

Pollock, Christal. "Raptor Gastrointestinal Anatomy and Physiology." *LafeberVet*, March 6, 2016, online.

Proctor, Noble S., and Patrick J. Lynch. *Manual of Ornithology: Avian Structure and Function.* New Haven, CT: Yale University Press, 1993.

Ralph, Carol Pearson, et al. "Analysis of Droppings to Describe Diets of Small Birds." *Journal of Field Ornithology* 56, no. 2 (Spring 1985): 165–74.

Rawal, U. M. "A Comparative Account of the Lingual Myology of Some Birds." *Proceedings of the Indian Academy of Sciences* 71, no. 1 (1970): 36–46.

Reid, Heather. "Wildlife Ophthalmology." Toronto Wildlife Centre, online.

Rothschild, Bruce M., et al. "The Power of the Claw." *PLoS One* 8, no. 9 (September 2013): e73811, online.

Rowland, Hannah M., et al. "Comparative Taste Biology with Special Focus on Birds and Reptiles." In *Handbook of Olfaction and Gustation*, 3rd ed., 957–82, edited by Richard Doty (New York: Wiley, 2015).

Saavedra, Irene, and Luisa Amo. "Insectivorous Birds Eavesdrop on the Pheromones of Their Prey." *PLoS One* 13, no. 2 (February 7, 2018): e0190415, https://doi.org/10.1371/journal.pone.0190415.

Saunders, James C., et al. "The Middle Ear of Reptiles and Birds." In *Comparative Hearing: Birds and Reptiles*, 13–69, James Saunders, et.al. (New York: Springer-Verlag, 2000).

Schaefer, H. Martin, Douglas J. Levey, et al. "The Role of Chromatic and Achromatic Signals for Fruit Detection by Birds." *Behavioral Ecology* 17, no. 5 (June 2006): 784–89.

Schaefer, H. Martin, V. Schaefer, and M. Vorobyev. "Are Fruit Colors Adapted to Consumer Vision and Birds Equally Efficient in Detecting Colorful Signals?" *American Naturalist* 169, no. 1 (January 2007): S159–S69.

Schneider, Eve R., E. O. Gracheva, and S. N. Bagriantsev. "Evolutionary Specialization of Tactile Perception in Vertebrates." *Physiology* 31, no. 3 (2016): 193–200.

Schneider, Eve R., M. Mastrotto, et al. "Neuronal Mechanism for Acute Mechanosensitivity in Tactile- foraging Waterfowl." *Proceedings of the National Academy of Sciences* 111, no. 41 (October 14, 2014): 14941–46.

Schnyder, Hans A. "The Avian Head Induces Cues for Sound Localization in Elevation." *PLoS One* 9, no. 11 (November 2014): e1121178, online.

Schorger, A. W. "The Crushing of Carya Nuts in the Gizzard of the Turkey." *The Auk* 77, no. 3 (July 1960): 337–40.

Siddique, Adnan. "A Comparison of Bird Digestive Systems by Diet." Research thesis, Ohio State University, Columbus, 2017.

Slagsvold, Tore, et al. "Prey Handling in Raptors in Relation to Their Morphology and Feeding Niches." *Journal of Avian Biology* 41, no. 4 (2010): 488–97.

Smith, Carolynn L. and Christopher S. Evans. "Multimodal Signaling in Fowl, *Gallus gallus*." *Journal of Experimental Biology* 211 (2008): 2052–57.

Smith, Charles R., and Milo E. Richmond. "Factors Influencing Pellet Egestion and Gastric pH in the Barn Owl." *Wilson Bulletin* 84, no. 2 (June 1972): 179–86.

Smith, Devon, et al. "Evolutionary Relationships Between the Amphibian, Avian, and Mammalian Stomachs." *Evolution and Development* 2, no. 6 (November-December 2000): 348–59.

Soliman, Soha A., and Fatma A. Madkour. "A Comparative Analysis of the Organization of the Sensory Units in the Beak of Duck and Quail." *Histology, Cytology and Embryology*, 2017, online.

Spring, Lowell W. "Climbing and Pecking Adaptations in Some North American Woodpeckers." *The Condor* 67, no. 6 (November 1965): 457–88.

Stallard, Brian. "Beak 'Handedness,' Crows Favor Left or Right Too." *Nature World News*, December 30, 2014, online.

Steiger, Silke S., et al. "Avian Olfactory Receptor Gene Repertories: Evidence for a Well- Developed Sense of Smell in Birds?" *Proceedings of the Royal Society* 275, no. 1649 (2008): 2309–17.

Stettenheim, Peter R. "The Integumentary Morphology of Modern Birds: An Overview." *American Zoology* 40, no. 4 (2000): 461–77.

Stevenson, James. "Experiments on the Digestion of Food by Birds." *Wilson Bulletin* 45, no. 4 (December 1933): 155–67.

Tsue, Terance, et al. "Hair Cell Regeneration in the Inner Ear." *Otolaryngology: Head and Neck Surgery* 111, no. 3 (September 1994): 281–301.

Tordoff, Michael G. "Calcium: Taste, Intake, and Appetite." *Physiological Reviews* 81, no. 4 (October 2001): 1567–97.

Tyrrell, Luke P., and E. Fernandez-Juricic. "Avian Binocular Vision: It's Not Just About What Birds Can See, It's Also About What They Can't." *PLoS One* 12, no. 3 (March 2017), online.

———. "The Hawk-Eyed Songbird: Retinal Morphology, Eye Shape, and Visual Fields of an Aerial Insectivore." *American Naturalist* 189 (June 2017): 709–17.

Wang, Bin, et al. "Keratin: Structure, Mechanical Properties, Occurrence in Biological Organisms, and Efforts at Bioinspiration." *Progress in Materials Science* 76 (2016): 229–318.

Wang, Kai, and Huabin Zhao. "Birds Generally Carry a Small Repertoire of Bitter Taste Receptor Genes." *Genome Biological Evolution* 7, no. 9 (2015): 2705–15.

Ward, Andrea B., et al. "Functional Morphology of Raptor Hindlimbs." *The Auk* 119, no. 4 (2002): 1052–63.

Wink, Michael. "Geese and Dietary Allelochemicals? Food Palatability and Geophagy." *Chemoecology* 4, no. 2 (January 1993): 93–107.

Withgott, Jay. "Taking a Bird's Eye View in the UV." *Bioscience* 50, no. 10 (October 2000): 854–59.

Yarmolinsky, David A., et al. "Common Sense about Taste: From Mammals to Insects." *Cell* 139, no. 2 (October 2009): 234–44.

Zaefarian, Faegheh, et al. "Avian Liver: The Forgotten Organ." *Animals* 9, no. 2 (2019): e63, online.

Zusi, Richard L. "A Functional and Evolutionary Analysis of Rhynchokinesis in Birds." *Smithsonian Contributions to Zoology*, no. 395 (1984).

FEEDING BEHAVIOR OF BIRDS

Askins, Robert A., et al. "Conservation of Grassland Birds in North America." *Ornithological Monographs*, no. 64 (2007), online.

Burin, Gustavo, et al. "Omnivory in Birds Is a Macroevolutionary Sink." *Nature Communications* 7 (April 7, 2016): online.

Forbey, Jennifer Sorensen. "Hungry Grouse in a Warming World." *Wildlife Biology*, 2013, 374–81.

Fredrickson, Leigh H. "Nutritional Values of Waterfowl Foods." In *Waterfowl Management Handbook,* 13.1.1. (Washington, DC: US Fish and Wildlife Service, 2018).

Glendinning, John I. "How Do Predators Cope with Chemically Defended Foods?" *Biological Bulletin* 19, no. 4 (December 2007): 252–66.

Graveland, J., and A. E. Berends. "Timing of the Calcium Intake and Effect of Calcium Deficiency on Behaviour and Egg Laying in Captive Great Tits." *Physiological Zoology* 70, no. 1 (January-February 1997): 74–84.

Graveland, Jaap, and Teun Van Gijzen. "Arthropods and Seeds Are Not Sufficient as Calcium Sources for Shell Formation and Skeletal Growth in Passerines." *Ardea* 55, nos. 1–2 (1994): 299–314.

Hafner, Heinz. "Ecology of Wading Birds." *Colonial Waterbirds* 20, no. 1 (1997): 115–20.

Hart, A. D. M., ed. "Methods for Estimating Daily Food Intake of Wild Birds and Mammals." London, UK: Department for Environment, Food and Rural Affairs, July 2002.

Hartley, Mitschka John. "Effect of Small-Gap Timber Harvests on Songbird Community." PhD thesis, University of Maine, Orono, 2012.

Hindmarch, Sofi, and John E. Elliott. "When Owls Go to Town: The Diet of Urban Barred Owls." *Journal of Raptor Research* 49, no. 1 (2015): 66–74.

Jackson, Sue, et al. "Chitin Digestion and Assimilation by Seabirds." *The Auk* 109, no. 4 (October 1992): 758–70.

Karasov, William H. "In the Belly of the Bird." *Natural History* (November 1993): 32–6.

Karel, Tara Haan, and Gary Man, eds. "Major Forest Insect and Disease Conditions in the United States: 2015." Washington, DC: US Forest Service, US Department of Agriculture, July 2017.

Linz, George M., and James J. Hanzel. *Sunflower Bird Pests.* Washington, DC: National Wildlife Research Center, US Department of Agriculture, 2015. pp. 175–86.

Marti, Carl D. "A Review of Prey Selection by the Long-eared Owl." *The Condor*, Autumn 1976, 331–36.

Mincey, Henry Dewayne. "Foraging Behavior and Success of Herons and Egrets in Natural and Artificial Wetlands." Thesis, Georgia Southern University, Statesboro, 2006.

Morrison, Michael L., et al., eds. "Avian Foraging: Theory, Methodology, and Applications." *Studies in Avian Biology* (Cooper Ornithological Society), no. 13 (1990), online.

Sawyer, Samantha Jean. "Effects of Carrion Decomposition on Arthropod Community Structure and Habitat Seeking Behavior." Thesis, Texas A&M University, College Station, 2017.

Smith, C. C., and O. J. Reichman. "The Evolution of Food Caching by Birds and Mammals." *Annual Review of Ecology and Systematics* 15 (November 1984): 329–51.

Speights, Jason R., and Warren C. Conway. "Wintering Yellow-bellied Sapsucker Time Activity Budgets." *Wilson Journal of Ornithology* 121, no. 3 (2009): 593–99.

US Department of Agriculture. *Grassland Birds*. Report No. 8. Washington, DC: Natural Resources Conservation Service, Wildlife Habitat Management Institute, October 1999.

Uprety, Yadav. "Preserving Ecosystem Services on Indigenous Territory." *Forests* 8, no. 6 (June 2017): 194.

Vale, Thomas R., et al. "Bird Communities and Vegetation Structure in the United States." *Annals of the Association of American Geographers* 72, no. 1 (March 1982): 120–30.

BIRD DIETS: INSECTS

Bell, Gary P. "Birds and Mammals on an Insect Diet." *Studies in Avian Biology* 13 (1990): 416–22.

Bernhardt, Glen E., et al. "Temporal Variation in Terrestrial Invertebrate Consumption by Laughing Gulls in New York." *American Midland Naturalist* 163 (2010): 442–54.

Blut, C., and K. Lunau. "Effects of Lepidopteran Eyespot Components on the Deterrence of Predatory Birds." *Behaviour* 152, no. 11 (July 2015): 1481–505.

Bollinger, E. K., and J. W. Caslick. "Red-winged Blackbird Predation on Northern Corn Rootworm Beetles in Field Corn." *Journal of Applied Ecology* 22, no. 1 (April 1985): 39–48.

Branson, David H. "Direct and Indirect Effects of Avian Predation on Grasshopper Communities in Northern Mixed-grass Prairie." *Environmental Entomology* 34, no. 5 (October 2005): 1114–21.

Brower, L. P., and L. S. Fink. "A Natural Toxic Defense System: Cardenolides in Butterflies Versus Birds." *Annual New York Academy of Science* 443 (1985): 171–88.

Dickson, James G., et al. *The Role of Insectivorous Birds in Forest Ecosystems.* Cambridge, MA: Academic Press, 1979.

Grass, Ingo, et al. "Insectivorous Birds Disrupt Biological Control of Cereal Aphids." *Ecology* 98, no. 6 (March 17, 2017): 1583–90.

Gunnarson, Bengt. "Bird Predation on Spiders." *Journal of Arachnology* 35, no. 3 (2007): 509–29.

Helms, Jackson A., et al. "Are Invasive Fire Ants Kept in Check by Native Aerial Insectivores?" *Biology Letters* 12, no. 5 (May 2016), https://royalsocietypublishing.org/doi/full/10.1098/rsbl.2016.0059.

Jennings, David E., et al. "Quantifying the Impact of Woodpecker Predation on Population Dynamics of the Emerald Ash Borer." *PLoS One* 8, no. 12 (December 9, 2013): e83491, online.

Joem, Anthony. "Variable Impact of Avian Predation on Grasshopper Assemblies in Sandhills Grassland." *Oikos,* September 1992, 458–63.

Kelly, J. F., et al. "Ecological Energetics of an Abundant Aerial Insectivore, the Purple Martin." *PLoS One* 8, no. 9 (September 25, 2013): e76616, online.

Kirk, David, et al. "Past and Current Attempts to Evaluate the Role of Birds as Predators of Insect Pests in Temperate Agriculture." *Current Ornithology* 13 (1996): 175–269.

Kourimska, Lenka, and Anna Adamkova. "Nutritional and Sensory Quality of Edible Insects." *NFS Journal of the Society of Nutrition and Science* 4 (July 16, 2016): 22–26.

Narango, Desirée, et al. "Nonnative Plants Reduce Population Growth of an Insectivorous Bird." *Proceedings of the National Academy of Sciences* 115, no. 45 (November 6, 2018): 11549–54.

O'Daniels, Sean T., et al. "Visual Cues for Woodpeckers: Light Reflectance of Decayed Wood Varies by Decay Fungus." *Wilson Journal of Ornithology* 130, no. 1 (2018): 200–212.

Schoener, Thomas W. "Large-Billed Insectivorous Birds." *The Condor* 73, no. 2 (April 1, 1971): 154–61.

Studier, Eugene H., et al. "Nutrient Composition of Caterpillars, Pupae, Cocoons.and Adults of the Eastern Tent Moth." *Comparative Biochemical Physiology* 100, no. 4 (1991): 1041–43.

Tremblay, A., et al. "Effects of Bird Predation on Some Pest Insect Populations in Corn." *Agriculture, Ecosystems and Environment* 83, nos. 1–2 (January 2001): 143–52.

Weiser, Jennifer I., et al. "Digestion of Chitin by Northern Bobwhites and American Robins." *The Condor* 99, no. 2 (May 1, 1997): 554–56.

Williams, Kathy S., et al. "Emergence of 13-Yr. Periodical Cicadas." *Ecology* 74, no. 4 (June 1993): 1143–52.

BIRD DIETS: PLANTS

Blem, Charles R., et al. "Rufous Hummingbird Sucrose Preference." *The Condor* 102 (February 2000): 235–38.

Diaz, Mario. "Food Choice by Seed-eating Birds in Relation to Seed Chemistry." *Comparative Biochemistry and Physiology* 113, no. 3 (March 1996): 239–46.

Fair, Jeanne M., et al. "Avian Communities Are Decreasing with Pinon Pine Mortality in the Southwest." *Biological Conservation* 226 (October 2018): 186–95.

Fleck, David C., and Glen E. Woolfenden. "Can Acorn Tannin Predict Scrub-Jay Caching Behavior?" *Journal of Chemical Ecology* 23, no. 3 (March 1997): 793–806.

Fricke, E. C., et al. "When Condition Trumps Location: Seed Consumption by Fruit-eating Birds Removes Pathogens and Predator Attractants." *Ecology Letter* 16, no. 8 (August 2013): 1031–36.

Johansen, Stacey M., et al. "Factors Influencing Seed Species Selection by Wild Birds at Feeders." *Wilson Journal of Ornithology* 126, no. 2 (June 2014): 374–81.

Keating, Jeffrey F. "Selection Responses of Avian Granivores to Various Morphological Food Characteristics." Masters thesis, Manhattan, KS: Kansas State University, 1989.

Koenig, Walter D., and Johannes M. H. Knops. "The Mystery of Masting in Trees." *American Scientist* 93, no. 4 (July-August 2005): 340–47.

Martinez del Rio, Carlos, et al. "Intake Responses in Nectar Feeding Birds." *Integrative and Comparative Biology* 41, no. 4 (August 2001): 902–15.

Reed, Haisworth F., and L. L. Wolf. "Nectar Characteristics and Food Selection by Hummingbirds." *Oecologia* 25, no. 2 (June 1976): 101–13.

Roessler, Elizabeth S. "Viability of Weed Seeds after Ingestion by California Linnets." *The Condor* 38 (March 1936): 62–65.

Schroger, A. W. "The Crushing of Carya Nuts in the Gizzard of the Turkey." *The Auk* 77 (1960): 337–40.

Smith, Christopher C., and Russell P. Balda. "Competition Among Insects, Birds, and Mammals for Conifer Seeds." *American Zoology* 19, no. 4 (1979): 1065–83.

Smith, Susan B., et al. "Fruit Quality and Consumption by Songbirds during Autumn Migration." *Wilson Journal of Ornithology* 119, no. 3 (September 2007): 419–28.

Stiles, Edmund W. "Patterns of Fruit Presentation and Seed Dispersal in Bird-Disseminated Woody Plants in the Eastern Deciduous Forest." *American Naturalist* 116, no. 5 (November 1980): 670–88.

Titulaer, Mieke, et al. "Importance of Seed Characteristics in Diet Preferences of Granivorous Birds: Pilot Study with House Sparrows." *Interciencia* 43, no. 7 (July 2018): 1.

Vander Wall, Stephen B. "The Evolutionary Ecology of Nut Dispersal." *Botanical Review* 67, no. 1 (January 2001): 74–117.

Washburn, Brian, and Thomas W. Seamans. "Foraging Preferences of Canada Geese Among Turfgrasses." *Journal of Wildlife Management* 76, no. 3 (April 2012): 600–607.

BIRD DIETS: ANIMALS

Binford, Laurence C. "Eastern Phoebes Fishing." *The Auk* 74 (April 1957): 264–65.

Eaton, Muir D., et al. "Fish Feeding Behavior in a Local Canada Goose Population." *Wilson Journal of Ornithology* 129, no. 4 (2017): 878–82.

Gavin, Michael, and Jennifer N. Solomon. "Active and Passive Bait fishing by Black- crowned Night Herons." *Wilson Journal of Ornithology* 121, no. 4 (2009): 844–45.

Gleason, Jeffrey S. "Mallards Feeding on Salmon Carcasses in Alaska." *Wilson Journal of Ornithology* 119, no. 1 (March 2007): 105–7.

Grubb, Teryl G., et al. "Winter Scavenging of Ungulate Carrion by Bald Eagles, Common Ravens, and Coyotes in Northern Arizona." *Journal of Raptor Research* 52, no. 4 (2018): 471–83.

Kapfer, Joshua M., et al. "Carrion-feeding by Barred Owls." *Wilson Journal of Ornithology* 123, no. 3 (2011): 6646–49.

Slagsvold, Tore, et al. "Prey Handling in Raptors in Relation to their Morphology and Feeding Niches." *Journal of Avian Biology* 41, no. 4 (July 2010): 488–97.

Varland, Daniel E., et al. "Scavenging as a Food-Acquisition Strategy by Peregrine Falcons." *Journal of Raptor Research* 53, no. 3 (2018): 291–308.

Werner, Scott J., et al. "Foraging Behavior and Monetary Impact of Wading Birds at Arkansas Baitfish Farms." *Journal of the World Aquaculture Society* 36, no. 3 (September 2007): 354.

CHALLENGES AND SOLUTIONS

Ackerman, Joshua T., et al. "Avian Mercury Exposure and Toxicological Risk Across Western North America." *Science of the Total Environment* 568 (October 2016): 749–69.

Barnes, David K. A., et al. "Accumulation and Fragmentation of Plastic Debris in Global Environments." *Philosophical Transactions of the Royal Society* 364, no. 1526 (July 2009), online.

Battisti, Corrado, et al. "Interactions Between Anthropogenic Litter and Birds." *Marine Pollution Bulletin* 138 (January 2019): 93–114.

Cruz-Martinez, Luis, et al. "Lead from Spent Ammunition, a Source of Exposure and Poisoning in Bald Eagles." *Human-Wildlife Interactions* 6, no. 1 (Spring 2012): 94–104.

Daane, Kent M., et al. "Biological Control of Arthropod Pests in California Agriculture." UCB-BC Interim Report, University of California, Berkeley, December 12, 2007, online.

de Castro Pena, João Carlos, et al. "Street Trees Reduce the Negative Effects of Urbanization on Birds." *PLoS One* 12, no. 3 (March 23, 2017): e0174484, online.

Epps, Clinton W. "Considering the Switch: Challenges of Transitioning to Non-lead Hunting Ammunition." *The Condor* 116, no. 3 (July 2014): 429–34.

Frias, J. P. G. L., and Roisin Nash. "Microplastics: Finding a Consensus on the Definition." *Marine Pollution Bulletin* 138 (January 2019): 145–47.

Haney, P. B., et al. "Cotton Production and the Boll Weevil in Georgia." *Athenaeum of University of Georgia*, March 2009, online.

Hladik, M. L., et al. "Environmental Risks and Challenges Associated with Neonicotinoid Insecticides." *Environmental Science and Technology* 52, no. 6 (March 2018): 3329–35.

Howell, Arthur H. *The Relation of Birds to the Cotton Boll Weevil.* Washington, DC: US Department of Agriculture, 1907.

Intergovernmental Science-Policy Platform on Biodiversity and Ecosystem Services. "Global Assessment Report on Biodiversity and Ecosystem Services." United Nations, May 2009, online.

Jambeck, Jenna R., et al. "Plastic Waste Inputs from Land into the Ocean." *Science* 347, no. 6223 (February 13, 2015): 768–71.

Jedlicka, Julie. "Integrating Songbird Conservation and Insect Pest Management in Organic California Vineyards." Santa Cruz, CA: Organic Farming Research Foundation, 2010, online.

Karnicky, Jeffrey. "What Is the Red Knot Worth? Valuing Human/Avian Interaction." *Society and Animals* 12, no. 3 (December 2004): 254–66.

Kerlinger, Paul. "Birding Economics and Birder Demographics as Conservation Tools." *Status and Management of Neotropical Migratory Birds* RM-229 (September 2012): 32–38.

Kirk, David A., et al., eds. "Past and Current Attempts to Evaluate the Role of Birds as Predators of Insect Pests." In *Current*

Ornithology, 175–269, Nolan and Ketterson, eds., (New York: Plenum Press, 1996).

Koenig, Walter D. "European Starlings and Their Effect on Native Cavity-Nesting Birds." *Conservation Biology* 17, no. 4 (July 2003): 1134–40.

Ledford, Heidi. "World's Largest Plant Survey Reveals Alarming Extinction Rate." *Nature* 570, no. 7760 (June 10, 2019): 148–49.

Losey, John E., and Mace Vaughan. "The Economic Value of Ecological Services Provided by Insects." *Bioscience Magazine* 56 (April 2006): 311–23.

MedlinePlus. "Methylmercury Poisoning." Bethesda, MD: US National Library of Medicine, September 2017, online.

Narango, D. L., et al. "Nonnative Plants Reduce Population Growth of an Insectivorous Bird." *Proceedings of the National Academy of Sciences* 115, no. 45 (November 2018): 11549–54.

Parencia, C. R. Jr. "One Hundred Twenty Years of Research on Cotton Insects in the United States." In *Agriculture Handbook* no. 515 (Washington, DC: US Department of Agriculture, March 1978).

Pokras, Mark, et al. "Lead Objects Ingested by Common Loons in New England." *Northeastern Naturalist* 16, no. 2 (July 2009): 177–82.

Potocka, Marta, et al. "Plastic Pollution Affects American Lobsters." *Marine Pollution Bulletin* 138 (January 2019): 545–48.

Purcell, Kathryn L. "Foraging Behavior of European Starlings." General Technology Report PSW-GTR-251. Fresno, CA: US Forest Service, 2015.

Rodenhouse, Nicholas L., et al. "Effects of Temperate Agriculture on Neotropical Migrant Landbirds." General Technical Report, GTR RM-229, 280–95. Fort Collins, CO: US Forest Service, 1993.

Sekercioglu, Cagan H. "Increasing Awareness of Avian Ecological Function." *Trends in Ecology and Evolution* 21, no. 8 (June 2006): 464–71.

Strohbach, Michael W., et al. "150 Years of Changes in Bird Life in Cambridge, Massachusetts from 1860 to 2012." *Wilson Journal of Ornithology* 126, no. 2 (2014): 192–206.

Thomas, V. G. "Lead-free Hunting Rifle Ammunition." *Ambio* 42, no. 6 (October 2013): 737–45.

Torres-Mura, Juan C., et al. "Plastic Material in the Diet of the Turkey Vulture." *Wilson Journal of Ornithology* 127, no. 1 (March 2015): 134–38.

US Environmental Protection Agency. "Mercury Emissions: The Global Context." Washington, DC: US Environmental Protection Agency, 2009, online.

HOW TO SUPPORT BIRDS

Cohen, Paul. *National Gardening Survey.* Jacksonville, TX: Garden Research, 2019.

Doughty, Robin. *Feather Fashions and Bird Preservation: A Study in Nature Preservation.* Berkeley: University of California Press, 1975.

Ganzel, Bill. "Farming in the 1930s." *Living History Farm* (website), 2003, online.

National Pesticide Information Center. "Pyrethrins." National Pesticide Information Center, November 2014, online.

Oregon State University. "A History of Pesticide Use." Oregon State University, October 2012, online.

Relyea, Rick A. "The Impact of Insecticides and Herbicides on the Biodiversity and Productivity of Aquatic Communities." *Ecological Applications* 15, no. 2 (April 2005): 618–27.

Robb, Gillian N., et al. "Food for Thought: Supplementary Feeding as a Driver of Ecological Change in Avian Populations." *Frontiers in Ecology and the Environment* 6, no. 9 (November 2008): 475–84.

Saunders, Sarah P., et al. "Local and Cross-Seasonal Associations of Climate and Land Use with Abundance of Monarch Butterflies." *Ecography* 41, no. 2 (April 2017): 278–90.

Short, P., and T. Colborn. "Pesticide Use in the US and Policy Implications." *Toxicology and Industrial Health* 15, nos. 1–2 (January–March 1999): 240–75.

Templeton, Scott, et al. "An Economic Perspective on Outdoor Residential Pesticide Use." *Environmental Science and Technology* 32, no. 17 (September 1998): 416A–23A.

US Fish and Wildlife Service. "Homeowner's Guide to Protecting Frogs." US Fish and Wildlife Service, July 2000, online.

Unsworth, John. "History of Pesticide Use." International Union of Pure and Applied Chemistry, May 2010, online.

Wilcoxen, Travis E., et al. "Effects of Bird-feeding Activities on the Health of Wild Birds." *Conservation Physiology* 3, no. 1 (December 2015), online.

Xerces Society. "How Neonicotinoids Can Kill Bees." 2nd ed. *Xerces Society for Invertebrate Conservation* 1 (2016), online.

PHOTO CREDITS

Unless otherwise attributed, all photographs are the work of the author.
Diet Profiles: All photographs from the following sources were supplied by Shutterstock (www.shutterstock.com).
Acadian Flycatcher: Frode Jacobsen. *American Avocet*: Dr. Alan Lipkin. *American Bittern*: Randy Bjorklund. *American Coot*: Enrique Aguirre. *American Crow*: Svetlana Foote. *American Dipper*: Tim Zurowski. *American Goldfinch*: Saptashaw Chakraborty. *American Kestrel*: Sergey Uryadnikov. *American Redstart*: Gerald A. DeBoer. *American White Pelican*: Krasnova Ekaterina. *Baltimore Oriole*: Brian Lasenby. *Barn Owl*: Danita Delmont. *Barn Swallow*: LP Primeau. *Barred Owl*: Robin Keefe. *Belted Kingfisher*: Ray Hennessy. *Black-capped Chickadee*: Peter K. Ziminski. *Black-chinned Hummingbird*: Danita Delmont. *Black-crowned Night Heron*: Serkan Mutan. *Black Tern*: AlexussK. *Blue Jay*: Mike Truchon. *Brewer's Blackbird*: Tom Franks. *Brown Creeper*: Robert L. Kothenbeutel. *Brown-headed Cowbird*: Elliotte Rusty Harold. *Bufflehead*: Roger Utting. *Bullock's Oriole*: Martha Marks. *Canada Jay*: Diana Carpenter. *Canvasback*: Brian E Kushner. *Carolina Chickadee*: Ami Parikh. *Carolina Wren*: Steve Byland. *Cattle Egret*: Jean Faucett. *Cedar Waxwing*: Annette Shaff. *Chimney Swift*: Paul Reeves Photography. *Chipping Sparrow*: Jeramey Lende. *Common Goldeneye*: Bildagentur Zoonar GmbH. *Common Grackle*: Manu M Nair. *Common Loon*: Ray Hennessy. *Common Merganser*: Daniel Bruce Lacy. *Common Murre*: Tarpan. *Common Nighthawk*: Carrie Olson. *Common Raven*: David Dohnal. *Common Tern*: Bildagentur Zoonar GmbH. *Cooper's Hawk*: Eivor Kuchta. *Dark-eyed Junco*: Kerry Hargrove. *Downy Woodpecker*: Mike Truchon. *Eastern Bluebird*: Steve Byland. *Eastern Kingbird*: C. Hamilton. *Eastern Phoebe*: Ray Hennessy. *Eastern Screech-Owl*: Tony Campbell. *Eastern Towhee*: Brian Lasenby. *Eastern Whip-poor-will*: Frode Jacobsen. *Eastern Wood-Pewee*: Natalia Kuzmina. *European Starling*: Nick Vorobey. *Ferruginous Hawk*: Bill Florence. *Gray Catbird*: Steve Byland. *Great Blue Heron*: James P. Mock. *Great Horned*

Owl: Lisa Hagan. *Greater Roadrunner*: Garrett Gibson. *Green Heron*: Krumpelman Photography. *Green-winged Teal*: Sheila Fitzgerald. *Hairy Woodpecker*: Martha Marks. *Herring Gull*: FotoRequest. *Horned Lark*: Szymon Bartosz. *House Sparrow*: Dave Montreuil. *House Wren*: Patrick Messier. *Indigo Bunting*: John L. Absher. *Killdeer*: Annette Shaff. *Least Sandpiper*: Carrie Olson. *Mallard*: jitkagold. *Marsh Wren*: Glenn Price. *Mountain Bluebird*: Agami Photo Agency. *Mourning Dove*: Kerry Hargrove. *Northern Bobwhite*: Tim Zurowski. *Northern Cardinal*: Bob Hilscher. *Northern Flicker*: Wayne Wolfersberger. *Northern Harrier*: Peter Schwarz. *Northern Mockingbird*: Thomas Morris. *Northern Pintail*: Wang LiQiang. *Northern Saw-whet Owl*: Glass and Nature. *Northern Shrike*: Piotr Krzeslak. *Northern Shoveler*: Paul Reeves Photography. *Osprey*: Ondrej Prosicky. *Ovenbird*: Liz Weber. *Peregrine Falcon*: Ondrej Prosicky. *Pied-billed Grebe*: Kent Ellington. *Pine Siskin:* BarciFoto. *Purple Martin*: Ivan Kuzmin. *Red Crossbill*: EvgenyPopov. *Red-breasted Nuthatch*: Karel Bock. *Red-headed Woodpecker*: Brian E. Kushner. *Red-winged Blackbird*: David Osborn. *Ring-billed Gull*: C. Hamilton. *Ring-necked Duck*: Gaston Piccinetti. *Ring-necked Pheasant*: Stephen Mellor. *Rock Pigeon*: Nick Vorobey. *Rose-breasted Grosbeak*: Stephen Mellor. *Ruby-throated Hummingbird*: Steve Byland. *Ruffed Grouse*: Steve Oehlenschlager. *Sandhill Crane:* Daniel Wright98. *Savannah Sparrow*: Arto Hakola. *Scarlet Tanager*: Brian Lasenby. *Semipalmated Plover*: Ivan Kuzmin. *Sharp-shinned Hawk*: Brent Barnes. *Song Sparrow*: Mircea Costina. *Snow Bunting*: Giedriius. *Sora*: Karel Bock. *Spotted Towhee*: Anatoliy Lukich. *Steller's Jay*: Stewart Myers. *Swainson's Thrush*: C. Hamilton. *Tree Swallow*: Wayne Wolfsperger. *Tufted Titmouse*: Brian Lasenby. *Turkey Vulture*: Hayley Crews. *Warbling Vireo*: Paul Reeves Photography. *Western Meadowlark*: Kerry Hargrove. *White-breasted Nuthatch*: Mircea Costina. *White-throated Sparrow*: Austin Seaman. *Wild Turkey*: QueenB19. *Wilson's Phalarope*: Frode Jacobsen. *Wilson's Snipe*: Carrie Olson. *Wood Duck*: Steve Oehlenschlager. *Wood Thrush*: Sandra Standbridge. *Yellow-bellied Sapsucker*: Dennis W. Donohue. *Yellow-billed Cuckoo*: Gerald A. DeBoer. *Yellow-breasted Chat*: Robert L. Kothenbeutel. *Yellow Warbler*: Ray Hennessy.

Additional photo credits: Page 9, *American Robin*: Gray Photo Service/Shutterstock. **Page 22**, *American Goldfinch*: Saptashaw Chakraborty/Shutterstock. **Page 38**, *Bald Eagle*: Colin Flashman/Shutterstock; *Northern Cardinal*: Bonnie Taylor Barry/Shutterstock; *Blue-Gray Gnatcatcher*: Michael G. McKinne/Shutterstock; *Ruby-throated Hummingbird*: Fiona M. Donnelly/Shutterstock; *Red Crossbill*: selimtumir/Shutterstock; *Pileated Woodpecker*: rhfletcher/Shutterstock; *Mallard*: TPROduction/Shutterstock; *Great Egret*: Brian Lasenby/Shutterstock. **Page 45**, *Ferruginous Hawk*: Bill Florence/Shutterstock; *Canvasback*: Harold Stiver/Shutterstock; *Mourning Dove*: JAREDWELLS007/Shutterstock. **Page 47**, *Northern Shoveler*: Brian Lasenby/Shutterstock. **Page 66**, *American Robin*: Anne Schwartz. **Page 69**, *Barn Owl:* Danita Delmont/Shutterstock. **Page 79**, *Laughing Gulls*: Gerald Marella/Shutterstock. **Page 121**, *Black-capped Chickadee*: Alexandra Rapaport. **Page 131**, *Common Tern*: R. Lavka. **Page 153**, *Northern Flicker*: Steve Byland/Shutterstock. **Page 165**, *Bluestem prairie grass*: Weldon Schloneger/Shutterstock. **Page 169**, *Field of native vetch*: Jennifer Larsen Morrow/Shutterstock. **Page 173**, *Texas thistle*: The Jungle Explorer/Shutterstock; *American Goldfinch*: Nan Bauer/Shutterstock. **Page 182**, *Black-billed Magpie*: Coulanges/Shutterstock. **Page 190**, *Winterberries*: Nancy J. Ondra/Shutterstock. **Page 204**, *Cooper's Hawk*: Elvor Kuchta/Shutterstock; *American Kestrel*: Sergey Uryadnikov/Shutterstock; *Burrowing Owl*: Martha Marks/Shutterstock; *Peregrine Falcon*: Michal Ninger/Shutterstock; *Barred Owl*: Vinnie Lauritsen/Shutterstock. **Page 309**, *Baltimore Oriole*: Mike Truchon/Shutterstock. **Page 313**, *Hummingbirds at feeder*: Colin Bristow/Shutterstock. **Page 322**, *Common Murre*: Tarpan. **Page 348**, *Tree Swallow*: Wayne Wolfsperger.

INDEX

backyard feeders, 7, 161, 175, 179, 224, 261, 312

bacteria, 22, 99, 100, 106, 109, 127, 160

bait, 155, 217, 271, 272

Bald Eagle, 228; anatomy, 31, 33, 105; competition, 220, 221; diet, 121, 209, 210, 219, 221; digestion, 100, 113; threats to, 273, 274, 287

Baltimore Oriole, 228, 313

Barn Owl, 26, 36, 62, 67, 69, 71, 75, 87, 110, 111, 206, 228

Barn Swallow, 109, 131, 154, 155, 228, 269

Barred Owl, 74, 75, 204, 207, 209, 271

Bar-tailed Trogon, 26, 87

bats, 16, 75, 135, 205, 209

batteries, 275

beak. *See* bill

bees, 138, 171, 173, 266, 288, 291, 295, 313

beetles, 73, 102, 119, 135, 136, 138, 139, 141, 142, 143, 148, 149, 150, 151, 157, 159, 160, 173, 179, 185, 211, 218, 222, 262, 269, 278, 279, 280, 291, 311, 312

begging, 77, 78

Belted Kingfisher, 121, 229

big toe. *See* hallux

bile, 100, 105, 109

bills, 19, 32, 34, 35–49, 50, 51, 52, 53, 73, 83, 153, 164, 182, 185, 186, 192, 202, 213, 219, 262; growth cycle, 35; hook at tip, 38, 39, 44; serration, 43, 47; sexual differentiation, 42; shapes, 36, 38, 40, 41, 186; terminology, 39; touch, 87–91, 218

"Bills of North American Hummingbirds," 41

bill-tip organ, 87

binocular vision, 57–61, 64, 65

bipedal, 10, 35

bird banding, 317

bird baths, 127

"Bird Crops," 97

Bird Diet Profiles, 244–258

"Bird Eye Shapes," 57

bird feeders, 7, 8, 9, 117, 122, 131, 161, 163, 171, 175, 176, 179, 209, 224, 295, 296, 297–313, 314

"Bird Gizzard," 102

bird observatories, 317

bird species, 19, 21, 23, 24–26

Bird Studies Canada, 316

"Bird Tongues," 50

bird-friendly gardens, 170, 289, 295–297

birding events, 314–317

"Bird's Digestive System, A," 93

"Birds' Ability to Taste Bitterness," 87

birds, and agricultural pests, 143; diversity of, 24

"Birds' Binocular Fields of View," 60

"Birds' Eardrums," 67

"Birds' Eye Movability," 61

"Birds' Olfactory Bulbs," 80

"Birds That Eat Agricultural Insect Pests," 156

bitter taste, 85, 86, 87

Black Tern, 230

blackbirds, 25, 67, 69, 77, 78, 129, 155, 156, 158, 159, 173, 178, 185, 266, 269, 307, 308, 309

Black-capped Chickadee, 57, 76, 122, 156, 163, 229, 304, 312

Black-chinned Hummingbird, 41, 229

Black-crowned Night Heron, 217, 230

Black-footed Albatross, 81

Black-headed Grosbeak, 86, 148, 230

blind zone, 59, 61

Northern Saw-whet Owl, 111, 246
Northern Shoveler, 47, 55, 124, 246
Northern Shrike, 122, 246
nostrils. *See* nares
number of taste buds, 83
"Nut Menu," 181
nuthatches, 25, 65, 105, 156, 163, 173, 182, 186, 188, 313
"Nutritional Value of Native Fruit," 191
"Nutritional Value of Seeds," 163
"Nutritional Value of Sunflower Seeds," 177
nuts, 37, 44, 96, 101, 102, 113, 116, 122, 161, 179–182, 183, 186, 187, 188, 189, 278, 279, 296
oaks, 179, 180, 182–185, 190
oilbirds, 75
olfactory bulb, 79, 80
omnivore, 97, 101, 114, 115, 262
operculum, 39, 45
organic gardening, 291, 293
Osprey, 25, 33, 34, 103, 105, 113, 126, 203, 210, 212, 217, 246, 285, 287
Ostrich, 15, 20, 57
outer ear, 66, 67, 68
Ovenbird, 247
overeating, 121
overgrazing, 166, 168
"Owl Pellets," 111
owls, 21, 26, 118, 122, 299; anatomy, 29, 33, 34, 45, 56, 57, 62, 64, 67, 96, 97; diet, 133, 203, 206–209; digestion, 102, 109; hearing, 67, 69–75, 81; pellets, 110–113; vision, 56, 59, 60, 65, 81; toxins, 270–272
pain receptors, 86, 300
palate, 84
pancreas, 106
papillae, 53, 54, 55
parasites, 20, 82, 109

parrots, 21, 25, 80, 81, 85, 186, 285
"Parts of a Bird's Ear," 68
"Parts of a Bird's Eye," 62
passerines, 76, 128; anatomy, 27, 31, 42, 54, 96, 97; diet, 23, 54, 128; evolution, 23; as prey, 209; threats to, 128; vision, 58
Pasteurella multocida, 110
pathogens, 109–110, 193
peanuts, 161, 302–303, 309, 311
pecking, 32, 61, 90, 128
pecking order, 77, 221
pecten, 62, 64
pectoral structure, 11
pelicans, 25, 44, 51, 54, 124, 126, 213, 275, 287
pellets, 102, 107, 110–113, 128, 132, 221, 272, 273, 277
penguins, 81, 86
perching, 23, 27, 28, 29, 30–31, 109, 205
Peregrine Falcon, 33, 46, 58, 87, 100, 204, 205, 209, 221, 247, 287
Permian Period, 13
Permian-Triassic Extinction, 13
persistent organic pollutants (POPs), 288
pesticides, 106, 131, 132, 160, 265, 267, 268, 283, 287, 288, 289
petrels, 25, 79, 81, 124, 213
pets, 109, 154, 203, 271, 272, 291
pH scale, 100
phoebes, 76, 113, 201, 215
photoreceptors, 62, 63, 65
physiology, 116, 124, 56–113
phytoplankton, 79
Pied-billed Grebe, 214, 215, 247
pigeons, 24, 85, 109, 262; anatomy, 45, 58, 97; crop milk, 46, 99; diet, 121, 126, 163, 185, 193, 261, 299; digestion, 100, 101; and feeders, 299, 305, 309, 310;

tomia, 35, 36, 39, 46

tongues, 7, 49–56, 96; barbs, 52, 54; dexterity, 51, 94; fringes, 53, 55; functions, 50, 52, 87, 126, 164, 305, 313; lingual nail, 55; mechanoreceptors, 90; taste, 82–87

torpor, 119, 120

touch, 44, 56, 87–91, 218; mechano-receptors, 32, 87, 88, 89, 90, 91

toxins, 259, 261–277, 280; in feed-ers, 303, 306; natural, 82, 86, 148, 160, 175, 303, 306

toxoplasmosis, 109

Tree Swallow, 43, 60, 154, 156, 193, 254, 348

Triassic period, 10, 13, 16

Trumpeter Swan, 118

Tufted Titmouse, 191, 254

Turkey Vulture, 78, 80, 81, 221, 222, 255, 277

tympanum, 68

Tyrannosaurus rex, 10, 11, 18

ultrasonic frequencies, 70, 75

ultraviolet light. *See* UV light

umami, 85, 86

underwater, 16, 45, 65, 212, 213, 214, 215, 216, 218

undigested food, 99, 116

uric acid, 107, 109

urine, 106, 107

UV light, 62, 63

"Variations in Bill Sizes," 38

Velociraptor, 10

vent, 93, 107

ventriculus, 93, 99, 100, 101, 110, 130

vermivore, 115

vertebrae, 11, 16, 62, 219

vibrations, 32, 68, 70, 78, 90, 91

Violet-crowned Hummingbird, 41

Visible Spectrum of Light, 63

vision, 66, 73, 74, 77, 81, 82, 88, 100, 118, 130; anatomy, 56–65;

blind area, 59; field of view, 57–59; fruit color, 189, 191; seed color, 189; underwater, 212

vitamins, 105, 136

volcanoes, 20

vultures, 21, 24, 34, 53, 78, 80, 97, 124, 219, 220, 221, 222, 223, 277

Warbling Vireo, 255

water, 17, 20, 29, 31, 33, 44, 48, 66, 89, 195–198, 200, 203, 210, 212–219, 265, 275, 291, 292, 294, 295, 313; as part of diet, 54, 55, 106, 116, 124–127

water plants. *See* aquatic plants

waterbirds, 37, 80, 88, 96, 109, 124, 142, 143, 203, 209, 214, 218, 221

webbed feet, 15, 17, 29, 31, 143, 214, 216

West Nile Virus, 291

Western Bluebird, 270

Western Meadowlark, 69, 134, 154, 156, 255

wetlands, 166, 195, 272

"What Birds Get Out of Their Food," 116

"What's Found in an Owl Pellet?," 112

white-bark pines, 188, 279–280

White-breasted Nuthatch, 65, 105, 156, 163, 182, 255

White-throated Sparrow, 61, 87, 256

whitewash, 109

Wild Birds Unlimited, 314

Wild Turkey, 25, 34, 45, 100, 101, 108, 124, 163, 173, 182, 183, 184, 185, 193, 209, 256

Willow Flycatcher, 281

Willow Ptarmigan, 130, 194

Wilson's Phalarope, 256

Wilson's Snipe, 256

wings, 11, 14, 15, 16, 17, 18, 19, 22, 29, 146, 209, 212, 213, 216, 217

ABOUT THE AUTHOR

Ed O'Brien

Kim Long is a writer, researcher, and graphic artist based in Denver. He has written more than fifty books covering subjects from tea to the history of political corruption, including two previous bird books, *Owls: A Wildlife Handbook* and *Hummingbirds: A Wildlife Handbook.* He was the editor of *The Weather Calendar* and contributes to the *Encyclopedia Britannica* as a field editor. He created *The Moon Calendar,* with more than 500,000 copies in print, published annually since 1981. Long has a BA from Wesleyan University (1971) and has additional academic credits in studio and graphic arts from Pratt Institute and the Herron School of Art.

ABOUT SKIPSTONE

SKIPSTONE is an imprint of independent, nonprofit publisher Mountaineers Books. It features thematically related titles that promote a deeper connection to our natural world through sustainable practice and backyard activism. Our readers live smart, play well, and typically engage with the community around them. Skipstone guides explore healthy lifestyles and how an outdoor life relates to the well-being of our planet, as well as of our own neighborhoods. Sustainable foods and gardens; healthful living; realistic and doable conservation at home; modern aspirations for community—Skipstone tries to address such topics in ways that emphasize active living, local and grassroots practices, and a small footprint.

Our hope is that Skipstone books will inspire you to effect change without losing your sense of humor, to celebrate the freedom and generosity of a life outdoors, and to move forward with gentle leaps or breathtaking bounds. All of our publications, as part of our 501(c)(3) nonprofit program, are made possible through the generosity of donors and through sales of 700 titles on outdoor recreation, sustainable lifestyle, and conservation. To donate, purchase books, or learn more, visit us online: www.skipstonebooks.org www.mountaineersbooks.org

SKIPSTONE
LIVE LIFE

MAKE RIPPLES

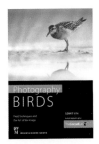